THE REPUBLIC
OF MANY
MANSIONS

THE REPUBLIC OF MANY MANSIONS

Foundations of American Religious Thought

by
Denise Lardner Carmody
and John Tully Carmody

UNIVERSITY OF TULSA

PARAGON HOUSE
New York

First edition, 1990
Published in the United States by Paragon House

Paragon House
90 Fifth Avenue
New York, NY 10011

Copyright © 1990 by Paragon House

Designed by Eve Kirch

Library of Congress Cataloging-in-Publication Data
Carmody, Denise Lardner, 1935–
    The republic of many mansions : foundations of American religious
thought / Denise Lardner Carmody, John Tully Carmody. — 1st ed.
        p.   cm.
    Includes bibliographical references.
    ISBN 1-55778-236-9 — ISBN 1-55778-392-6 (pbk.)
    1. Religious thought—United States. 2. Religious thought—Modern
period, 1500–   3. Puritans—United States. 4. Edwards, Jonathan,
1703–1758. 5. Freedom of religion—United States. 6. Jefferson, Thomas,
1743–1826. 7. Pragmatism. 8. James, William, 1842–1910. 9. United
States—Religion. I. Carmody, John, 1939–
II. Title.
BL2525.C365 1990
200'.973—dc20   90-30737
                                                                      CIP

Manufactured in the United States of America

The paper used in this publication meets the minimum requirements
of American National Standard for Information Sciences—Permanence
of Paper for Printed Library Materials, ANSIZ39,48-1984.
10 9 8 7 6 5 4 3 2 1

For Nancy and Ted Kachel

Contents

PART THREE AMERICAN PRAGMATISM

Preface

In this book we speculate about three ideas that arguably lie at the foundations of American religious thought: the Puritan conception of human nature, the Enlightenment conception of religious liberty (leading to the disestablishment of any church from a privileged position), and the pragmatic conception of truth. To speculate about each of these ideas, we begin with a representative figure. For Puritanism, we have chosen Jonathan Edwards. For the view of religion that the United States drew from the Enlightenment, the figure is Thomas Jefferson. Pragmatism is represented by William James. After exposing some of each thinker's views, we generalize to create a rough impression of what the idea in question meant to the American mainstream.

As a counterpoint to the mainstream, we have also examined what we call the margins. If the mainstream in American religious thought, and American culture at large, has been white, Protestant, and perhaps male, the margins have housed Jews, Catholics, African Americans, Asians, Protestant sectarians, and perhaps women. By reflecting on *their* senses of human nature, disestablishment, and pragmatism, we flesh out our analysis of all three notions and suggest further how they have cohered and what they have meant to the American population at large. We owe many thanks to Don Fehr of Paragon House Publishers for initiating this project and shepherding it through to production, and to the specialists in American religion whose writings have instructed us through the years.

Chapter 1

Introduction

Religious Thought

Most etymologies of the word "religion" link it to the Latin word for tying or binding. By "religion," a person is bound—to the sacred obligations the tribe considers important, to the requirements of mature humanity, to God. The implication is that this tie is the most significant characteristic of human beings. Traditionally, virtually all peoples equated their religious myths and rituals with their selfhood. One could not separate their culture, who they were (as Lakota or Bengalis, as Greeks or Azerbaijanis), from what they thought about the construction of the world, the origin of their particular tribe, the destiny that the ultimate powers presiding over human affairs had laid out for them.

Religious *thought* therefore has been reflection about matters of ultimate significance. In most traditional cultures, it has been nearly coincident with wisdom. To think about what most mattered might be difficult, even troubling, in youth, but it was delightful in old age. One could do nothing more satisfying for one's own soul, or more beneficial to one's people, than to become a person who had puzzled out the mysteries of human existence. Usually the wise person went about such puzzling with a great deal of help from prior elders and long-standing traditions. Usually becoming wise was a matter of seeing how what one had been taught as a youth, what one had been initiated into, did in fact make great sense and

1

provide deep consolation. The difference between youth and old age was only experience. If the life cycle had gone well, one had come to appreciate why it was good to follow one's people's customs about food, drink, marriage, education, ritual activity, dealings with outsiders, and the rest.

Does this mean that there was no room for criticism or innovation in the religious thought of a typical traditional (pre-modern) group? No, but it does mean that the burden of proof fell on the critic or innovator, because the assumption was that what had preserved the people down to the present age probably continued to be worth heeding. Thus, when traditions such as Judaism and Christianity came under radical criticism, from the seventeenth century on, the effect was traumatic. On the one hand, the best of the critics could bring forward persuasive reasons (many of them lodged in the discoveries and theories put forward by the newly emancipated natural sciences) for rethinking traditional positions. Perhaps the world had not arisen as the first chapters of the book of Genesis in the Bible suggested it had. Perhaps the established ideas about a kosher diet or about the authority of priests and ministers ought to be reconsidered in light of new social and economic conditions. On the other hand, what would happen to the solidarity of one's people (as Polish Jews, or Italian Catholics, or Swiss Protestants, or Russian Orthodox) if old social patterns were torn down and democracy or freethinking were given free play? Would there not be great confusion, upheaval, and spiritual loss? The problem of negotiating change so that a group both preserved the traditions that had served it well in the past and honored the truths becoming apparent in present experiences was very weighty. The more one wants a culture that is profound and beautiful, a social group that is confident about its place in the overall scheme of things and full of peace and joy, the more one can sympathize with the elders who thought that relinquishing the rules about a kosher diet or the customs about how to run the Sunday worship service would do more harm than good. Equally, however, the more one has chafed under outmoded notions, feeling that they were crushing creativity and freedom, the more one can sympathize with critics and reformers.

Religious ideas tend to gain their weathered look by having passed through the storms of debate generated by the conflict between conservatives and progressives. For while it might seem that ideas about God, human nature, the ultimate sanctions for customs, worship, and the like ought to be immune from casual change, in fact such ideas are influenced by every bit of significant change that an individual or a group undergoes. Let there be a new hypothesis about the origin or construction of nebulae and a reevaluation of the traditional theology of creation is immediately suggested. Let there be a new finding in the area of genetic engineering and a new ethical question is sure to arise. When a nation begins debating its ways and means of educating its youth, because of dismal statistics about literacy or fears it is losing its competitive edge in international business, that nation is nearly certain to hear some reflective people reminding it that the deeper question probably concerns its priorities: How important does it consider its obligation to launch the next generation toward a productive and happy life? How does this obligation compare to the obligation to defend its shores against external enemies, or to rid its ghettos of drugs, or to provide full medical care for its elderly? If one continues with questions of this sort, and does not turn aside because of fatigue, fear, or challenges to the superficial thinking that dominates most political activity, one is bound to come upon explicitly religious issues. For what have human beings been given existence? In what terms ought a society to calculate the good life? Who are the models of ripe humanity that one's group ought to follow? Does anything that mortal human beings do really matter in the final analysis, since all of us are bound to end up in the grave?

Religious thought has its real home in questions of this latter type. In our opinion, the religious thought that has been most influential throughout human history has never been far from poetry and mysticism. In the final analysis, the human mind in and of itself cannot handle the task that wisdom sets it. Wisdom is necessary because people need direction, because as one ages one wonders what makes life (which so often is painful) worthwhile, because nature and human beings alike never cease giving one reason to wonder, even to be shocked, by either their beauty or their cruelty. Yet what people seek when they pursue wisdom takes them into the whole of their situation and condition. They want to know how the world got going, where it is going to end, what can justify trying to live honestly and kindly, what resources might enable them to overcome pain, injustice, death, and moral ugliness (sin: evil freely chosen). But people can never know such things, can never get answers to such questions, in linear, factual terms. There is no proposition that can carry all the experiential weight (emotional, intellectual, physical) enfolded in the wonder and pain behind our deepest puzzling. So the "answers" that have been most prized in human history are the sayings that give the mysteriousness of the human condition its due. Such sayings have told people to quiet their minds and listen to the silence that might be the speech of their God. They have told people to love (profoundly, selflessly) and do what they felt best. They have said that the way that can be spoken about cannot be the real, ultimate way to think about, to try to deal with, ultimate reality.

From these sayings, which have tended to be enshrined in writings called sacred (scriptures), religious thought has received the counsel to make itself theology: faith seeking understanding. One had to believe in the priority of the mysteriousness of the human condition, had to accept one's death and finitude, if one were ever going to think correctly and wisely about the human condition. Be it childrearing, education, politics, economics, health care, or the arts, one would only think wisely if one situated one's reflection in the context of how in fact the most admirable people had managed to survive, become admirable, or end up with a well-deserved reputation for honesty and love. Only the mind tied, bound, to the most basic fact about the human condition, its mysteriousness, would ever be truly religious, and thus dependable when it came to matters of greatest moment. Thus for most traditional peoples religious thought bore on the acts of faith necessary for the group to make its way from birth to death hopefully, expecting more good than evil.[1]

American History

If one considers applying these notions associated with "religious thought" to Americans, one finds that they apply, but only with notable qualifications. The history of human beings in what is now the United States began over ten thousand years ago, when Asiatic peoples crossed the Bering Strait and started to fill the continent. The majority of these native Americans lived in tribes whose religious thought was mythic, ceremonial, and shamanistic. It was mythic in the sense that stories dominated people's minds—stories of how the world had arisen, or how the buffalo came to serve the people's needs, or where the human spirit went at death. It was ceremonial, in the sense that the great experiences unifying the tribe tended to be the rituals it enacted regularly. In their singing and dancing and remembering the stories by which they situated themselves in the world, these peoples reaffirmed constantly their identity as Hopi or Shawmut or Pawnee. Native American religious thought was shamanistic in the sense that the ecstasy—the going out of ordinary consciousness to a different, spiritual world—characteristic of shamans provided the most personal verifications of traditional tribal beliefs. In giving their people ethical guidance, or curing the sick, or guiding the souls of the dead to their resting place, native American spiritual leaders shared characteristics associated with shamans the world over.

The whites who came to North America in the sixteenth century were mainly Christians, first Spanish and French Catholics and then, early in the seventeenth century, British Protestants. Despite the influence of the Protestant Reformation, the faith of these whites was more traditional than modern. Thus, for the first two hundred years of white experience in what is now the United States, the centrality of Christ for salvation was taken for granted. "Salvation" meant mainly rescue from the disfavor of God caused by sin. "Sin," in turn, meant mainly offense against God. White religious thought certainly dealt with many other topics, but its center tended to be the question of how to gain a proper relationship with God, which could keep one from suffering hellfire and gain one admittance to heaven.

In the colonies that became the matrix of the United States, the great early influence was the brand of Protestant (Reformed) theology known as Calvinism. John Calvin (1509–1565), a second generation Reformation giant, had led a Reformed community in Geneva, Switzerland, and written the leading Reformed text, *The Institutes of Christian Religion.* Despite the presence of Anglicans, Quakers, Catholics, and others whose notion of "reformed" religion was not strictly Calvinistic, the convictions about the depravity of human nature and the need for divine grace that Calvinism placed at the center of Christian life dominated the Puritanism that was the most powerful early American ideology. Indeed, the impact of the New England thinkers who articulated that Puritanism was such that virtually all treatments of the origins of American culture give Puritanism center stage. Begun in England as a movement to purify the Anglican church of Roman Catholic usages, Puritanism evolved on American soil into a full theory and practice of the Christian life. In the seventeenth century it articulated both how the individual ought to pursue a devout life and how the community, religious and civil (one could distinguish the two but not separate them), ought to govern itself.

By the time of the American Revolution the Enlightenment movement that had matured in Europe had become a great influence on leading American thinkers. From George Washington and Benjamin Franklin to Thomas Jefferson and James Madison, the emancipation of reason from religious authority that had been the hallmark of the European Enlightenment had gained solid support in the American colonies. The English philosopher John Locke was the greatest initial influence, and many of the founding fathers of the United States were convinced that freedom of conscience (to believe and worship as one wished) was one of the most fundamental human rights. Equally, many of the founding fathers were more comfortable with a Deistic religion, according to which the God of the Bible ought to be supplanted by a more general deity (called by some the "Architect of the Universe"), than with a traditional Christianity that considered Jesus Christ to be the divine Word of God enfleshed.[2]

Even before the American Revolution, during the Great Awakening that stirred New England in the 1740s, the seeds of the revivalism that would become a regular feature of the American religious landscape were sown. After the Revolution, as the country expanded westward, an evangelical and revivalist Christianity was probably the most powerful religious force. What people tried to "revive" was the intensity of their religious faith, and so of their experiential grounds for optimism or hope that they would be saved. They tended to be "evangelical" in looking to the Christian gospel (*euangellion* in Greek) for such a revival of their faith, and in prefering the plain, literal words of the Bible to any learned interpretations.

By the time of the American Civil War the impact of both black slaves, originally imported from Africa, and non-British Europeans had become so powerful that it could not be ignored. Slaves had become essential to the agrarian society that prevailed in the South, while Irish, German, and Jewish immigrants had all diversified the character of the urban centers of the North. No longer was the United States simply a venture in redoing British culture without the tyranny of a monarchy. Now it had become a venture in unifying diverse ethnic groups sufficiently to manage a national life. Native Americans continued to be either abused or ignored, and African Americans were not considered fully human, but the non-British immigrants were challenging many established patterns. Within a few generations, they had become political powers in the northeastern and midwestern cities. After the Civil War, immigration (much of it from Eastern Europe) greatly increased, so that by the end of the nineteenth century the United States had become a welter of different tongues and ethnic traditions.

During the twentieth century the United States continued to accept immigrants, to finalize its borders, and to gain greater influence in world affairs. A theme as old as the New England colonies, God's "providential" work for Americans, inspired leaders such as President Woodrow Wilson to think that the United States was the world's great hope. Just as many European colonizers had gone to Africa, India, and Asia thinking that whites had the obligation to instruct lesser cultures, so many American leaders assumed that American righteousness justified the application of American might to world affairs. The American role in the two world wars of the first half of the twentieth century consolidated this assumption, as did the American stance in the cold war of the 1950s and 1960s that pitted democratic against communist forces.

Through this long history, the initial white imperative to religious thought changed considerably. Whereas in the beginning the question was how best to think about the salvation offered in Jesus Christ, various modern intellectual movements, and the nation's own diversification, changed America's religious culture. Asian and Latin-American immigrants further complicated the American scene, as did the increasing internationalization of business and world affairs. New technologies greatly altered human beings' relations with nature, while the intellectual elite became disaffected from religion.[3] The result was that American religious thought tended to slip away from its original focus on Jesus Christ and concentrate on how to speak to a pragmatic, this-worldly citizenry about the ultimate implications of its secular culture or technological outlook. Jesus Christ has continued to be the great interest of passionate Christians (many of them evangelicals), but today American religious thought as a whole is not centered on Christ.

The Mainstream and the Margins

The easiest way to write the story of American religious history is to concentrate on the white, Anglo-Saxon, Protestant group that dominated the colonial venture, engineered the Revolution, established the Constitution, and until recently dominated political, economic, and cultural life. Whether or not this group continues to determine American cultural trends (and one could make a strong argument that it does), it seems beyond dispute that it has wielded the formative influences in American history, both civic and religious.

On the other hand, when historians look more closely at the white, Anglo-Saxon, Protestant group that is the best candidate for the title "The American Mainstream," they find considerable diversity. Just to mention the religious aspects of this diversity, one encounters Congregationalists, Presbyterians, Baptists, Anglicans, Episcopalians, Methodists, and numerous other churches. Each has a history justifying its establishment as a distinctive group, and each has a distinct theology and contribution to the overall complexion of American religion. Who, then, constitutes the Protestant "mainstream?" How precisely can one determine the power wielded by Episcopalians and Presbyterians in contrast to the power wielded by

Baptists and Methodists? Is the notion of a "religious mainstream" not as much a hindrance to appreciating what actually has gone on in American religious history and thought as it is a help?

This question is only amplified when one turns to the impact of the groups that were not white, Anglo-Saxon, or Protestant. African Americans and Catholics, Jews and Asians, Eastern Europeans and Latin Americans—all have certainly fallen outside the American mainstream, at least during their early years in this country, but sometimes their influence on a given city has been greater than that of the supposedly white Protestant establishment. In coming to appreciate the diversity of what it has meant to be a religious American, scholars have recently cast considerable doubt on both the notion that America created a "melting pot" that boiled away ethnic or religious differences and the notion that a white Protestant mainstream was the center of all the significant evolution.[4]

The final complication we have to mention concerns the role of religious women in American history and culture. With the rise of interest in women's history, the study of American religion has broadened to include the contributions made by women in all the American eras—Colonial, Revolutionary, Civil War, the twentieth century. In some cases such women appear to have accepted the main tenets of their religious group, and so to have more supported the general impact of Presbyterian, or Catholic, or Jewish, or African-American religion than to have diversified it. In other cases women have modified their own tradition, challenged it, or started a new tradition. For example, Ann Lee founded the Shakers and Mary Baker Eddy founded Christian Science. So nowadays it is necessary to qualify statements about the impact of a given idea, or thinker, or movement by asking whether American women received it and used it differently from the ways that American men did.[5]

Despite all the difficulties posed by the concepts of the mainstream and the margins, books such as this are nearly bound to employ them. If one wants to discuss notions that seem to have been at the heart of American religious thought, one is bound to concentrate on the groups that advanced such ideas and saw to it that they gained prominence. Fortunately, the influence of an idea is not directly tied to the actual power that a group associated with it may have had at a given time or place. Ideas such as those that we are going to study (the Puritan notions of human nature and religious calling, the Enlightenment conceptions of religious freedom and God, and the Pragmatic idea of the primacy of experience and action) spun away from the groups that originally launched them in America, taking on a life of their own. One can argue that they became part of the cultural mainstream without necessarily arguing that their original sponsors controlled all of their influence. In fact their original sponsors were white, Anglo-Saxon, Protestant, and male, but these ideas have nevertheless become part of the life of African-American, Catholic, Jewish, female, and Asian communities.

The interplay between the mainstream and the margins therefore has been subtle, especially concerning ideas. Not all Americans have accepted what the Puritans, or those shaped by the Enlightenment, or the Pragmatists said, but all Americans have been greatly influenced by what they had to say. For example, since the creation of the Constitution, all Americans have lived in a nation that does not have an established religion. That was a novelty in the eighteenth century, and it has led to the distinctively American concern regarding the separation of church and state. As another example, since the beginning of the twentieth century all Americans have had to deal with an articulated conviction that deeds and results are more significant than theories. Perhaps this conviction goes back much further in American history, but after the work of philosophers such as C. S. Peirce, William James, and John Dewey it gained new force. Even newcomers such as the Asians and Latin Americans who have appeared in the second half of the twentieth century have had to contend with this conviction, so powerfully has it shaped American attitudes toward work and politics (and religion).

One cannot expect precision when dealing with the relationship between the generation and the reception of a significant idea in the mainstream of a culture and its reception on the margins. Still, it is useful to consider the idea from both points of view, because this brings it into sharper focus. And if it is a significant idea, this sharper focus in turn becomes a key to understanding the culture in question. In addition to sharpening the intrinsic interest the idea may carry, clarifying it enables one to fashion hypotheses about the character of the culture in question— the convictions, the ways of regarding the world, that give that culture its unique identity. So people writing about the English, or the Italians, or the Spanish, or the French find themselves searching for typical traits, typical ways of construing social relationships, and so forth. Similarly, people writing about the Chinese or the Americans find themselves searching for ideas and beliefs that, if not completely distinctive, nonetheless typify the way that Chinese or American culture usually works.

That is our interest in the interactions between the mainstream and the margins generated by major religious ideas that have shaped American culture. We hope that by first presenting a significant idea in the terms that it originally possessed (and has tended to retain) in the mainstream, and then reflecting on how that idea has looked when viewed from the margins, we may develop a provocative essay about American religious thought. One might use different ideas than those we have chosen to use, and one might think differently about the varying groups that had to come to grips with these ideas. But unless one is dealing with religious ideas that changed the lives of both the power holders and those on the fringes of official power, one is not writing a book that says anything significant about American religious thought.

In a later section we describe more precisely how we intend to structure our essay. Here it should be enough to have planted the seed of our dialectical procedure. We are interested in the religious ideas that have helped to make American culture what it has become. We are interested in the reasons why such ideas came into being and how they expanded or flattened when groups other than those who launched them or believed in them had to deal with them. The end product of our reflections should be a challenge to reexamine such central ideas as the prevailing American conceptions of human nature, community, God, and truth, all of which hold great significance for the future of American culture.

Puritanism, Enlightenment, and Pragmatism

The three sources of leading religious ideas that we consider are Puritanism, Enlightenment, and Pragmatism. Puritanism dominated the first 150 years of American religious life, in the sense that in that period it produced the most influential view of human nature, including the fittingness of human beings' entering into covenants (contracts). Some analysts offer the opinion that Puritanism got so deeply into the marrow of American culture that long after the New England communities where it had flourished ceased to exist as religio-secular unities their Puritan sense of human selfishness continued to shape American literature, America's ventures in education, and American political instincts.[6]

The impact of the Enlightenment may have been narrower, in that only the intellectual elite of the revolutionary generation was enthusiastic about the views of God and human conscience proposed by the Enlightenment thinkers. On the other hand, inasmuch as that elite included the founding fathers who set the new nation's cultural course, the impact of the Enlightenment has run very deep in the United States. By separating the religious and civic spheres, at least when it came to determining constitutional rights, the framers of America's basic law determined that American culture would be secular and pluralistic. This ran against the grain of premodern religious and political thought, as it runs against the grain of prevailing Muslim religious and political thought today. It opened the United States to the likelihood that its culture would never have the depth and unity of cultures that could gather their citizens under the standard of a single set of convictions about divinity and human destiny. And it prepared the way for later intellectual elites that would repudiate the notion of God and despise popular religion, because they found them irrelevant to the daily business of scientific research, or artistic creation, or higher education, or running governmental offices, or furthering industrial progress.

Last, the influence of the Enlightenment shows negatively in the backlash associated with conservative if not fundamentalist religion. Throughout American history millions of people have been at odds with the secular assumptions of their nation's constitutional code, because they have found their center in the Bible and church circles that taught them to confess Jesus Christ as their Lord and Savior. They could be grateful to their land for letting them exercise their religious faith as they saw fit, but they had to feel alien to the unreligious options that others exercised, and to the constitutional proposition (as they saw it) that freedom to choose is more important than obeying God. All of this became convoluted, and many conservative religious people accounted themselves the most patriotic Americans. But deep in the fabric of American culture was woven an unavoidable tension between the nonestablishment of religion that the founding fathers derived from the Enlightenment, and the primacy of God that the Puritans and their evangelical successors derived from their biblical faith.

Pragmatism provides our third cluster of ideas that have shaped American culture and character considerably. As associated with American philosophers of the late nineteenth and early twentieth century, Pragmatism is a sophisticated view of the primacy of action over thought and the legitimacy of determining truth by analyzing what works. In this case "what works" admits of many shadings, and Pragmatism need not be merely utilitarian—merely concerned with an obvious or vulgar success that one would measure in terms of money, social status, or medals of various sorts. The roots of Pragmatism may lie in biblical culture, inasmuch as both the Old and the New Testament show a preference for deeds over abstract ideas. Thus 1 John 3:17–19 became a beloved text: "But if any one has the world's goods and sees his brother in need, yet closes his heart against him, how does God's love abide in him? Little children, let us not love in word or speech but in deed and in truth. By this we shall know that we are of the truth, and reassure our hearts before him." The New England Puritans were much concerned to reassure their hearts before God, sensitive as they were to the selfishness in the human heart that always rendered its salvation problematic. Many of them therefore liked the notion of a "practical syllogism," according to which one could argue that salvation showed itself in virtuous living, that they themselves were living virtuously, and so that they themselves could be hopeful about salvation.

Another possible source of American Pragmatism lay in the failure of the Enlightenment thinkers to secure the trustworthiness of human understanding. Whether one read David Hume or Immanuel Kant, one found human understanding to be unequal to the task of providing sure judgments about the existence of God, the immortality of the soul, the freedom of the human will, and other convictions that had been crucial to traditional European culture. Kant summarized the findings of the Enlightenment thinkers by postulating such convictions as necessary for morality—for the virtuous action on which society depended. This in turn gave the priority to action, praxis, what people actually did, when it came to determining where they stood, what was their worth. More significant than what they said or thought were their deeds, so in their deeds must lie the strongest truth about their lives.

When one combines this intellectual background with the practical tasks Americans faced in building a huge new nation, it is easy to see why focusing on action became a hallmark of the American mentality. Americans came to think of themselves as doers, achievers, people who rolled up their sleeves, got their hands dirty, and solved problems. Only when the world became truly international, and nature became truly ecological, and it became recognized that America's own cultural problems were impossibly complicated did the pragmatic mentality on which the nation had depended come up for serious reconsideration. Even then, neither the priority that some branches of Christianity had given to contemplation,[7] nor the priority that other cultures had given to thought, became serious alternatives for the majority of Americans. Even then, the American instinct was that one solved problems such as widespread addiction to cocaine by throwing money into practical programs and patching up a few tears in the American sense of values. To say that a wholesale conversion to the primacy of the spiritual life (thinking about wisdom, dedicating oneself to scientific or artistic creativity, praying to God) was the more profound answer would only bring one looks of incomprehension, whether in the White House or on Main Street.

We shall be interested in both the origins and the inner consequences of the ideas that we are associating with Puritanism, the Enlightenment, and Pragmatism. In this book we shall examine both how they took shape in representative figures such as Jonathan Edwards, Thomas Jefferson, and William James, and how they fit with convictions flourishing outside the white, Anglo-Saxon, Protestant, male mainstream. Although it will be useful to clarify the original intent of the ideas we reflect upon, our deeper interest will lie with the ideas themselves: their assumptions, their further consequences, the gains and losses one can associate with them. As they impact upon a given culture, ideas lose their detached quality and become forces for stability or change, for hope or discouragement, for depth or triviality. Inasmuch as American culture has not been distinguished for its contemplative depth, such ideas as the depravity of human nature, the priority of individual liberty over religious consensus, and the primacy of action have worked more effects than most Americans have realized. If we can heighten awareness of such effects, and increase in our readers the attractiveness of contemplation, we shall count our labors worthwhile.

———

This book, therefore, examines the appropriation of certain religious ideas that, arguably, have greatly contributed to the molding of the American character. It is not so much a historical analysis of the rise of Puritan ideas about human nature, or of Enlightenment ideas about disestablishing religion, or of Pragmatic ideas about religious pluralism, as it is a reflective *engagement* with such ideas.

After exposing the origins of the ideas with which we are concerned, we shall concretize them by focusing on representative figures whom they informed, and who in turn furthered them. The three such representative figures we have chosen are Jonathan Edwards, Thomas Jefferson, and William James. Jonathan Edwards, preacher and theologian, is usually accounted the greatest American theologian—certainly the most original and seminal figure. In his hands, Puritanism became a prod to a sensitive and profound exploration of human nature. Because Edwards was so brilliant, and so closely associated with the Great Awakening that is perhaps the most striking phenomenon in American religious history, he stands as a watershed. After him, anyone seeking to understand either Puritanism or American views of human nature and destiny had to come to grips with what Edwards had written.

Thomas Jefferson needs little introduction. Author of the Declaration of Independence, first secretary of state, third president, and founder of what he hoped would be a model university in Virginia, Jefferson was the most versatile intellectual of his day. In him one found the complete representative of the Enlightenment, of the American Revolution, and of the efforts of the new nation to place individual rights, especially those focused on religious liberty, at the center of American culture. When Jefferson wrote that he wanted to be remembered for three things: writing the Declaration of Independence, authoring Virginia's statute on religious liberty, and founding the University of Virginia, he gave his own assessment of the priorities in his life. He thought of himself as a spokesman for ideas, among which freedom from tyranny (whether the tyranny of the monarchical state or the tyranny of the established church) was paramount. Jefferson's further conviction was that unless Americans were sufficiently educated to bear the burdens that a democracy placed upon its citizens, the enterprise known as the United States would not prosper. He therefore relied upon the capacity of human beings to learn why they should prefer democracy to other political systems and honor liberty of conscience as a first good. In these convictions he was a brilliant descendant of the Enlightenment and a beacon to idealistic Americans of all succeeding generations.

William James, coming from a prominent Boston family, distinguished himself first as a psychologist and then as a philosopher. Inasmuch as he popularized the ideas of Pragmatism, writing so brilliantly that he made the convictions of this movement about the primacy of experience, the crucial place of action in determining truth, and the pluralism of humanity's experience of divinity widely known and respected, James was the great mediator of Pragmatism to the mainstream of American culture. After him John Dewey extended ideas rooted in Pragmatism to education, and other aspects of American culture, but James was the one who first tussled with the implications that Pragmatism bore for traditional religious faith. Accepting the dethronement of Puritanism that was implicit in the work of Jefferson, and the marginalization of Christian ideas that had occurred among the intelligentsia during the second half of the nineteenth century, when natural science began to reveal its extraordinary potential for changing people's sense of the universe, James struggled to work out a defense of religious experience that would play true to its vast influence and depth.

When he wrote of the varieties of religious experience, James showed himself sensitive to the revelations that the mystics and saints had received—revelations pertinent to any fair-minded assessment of human nature. On the other hand, James had less sympathy for the understanding of God and the world that undergirded most of the traditional interpretations of religious experience. So he labored to elaborate a new metaphysical standpoint, according to which variety would have rights at least equal to those of unity. In other words, James found the notion of divinity acceptable but not the notion of monotheism. People certainly experienced something otherworldly, something well labeled a holiness or divinity, but it was not certain that such people experienced the One God spotlighted by the Bible.

It will be our pleasure to consider ideas such as those we have associated with Edwards, Jefferson, and James, trying to clarify both the implications they carried in those giants' own day and the implications they carry nowadays. It will also be our pleasure to consider how these ideas have sounded when caught by the ears of people on the margins of the mainstream that Edwards, Jefferson, and James represented. What have Catholics and Jews made of the depravity of human nature associated with Jonathan Edwards and Puritanism? How does the disestablishment of religion associated with Jefferson ring today in the ears of Muslims, Buddhists, and others coming to America from cultures that have not accepted the modern split between the religious and the secular? When women and African Americans consider the variety of religious experience, or the Pragmatic proposition that truth emerges in action, what do they tend to think? By trying to retrieve or imagine such reactions from the margins, we hope to get a second appreciation of the ideas that Edwards, Jefferson, and James helped make formative of the typical American's personality.

The point to our overall exercise probably is patent, but perhaps it still deserves commentary. Inasmuch as ideas such as those we study have been potent in the past, they reveal much of the pathway that the United States traveled on the way to its present cultural configurations regarding religion. Since these ideas are intrinsically interesting—thoughts begotten and carried along in formidable traditions, such as Puritanism and the Enlightenment, thoughts that would command attention regardless of their parentage—they can stimulate us to think hard about how we ourselves want to understand human nature, or want to understand the proper function of religion in civil life, or want to understand the relationship between contemplation and action.

For many people in America, these latter considerations are luxuries. Only those not pressed by practical affairs are likely to have the leisure in which to probe them. For a few other Americans, however, thinking about either the foundations of the typically American construct of religious experience or about human nature, individual and social, is the sine qua non of responsible citizenship. Unless at least a critical mass of people have well-founded opinions about why their fellow citizens should or should not be trusted to have good spontaneous instincts, or about why it is wise to make government the friend of religion in general but the patron of no religious tradition in particular, or about why one is more likely to learn the real proportions of the world by plunging in than by sitting back to reflect, then the whole country is liable to muck about with no direction. Indeed, it is liable to lack even a rudimentary mechanism for evaluating its trials and errors.

So our own satisfaction in this enterprise is the stimulus to entertain and perhaps clarify the matters that must be considered if any American citizen is to come to a reasoned appreciation of the religious heritage and present prospects lying before him or her. We have enjoyed thinking in the footsteps of the three trailblazers we shall study, and we have enjoyed thinking from the margins about what else ought to be said.

NOTES

1. For a representative study of the term "religion," see Winston L. King, "Religion," in *The Encyclopedia of Religion*, ed. Mircea Eliade (New York: Macmillan, 1987), vol. 12, pp. 282–293. On how scholars have tended to deal with American religion, see Henry Warner Bowden, "The Historiography of American Religion," in *Encyclopedia of the American Religious Experience*, ed. Charles H. Lippy and Peter W. Williams (New York: Charles Scribner's Sons, 1988), vol. 1, pp. 3–16.

2. See Edwin Scott Gaustad, *Faith of Our Fathers* (San Francisco: Harper & Row, 1986).

3. See Michael J. Buckley, S.J., "Experience and Culture: A Point of Departure for American Atheism," *Theological Studies*, vol. 50, no. 3 (September, 1989), pp. 443–465.

4. See R. Laurence Moore, *Religious Outsiders and the Making of Americans* (New York: Oxford University Press, 1986).

5. See Rosemary Radford Ruether and Rosemary Skinner Keller, eds., *Women & Religion in America*, 3 vols. (San Francisco: Harper & Row, 1981).

6. See Daniel Walker Howe, "The Impact of Puritanism on American Culture," in *Encyclopedia of the American Religious Experience*, vol. 2, pp. 1057–1074.

7. For examples of a nonpragmatic approach to Jesus Christ, see John Meyendorff, "New Life in Christ: Salvation in Orthodox Theology," *Theological Studies*, vol. 50, no. 3 (September, 1989), pp. 481–499.

Part One

THE
PURITAN
FOUNDATIONS

Chapter 2

Jonathan Edwards and Human Nature

New England Puritanism

The settlers who came to the New England colonies in the first half of the seventeenth century were most formed by their repugnance for Anglican ceremonies. English Puritanism had begun as a movement to purify the established church of styles of worship and government that the purifiers deemed unbiblical and/or papist. Whereas the established, Anglican church was attempting a middle road between Roman Catholic ceremonies and the changes introduced by the continental Reformers (above all by the Calvinists), the Puritans wanted a simpler, plainer path hewing to what they took to be pristine Christian rituals.

John Calvin was the theological father of the Puritans, and in his writings they could find a clear rationale for making the Bible the supreme authority in Christian life, for downplaying the authority of bishops and monarchs, and for considering human nature so depraved that, apart from the grace of God given in Jesus Christ, it was fit only for hellfire. The Calvinist God was the sovereign controller of the universe, guiding all things by his providential will. Worship of this God begot not only awe at his majesty but also freedom from all human tyrannies. One had to believe that the love of God would triumph over God's wrath, but the Bible gave one many reasons for such a belief. And one had to covenant together with like-minded Christians ("saints"), if one wanted the security of belonging to a community dedicated to obeying the sovereign will of the divine King. Certainly the Calvinists paid attention to the priestly and prophetic roles of the deity and his Christ, but most prominent was the kingly role. It fell to church leaders to dispense such discipline as the saints required to serve their King well, and those truly on the path to salvation would receive correction gladly, in good heart, knowing it could only benefit them.

When Charles I gained the English throne in 1625, many English Puritans lost heart. Charles supported the church party led by William Laud, which wanted to soften the strictness of Calvinist tenets about human nature and salvation. Their position was known as Arminianism, because it derived from the teachings of Jacob Arminius (1560–1609), a Dutch reformer who had challenged Calvinist positions about human freedom and proposed a more optimistic view of human nature. The Puritans who emigrated to New England objected to Laud's Arminianism, deciding to seek a situation in which they could exercise their faith in all the strictness they felt it required.

The New England Puritans gave considerable authority to the lay members of the local church, and from their original political arrangements came the tradition known as Congregationalism. The congregation called the minister to serve in their church, had a say in the ordination of ministers, and provided the minister his salary. The notion was that the local church rested on the religious experiences of its members as its basic foundation. Conversing together about their religious experiences, members convenanted to form a church when they determined that at least seven of them had been worked upon by divine grace. The tradition developed that full church members would be those who had related their experience of the work of grace in their souls. The guiding conviction was that without such grace no one could obey the commandments of God and receive salvation.

The experience of grace might have an ecstatic or dramatic character, but as the reports ("relations") available from the 1630s and 1640s suggest, the more significant note was the person's ongoing tendency to find hope for salvation in the impact that scriptural passages had upon him or her. So, the "saints" who constituted the inner core of the local church were those who were moved by Scripture and supported in their efforts to obey God's commandments. Those who could not relate experiences of such movement could not be full church members. All citizens were taxed to support the local church, and all were expected to attend church services, but only the saints were full members. The very basis of the original

Massachusetts towns was the members' covenanting together to form a society bound by obedience to God. From this obedience could come the mutual respect and love that would make their town prosper.

The fact that significant numbers of the town members could not or would not become full church members created both theological and political problems. As time passed and the children and grandchildren of the original convenanters became potential church members, it became clear that church leaders had to rethink what they were doing. The question of baptism concretized some of the issues. Baptism was the sign of the new covenant that Christ had created between God and human beings. What did it mean if people baptized as children never showed in their adult lives the evidence of divine grace? If they did not keep God's commandments, or if they did not feel the movements of grace, or if they were not strengthened by reading Scripture and hearing it expounded in church sermons, what did their faith or church membership amount to? A "Half-way Covenant" fashioned in Massachusetts in 1662 sought a compromise answer. Those baptizing their children had to "own" the original covenant in the minimal sense of acknowledging the obligations that their own parents had contracted on their behalf, such as accepting church doctrine and living without scandal. They might not have the inner experiences of grace, but if they did not disturb the outer arrangements that the saints prescribed for church order, they could be considered partial church members (and thus unsuspicious citizens).

To generate piety in their members, churches encouraged daily devotions and weekly spiritual meetings. They also sponsored regular Sunday sermons, the main burden of which was how to continue to grow in divine grace. The great danger, as the leading preachers saw it, was hypocrisy. People could profess full faith but not actually possess it. They could even deceive themselves, not knowing their own state of soul. Thus ministers urged members to examine their consciences and follow the rhythm of dying to sin and rising to grace that the death and resurrection of Christ had made normative for Christian faith. The great task of life was disposing oneself to the divine grace that alone could work one's salvation. Inasmuch as this grace was thought to show itself in signs, both interior and exterior, the discernment of the signs of grace was a major Puritan preoccupation.

As early as 1636 some members of the Massachusetts Bay Colony challenged its focus on the signs of grace, arguing that such a focus begot a stress on works that ran counter to the gospel, as the Protestant Reformers had interpreted it. In the Reformers' interpretation, it was not what people did ("works") that brought them salvation but only their faith, which could never be fully calculated. Anne Hutchinson was banished from the Bay Colony for her challenges, which were considered "antinomian" (lawless). Another challenger, Roger Williams, moved to Providence, in what became Rhode Island, to establish a community open to people of all religious convictions (not just those citizens willing to subscribe to the Massachusetts orthodoxy). Williams became a Baptist, arguing that only the saints (mature Christians of manifest religious experience) should undergo the formal sign of covenant with God.

During the second half of the seventeenth century many New England Puritans began to consider the previous years a golden age, when piety was more fervent and the ideals of the covenant were better realized. Ministers frequently preached what came to be known as "Jeremiads": sermons in the tradition of the prophet Jeremiah that lamented the backsliding of the present generation. After 1691 the English imposed toleration on the Bay Colony, so it could no longer make membership in the Congregational church a condition of citizenship. That meant that Baptists and Quakers could not be banished from the colony because of their deviant faith (though they could be taxed to support the established Congregational church). Thus a crack appeared in the fusion of citizenship and church membership that the Puritans had made the basis of their covenant with one another.[1]

The Life of Jonathan Edwards

Jonathan Edwards (1703–1758) was the son of Timothy Edwards, a Puritan pastor in East Windsor, Connecticut. His mother, Esther Stoddard, was the daughter of Solomon Stoddard, an eminent pastor in Northampton, Massachusetts. Jonathan was the fifth of 11 children (and the only boy). He grew up in a household dominated by Puritan ideals, and it seemed fated that he would follow the family tradition of entering the ministry. However, his early interests included natural science, especially the physics of Isaac Newton, and he was a keen observer of natural phenomena, including the habits of insects. Throughout his life, he maintained an interest in the philosophy of nature and tried to keep abreast of the latest scientific discoveries.

Jonathan was educated at home and then, at age 13, sent to Yale College in New Haven, Connecticut. He graduated in 1720, at the age of 16, and remained at Yale for two more years, for theological studies. During 1722–23 he served a church in New York, and in 1723 he received his M.A.

degree. The years 1724–26 found him working as a tutor at Yale, but in 1727 he became associated with his grandfather in the pastorate of the church in Northampton. There in 1727 he married Sarah Pierrepont, whom he came to regard as an exemplary Christian, and together they had 11 children.

In childhood Jonathan Edwards struggled with the Calvinist notions of predestination that predominated in New England Puritan congregations. According to these notions, God assigns some people to hell and some to heaven, partly in virtue of God's free choice and partly in virtue of God's knowledge of people's merits. This predestination cannot compromise the divine justice, but it brings home the elementary fact that of themselves (apart from divine mercy and grace) human beings deserve to suffer the punishments of hellfire. In other words, of themselves human beings are deeply wicked, so that in speaking of human nature (in distinction from what human beings receive by grace) one has to stress both rebellion against God and depravity. Gradually Jonathan worked out an intellectual compromise with this Puritan orthodoxy, but his first instinct had been to question its justice. The crucial event in his passage was a conversion experience in 1721, which impressed upon him the reality of the sovereignty of God and the splendor of God's glory. In other words, because he had glimpsed or tasted the reality of God—how God is separate from and far above every creature—the need to place the fate of human beings in God's hands seemed delightful rather than oppressive. This experience led Edwards to distinguish between merely notional understanding of God, which is limited to correct concepts, and an experiential understanding directly imparted to the soul in times of grace. The distinction would play an important role in Edwards's defense of the Great Awakening in the years to come.

By 1734, when he had long reflected on his conversion experience, Edwards was convinced that the supernatural light in which it had consisted was what gives worth to a human being and constitutes salvation. Thus, without the experience of such supernatural light one's salvation had to be in question. His conversion also convinced Edwards that whatever God does is correct: as done by God, any divine action has to be excellent. The divine being is simply goodness and love, so the divine action must also be for the best. Therefore, in his sermons Edwards urged his parishioners to try to love God purely, for what God is in himself (Edwards used what one might now consider patriarchal language, construing the divinity as masculine), rather than for the benefits that God might bestow upon his creatures, including even the great benefit of salvation. In a related fashion, in his ethical teachings Edwards placed the Christian ideal in a universal benevolence that would imitate the God who makes his rain to fall and his sun to shine on just and unjust alike.

Edwards read assiduously throughout his career and wrote equally assiduously. Among his favorite sources were such English philosophical scientists as John Locke and Isaac Newton. These authors, along with the school known as the Cambridge Platonists, led Edwards to stress that things only exist to the degree that they are ideas in the mind of God. The sovereignty that one should associate with the divine will regarding salvation has its parallel in the primacy of the divine mind in assuring the existence of creation. Using the psychology that Locke had developed, which stressed the role of sensation in generating human knowledge, Edwards worked out a view of religious knowledge that made it quite directly dependent on the direct revelation of God. When God makes such a revelation, as when God moves the will toward conversion, the human recipient cannot resist. All of the priority belongs to God, as befits the divine supremacy. This was traditional Calvinist teaching, and the theology that Edwards steadily elaborated tended to imitate Calvin's in reasoning from a fundamental awe before the divine majesty. Edwards believed that God's will is that human beings be saved, and that the experience of salvation constitutes the greatest fulfillment the human personality can know. Thus he was able to preach with complete conviction about the beauty of serving God.

At the death of Solomon Stoddard in 1729 Edwards assumed sole charge of the church in Northampton, which at the time was second only to Boston in ecclesiastical significance. He became known as a powerful theologian, and one of his inferences from the sovereignty of God was that when human fortunes go bad the cause has to be religious failure and the remedy repentance. The covenant that God had made with New England was like the Mosaic covenant in justifying this linkage between sin and punishment. In 1734 Edwards's preaching, especially a sermon dealing with justification by faith alone, led to a revival of religious commitment in Northampton and along the Connecticut Valley. Some historians account this revival the beginning of the Great Awakening in New England. Overwhelmed by witnessing more than three hundred people make professions of faith, Edwards described the entire experience in a work (*A Faithful Narrative of the Surprising Work of God*) published in 1737, adding to the influence of the original event by advertising it widely. His description was read in England as well as the other American colonies, and it established his skill at detailing the psychology of conversion.

During the years 1740–42 the preaching of the English evangelist George Whitefield precipitated the Great Awakening that shook all the colonies. Edwards's most famous sermon, "Sinners in the Hands of an Angry God," preached in 1741, contributed to this national movement, although he did not approve of its emotional excesses. In the controversies that either preceded the Great Awakening or flared up because of it, Edwards tended to defend the validity of the revivalist phenomenon, arguing from his Calvinist convictions about the supremacy of God, and his own experience of conversion, that feeling the grace of God, knowing the supernatural light personally, is all-important. In terms of the labels that arose at the time, he associated himself with the "New Lights," against the "Old Lights" who feared the enthusiasm of the converts and their potential for upsetting established church order and authority. Edwards was much absorbed by the theological issues spotlighted by the Great Awakening, and his great works on the religious affections, free will, and original sin all bore the stamp of that signal phenomenon.

Personally, things deteriorated for Edwards in Northampton in 1750 when he was dismissed from his pastorate because he had offended leading church families. He was perceived as too rigorous, having condemned the partying and sexual curiosity of some young people and refused communion to those who had not professed themselves converted. In this latter action he had retracted the tolerance that Stoddard had shown toward the Halfway Covenant, and a thin majority of his congregation voted for his dismissal. From 1751 to 1757 he labored as a missionary to the Indians in Stockbridge, Massachusetts, where he continued to work on his major theological writings. In 1757 he accepted the presidency of what became Princeton University in New Jersey, but he died of smallpox vaccination shortly after assuming office there.[2]

Original Sin

If we turn now to some of Edwards's main intellectual concerns, his reflections on original sin may be a good starting point. They bear directly on the Puritan view of human nature that is our overriding interest here, and they plunge us into the middle of Edwards's life and thought. The full treatise that Edwards wrote on original sin was only finished in 1757, but his ideas on the subject had been in process for many years. From youth he had struggled with the notion of predestination, which implied a judgment regarding the wickedness of human nature, and in embracing the

Calvinist view that human nature is depraved, Edwards set his face against any Arminian abridgments of Calvin's severity. Thus when Edwards read the work of the British theologian John Taylor, *The Scripture-Doctrine of Original Sin*, which was published in 1738 (or 1740), he was dismayed. Taylor seemed to be destroying one of the basic foundations of Christian religion, and Edwards felt that a strong rejoinder was necessary. Taylor even figured in the controversy in Northampton that resulted in Edwards's dismissal in 1750. In the background of Edwards's stance against opening communion to those who had not proclaimed themselves converted lay his convictions about original sin (the unworthiness of those who did not surely possess divine favor). Clyde A. Holbrook has suggested both the sequence of events in Northampton and Edwards's feelings about their significance: "During the quarrel with his church, Edwards had attempted a careful defense of his position on the subject of qualification for communion and was answered soon thereafter by the Reverend Solomon Williams. Edwards might well have saved himself the trouble of a reply to Williams for all the good it would do his cause, but ever tenacious of what he considered an important doctrine, he published *Misrepresentations Corrected and Truth Vindicated* two years after the irrevocable decision had been taken against him. He had detected in Williams' tract ideas, which at certain points coincided with those of Taylor, 'the author who lately has been so famous for his corrupt doctrine' and whose scheme of religion 'seems scarcely so agreeable to the Christian scheme, as the doctrine of many of the wiser heathen.' In a letter to his former parishioners, apprehended to the *Misrepresentations Corrected*, he went on to warn his former flock that if the church fell in with Williams' views it would also have accepted 'the strange opinion of Mr. Taylor,' whose conception of Christianity 'utterly explodes the doctrines you have been formerly taught, concerning eternal election, conversion, justification; and so, of a natural state of death in sin; and the whole doctrine of original sin.' "[3]

Thus Edwards's involvement with the doctrine of original sin was quite practical. He saw it as playing a central role in the behavior of Christians like his former congregation in Northampton, and he was certain that thinking wrongly about original sin would materially increase people's danger of damnation.

We have to remind ourselves that Edwards wrote in a time that took religious doctrine seriously. From the earliest Christian days, when creeds had arisen to express true faith and distinguish it from false, thinking correctly about the significance of Christ had been highly prized. One may consider the punishment of heretics (those whose faith was considered deviant) a dangerous matter, and the Spanish Inquisition has few serious defenders, because it reveals how sadistic the dogmatic mind can become. Moreover, the history of religious wars in Europe alone is enough to give any sober person reasons to be leery of strong claims for the importance of "orthodoxy." Still, the losses that accompany switching from strong claims about orthodoxy to an easy tolerance of various opinions also have to be reckoned. For an intense Christian like Jonathan Edwards, such losses certainly included the clear path to salvation and the honor owed to the God who had done human beings the great mercy of revealing his will to save them. In other words, to miss the mark concerning so central a matter as the depths of the sin that Christ died to overcome was for Edwards a great wickedness in its own right, and one sure to bring all sorts of mischief in its wake. Orthodoxy therefore could never be a matter of indifference. For Edwards, attacks on it would always have to be rebuffed.

When it came to explaining the proper understanding of the doctrine of original sin, Edwards relied on two major arguments. The actual behavior of human beings showed them to be wicked in heart, and the biblical teachings about the sin of Adam showed that all human beings had been ruined by Adam's fall. If one prescinded from the mercies of God, as those came to fullest flower in the work of Jesus Christ, one had to say that the human condition was hopeless. As Edwards himself arranged the two orders of grace and sin, sin remained something natural to human beings: "The reader is desired to bear this in mind, which I have said concerning the interposition of divine grace, its not altering the nature of things, as they are in themselves; and accordingly, when I speak of such and such an evil tendency of things, belonging to the present nature and state of mankind, understand me to mean their tendency *as they are in themselves*, abstracted from any consideration of that remedy the sovereign and infinite grace of God has provided.

"Having premised these things, I now proceed to say, that mankind are all naturally in such a state, as is attended, without fail, with this consequence or issue; that they universally run themselves into that which is, in effect, their own utter eternal perdition, as being finally accursed of God, and the subjects of his remedy-less wrath, through sin. From which I infer, that the natural state of the mind of man is attended with a propensity of nature, which is prevalent and effectual, to such an issue; and that therefore their nature is corrupt and depraved with a moral depravity, that amounts to and implies their utter undoing."[4]

This is a reading of Scripture and traditional Christian faith with a handsome lineage. One could bring forward sentences from Saint Augustine, Martin Luther, and John Calvin that run to much the same conclusion. What is the religious psychology behind it? Two points stand out. First, Edwards finds the behavior of human beings, including the behavior that he knows most intimately, his own, to be dominated by selfishness. If we look at human motivation, we find acts of desire outweighing by far acts of dispassionate, disinterested love seeking only the glory of God or the welfare of other people. Second, Edwards is always concerned with praising the goodness and sovereignty of God, compared to which the human factor in any situation is quite secondary. Because it magnifies the goodness of God to attribute all glory to him in the salvation of human beings, it must be true that human beings cannot save themselves. The work of Christ must have "substituted" for human sin, because that would more greatly redound to God's honor. This argument would not be persuasive without the biblical evidence that the work of Christ was fully a mercy of God and in no way something merited by human beings, but taking into account such biblical evidence, it suggests why human beings needed so outlandish a display of God's mercy as the crucifixion of Christ. They needed it because human nature on its own, apart from the grace of God, is so wicked that it can only ruin itself.

Much more remains to be said about this instinct of Jonathan Edwards and other Calvinists, including rejoinders from those who historically called them heretics for so denigrating God's work in creating human nature, but for the moment it is enough to have glimpsed the logic of Edwards's views and so some of the reasons for his passionate convictions about original sin.

Freedom of the Will

Granted the Calvinist doctrine of original sin, what remains of human liberty? The Arminians, whom Edwards considered mortal foes, were logical in denying both the severity of original sin that Edwards saw taught in the Bible and the imprisonment of human freedom that Calvinists inferred. For the Arminians, human beings were able to respond to the divine initiatives, and so to contribute to their salvation. Original sin had not taken away their basic capacity to say yes or no to God.

Edwards would have none of this. For him the doctrine of original sin, allied with a proper appreciation of the sovereignty of God, meant that salvation had to be completely a work of God. In consequence, salvation could not be in any part the product of free choices of human beings. As his own experience of conversion suggested, when divine grace enlightened the human mind and moved the human will, it was irresistible. God could not be thwarted, and the human will could not produce by itself God's effects. So there were serious limitations to human freedom, as Edwards took pains to show.

Edwards had been thinking about writing a treatise against the Arminians for many years, but only after his dismissal from Northampton and his establishment in Stockbridge did he put his hand to this task. The crux of the matter, as he saw it, was the Arminian conviction that the human will (person) is free to participate in the work of salvation. To Edwards's mind this compromised the graciousness of salvation. Once again, this analysis was not merely speculative. Edwards tied the Arminian convictions about the freedom of the will to the laxity, the lack of full appreciation of the human need for divine grace, that had afflicted his Northampton congregation. Only if people realized their utter depravity, and so their complete dependence upon God, would they rouse themselves to the professions of faith necessary in his mind for admission to the Lord's Supper. Only if their assertions of the sovereignty of God passed from the merely notional to the experiential would they enjoy the vital faith necessary to please God and ensure their salvation. In Edwards the pastor and the theologian were never separated. Doctrine was not a matter of academic discourse, but a matter bearing directly on lived religion.

In discussing the background of the discourse on the freedom of the will, Paul Ramsey has provided a glimpse of Edwards's working habits: "Dwight estimates that in the actual composition of the *Inquiry* [into free will] Edwards spent only four months and a half, and concerning this he exclaims, 'So far as I am aware, no similar example, of power and rapidity united, is to be found in the annals of Mental effort.' With no desire to expunge this record from the annals of mental effort, perhaps we should not regard it as such an astonishing accomplishment, recalling that the author had given the subject his strongest, if intermittent, attention for many years prior to 1752–53, and remembering also that he habitually spent more than twelve hours a day in some form of study and that his usual method of study was to formulate and arrange his thoughts upon some problem *by writing*."[5]

In attacking the Arminians on the question of freedom of the will, Edwards first enters the difficulties he has, on philosophical or natural-scientific grounds, with their explanations of the basis of free will. Then he comes to the positive reasons for his own position that the human will has no freedom (at least of the Arminian sort) regarding the divine grace that is essential for salvation. The most important of these positive reasons is the certain foreknowledge that God possesses. If God knows beforehand what the volitions (the choices) of moral agents are, then the freedom (from necessity) enjoyed by those moral agents is severely constrained. To put this in Edwards's own words: "That the acts of the wills of moral agents are not contingent events, in that sense, as to be without all necessity, appears by God's certain foreknowledge of such events. In handling this argument, I would in the first place prove, that God has a certain fore-knowledge of the voluntary acts of moral agents; and secondly, show the consequence, or how it follows from hence, that the volitions of moral agents are not contingent, so as to be without necessity of connection and consequence. First, I am to prove, that God has an absolute and certain foreknowledge of the free actions of moral agents. One could think, it should be wholly needless to enter on such an argument with any that profess themselves Christians; but so it is; God's certain knowledge of the free acts of moral agents, is denied by some that pretend to believe the Scriptures to be the Word of God; and especially of late."[6]

The fact that God foreknows events flows from the divine omni-science, which in turn is a feature of the divine status as source of all that exists. For Edwards it is plain, from Scripture and reason alike, that God would be no God were he not in control of creation—were he not to have caused it, by his free intentions, and not to know its every particular and eventuality. How one squares this with sufficient human freedom to make human beings, and not God, the author of sin is a further question, which Edwards takes up later. But it is interesting to note that the first positive move that Edwards makes in defense of the Calvinist position regarding freedom of the will is to assert the divine foreknowledge. In any matter of human volition, God has to have the priority—has to know before the human agent what is going to happen, and so to diminish the freedom with which the human agent operates. This in turn leads to the conclusion that what God knows happens necessarily. There is no contingency (no free-dom from necessity) in the events foreknown by God, including the ac-tions of human agents.

But does this not lead to a fatalism, a scheme in which everything has been worked out in advance of human agency? Edwards denies such an inference, but apparently by interpreting "fatalism" as the pagan doctrine that would picture the world as running independently of a divine source: "If they [ancient Stoic philosophers] held any such doctrine of fate as is inconsistent with the world's being in all things subject to the disposal of an intelligent, wise agent, that presides, not as the soul of the world, but as the sovereign Lord of the universe, governing all things by proper will, choice and design, in the exercise of the most perfect liberty conceivable, without subjection to any constraint, or being properly under the power or influence of anything before, above or without himself; I wholly renounce any such doctrine."[7]

But of course this does not meet the charge that the necessity suggested by the divine foreknowledge makes God the real author of human actions, including the evil actions called sins. Edwards struggles to escape this conclusion, and makes a useful distinction between being the author of sin and one who permits sin. The example of the crucifixion of Christ (one of many examples that Scripture suggests) shows that God may permit something that is contrary to his Law, for the sake of a greater good that God alone appreciates before the fact: ". . . the crucifixion of Christ was a thing contrary to the revealed or preceptive will of God; because, as it was viewed and done by his malignant murderers, it was a thing infinitely contrary to the holy nature of God, and so necessarily contrary to the holy inclination of his heart revealed in his Law. Yet this don't [sic] at all hinder but that the crucifixion of Christ, considered with all those glorious consequences, which were within the view of the divine omniscience, would be indeed, and therefore might appear to God to be, a glorious event; and consequently be agreeable to his will, though this will be secret, i.e. not revealed in God's law. And thus considered, the crucifixion of Christ was not evil, but good."[8]

This may be fine as an argument to vindicate the wisdom and goodness of God in developing a plan (of salvation) pivoted on the apparent evil (but actual good) of the crucifixion of Christ, but where does it leave the perpetrators of the evil deed—the murderers of Christ? Were they responsible for their acts, and so at least somewhat free? Edwards does not deal with this issue at this juncture,[9] and so leaves the reader to wonder whether any but a fictional human responsibility for sin has been proven, due to the fact that the capacity of human beings to act either for or against the stated (though never the actual) intent (Law) of God has not been established. If the actual will of God can never be thwarted, how can human beings be responsible for their sins, and why is God not finally the author of their sins? This question has bedeviled speculative theologians other than Edwards, but when he took up the issue of human freedom, Edwards had to know that unless he answered it well his arguments would not seem persuasive.

To this point, the Jonathan Edwards we have seen is both a literalist about Scripture and a keen reasoner in the mode of the Calvinist scholastics. Edwards does not bring to Scripture the sense of metaphor that present-day biblical studies regularly employ, nor does he show the sensitivity that patristic exegesis, which distinguished several different "senses" the text might carry, brought to its task. On the whole, he is interested in the ideas that the biblical page seems to be presenting, and he deals with such ideas as though they were being proposed as fully rational arguments. This was the mode of theologizing congenial to the scholastics, both Catholic and Protestant. For them the argument was the main thing and keen logic was highly prized. One result was a neglect of the mysteriousness of the divine agency. None of the scholastics, including Edwards, would have denied that God, being infinite and omniscient, exceeds human understanding, but few of them took this exceeding of human understanding into account when they dealt with the interactions between creatures and God. Those most reasonable ended up making dozens of distinctions that finally clarified very little. In hindsight, they would have been better off confessing that one cannot know precisely how the divine omniscience and omnipotence correlate with sufficient human understanding and freedom to make human beings responsible for their sins, but that it is essential to orthodox faith and moral health alike to affirm both parts of the equation: the divine control of the world (which alone assures ultimate meaningfulness and justice) and human freedom (which alone makes human beings capable of the love essential to salvation).

It is no demeaning of Edwards's achievement to point out that he was limited by the contemporary rules of the work he was doing. Within the assumptions of his day, he worked brilliantly. As well, he introduced points of view that many of his contemporaries did not associate with speculative theology, especially regarding the religious affections. We now turn to his work on this latter subject.

Religious Affections

From the time of his conversion, Edwards had been intensely interested in the movements of grace in the believer's spirit. Convinced that full religion implied much more than a notional assent to faith, he desired to learn all he could about what faith felt like, how it actually worked in the spirits of the just, the ways that the Spirit of God seemed to provide empirical supports. The phenomena associated with the Great Awakening in New England offered Edwards a wide field for such study. Against the background of the Puritan interest in signs of election and salvation, Edwards honed a fine religious sensibility and became an outstanding psychologist of the Christian spiritual life. His work *A Treatise Concerning Religious Affections* may be the most lasting of his theological contributions, and while it is informed by the theological convictions we have found him to possess regarding original sin and the freedom of the human will, it avoids dogmatism and remains sufficiently close to experience not to distort what Edwards takes to be the workings of grace.

Concerning the context in which Edwards wrote, John E. Smith has noted that "the period . . . was dominated by the phenomenon known as revivalism, and especially that segment of it which in America we call the Great Awakening. There were in fact a series of awakenings, some great, others small, beginning with Solomon Stoddard's five 'harvests' of souls in Northampton between the years 1679 and 1718 and proceeding through the fervor of 1734–35 to the climax of the Great Awakening in the 1740s. . . . Edwards was in the center of the most important of the eighteenth century revival activities. He preached 'affecting' sermons, including the famous one at Enfield in 1741 ["Sinners in the Hands of an Angry God"] (which is erroneously supposed to be more representative of Edwards' thought than it actually is); he filled the pastoral office, helping to interpret the experiences of his parishioners, lending aid in decisions involving 'cases of conscience,' as they were called, corresponding with ministers abroad, giving counsel and advice concerning religious experiences."[10] Smith points out that in addition to the *Affections,* which he produced in 1746, Edwards wrote three other works describing and analyzing the revivalist phenomena of his day, in 1737, 1741, and 1742. By the time that he approached the *Affections,* Edwards was not only highly experienced but disciplined. He had already established the facts regarding contemporary reports, as well as his conviction that the revivals had brought to many people a new sense of or conviction about the truth of the gospel. Finally, he had already sifted the data and applied such distinctions as that which Calvinists employed to separate operations of the Spirit that were saving from operations that were common (ordinary). In other words, he had distinguished between the essential and the accidental aspects of revivalism and so prepared a defense against detractors, whose criticisms, in his view, often missed the truly significant matters. To Edwards's mind, the truly significant matters were the peace, joy, love of God, and light of knowledge that the revivals regularly produced. When such key signs (already intimated by Saint Paul in Galatians 5) were present, the person open to the possibility that God could act in people's hearts to transform them had to think that the divine agent was at hand.

Edwards begins his treatise with a commentary on 1 Peter 1:8 that establishes the nature and importance of the affections (feelings, experience) in religion. Then he describes phenomena that may be present in revivals but cannot serve as authentic criteria for determining whether or not God is at work offering saving grace. The third and major portion of the text deals with the twelve signs that according to Edwards distinguish religious affections as truly gracious (rather than simply ordinary)—twelve characteristics of God's saving action.

The first sign depends on the principle that gracious affections come from influences that are spiritual, supernatural, and divine—not carnal, not natural, not human; more than what these latter influences can explain. The crux is regeneration: the arising of a life truly filled with God. Compared to this crux, dramatic emotional displays and even supposedly "miraculous" happenings are irrelevant. The second sign is that the person loves the sovereignty of God and the excellence of the divine glory.

The third sign of holy affections is that they are founded on "the loveliness of the moral excellency of divine things. Or (to express it otherwise), a love to divine things for the beauty and sweetness of their moral excellency, is the first beginning and spring of all holy affections."[11] The fourth sign is that the affections arise from the right enlightenment of the mind, so that it understands divine things. The fifth sign is a reasonable and spiritual conviction, in the human judgment, of the reality and certainty of divine things. The sixth sign is evangelical humiliation—"a sense that a Christian has of his own utter insufficiency, despicableness, and odiousness, with an answerable frame of heart."[12] The seventh sign is a change of nature (or character): the person behaves for the better. The eighth sign is the sort of meekness, love, quietness, forgiveness, and mercy that appeared in Christ.

The ninth sign is a Christian tenderness of spirit. The tenth sign is a certain symmetry and proportion—the affections pull together and make something both whole and beautiful in the personality. The eleventh sign is that the higher the affections rise, the more appetite they show for spiritual attainments (they are not complacent but reach out to the full holiness of God). The twelfth sign is that holy affections produce a practice that fits the Christian sense or rules of the good life (whether at home, in business, or socializing, the person does the Christian thing, does not violate Christian ethics).

Edwards gives quite detailed arguments and illustrations for these signs, and whereas some remain ambiguous or ethereal, on the whole the portrait he paints of the genuinely religious person is quite plain. Only if the character has been elevated and the behavior purified, should one judge that the Spirit of God has certainly been at work. Only if the person has become truly spiritual can one speak of regeneration.

David Brainerd

In 1749 Edwards published a life of David Brainerd, a missionary to the Indians, who had died in Edwards's home of tuberculosis. Brainerd had left lengthy writings about both his work and his interior life, and Edwards found these writings useful for his own polemics against those he felt were misinterpreting the Great Awakening. Brainerd was a rather dour personality, but his perseverance in difficult work without many signs of success impressed Edwards as an example of true virtue. In addition, Brainerd had recorded the experiences of his converts and paid close attention to the spiritual signs attending their experiences of faith. All of this was grist for Edwards's mill. In effect, David Brainerd became a case study in which Edwards could concretize his own views about genuine religion. Brainerd had died in 1747, and by the time that Edwards published his life of Brainerd his days as pastor in Northampton were numbered. After being expelled from Northampton, Edwards followed Brainerd's example as a missionary to the Indians. The fact that he himself experienced if anything even less success than Brainerd further linked their lives, as did the fact that Edwards's daughter died of tuberculosis after having nursed Brainerd in his last days. The medical knowledge of the day did not include an awareness of the contagious character of tuberculosis, and Edwards never blamed Brainerd for his daughter's death. Indeed, he buried her by Brainerd's side.

We shall consider momentarily some of the lessons that Edwards drew from Brainerd's life, but first we should indicate the great influence that this work of Edwards achieved. In part because Edwards did not make clear Brainerd's failure as a missionary (his achieving few conversions), but instead stressed his great spiritual strength, especially in light of his youth (Brainerd died at 30), others interested in missionary work often took Brainerd as a great model. Indeed, Edwards's *"Life of Brainerd* soon became a spiritual classic and a model of missionary histories. In the words of Thomas H. Johnson, it was 'the first biography written in America that achieved wide notice abroad as well as at home.' Gideon Hawley, another missionary protegé of Edwards, carried in his saddlebag a copy of the *Life*, to which he referred when unable to stand the strain of another day. 'I need, greatly need something more than human to support me,' he wrote in 1753. 'I read my Bible and Mr. Brainerd's Life, the only books I brought with me, and from them have a little support.' John Wesley was so impressed that he published a condensed version (1768). 'Let every preacher read carefully over the "Life of David Brainerd," ' he instructed in the handbook for the Methodist ministry. Although Wesley could be critical of Brainerd for 'applauding himself and magnifying his own work,' his example was upheld. 'Find preachers of David Brainerd's spirit,' he wrote in his journal (1767), 'and nothing can stand before them.' Francis Asbury (1745–1816), who in 1771 became the first missionary of Methodism to America, later referred to Brainerd as 'that model of meekness, moderation, temptation and labor, and self denial.' "[13]

In introducing his book on Brainerd, Edwards praised Brainerd's character and faith, but he also entered one caution. Brainerd suffered fits of melancholy, which Edwards wanted to disassociate from the heart of the man's spiritual achievement. In saying this, Edwards wanted to refute those who claimed that all religion depended on dejection of spirit. The point was not that Brainerd suffered low periods, but that he persevered regardless of how he felt, and that in both his own life and his estimates of the religious lives of those to whom he ministered he revealed the sensitivity to the divine that Edwards thought was the great result of the awakening that had come to New England. Neither the enthusiasts, who placed great weight on high spirits (being uplifted by God), nor the Old Lights who disparaged all claims that the Awakening was a momentous work of God, were correct. David Brainerd was a concrete example of the balanced, middle position that Edwards felt was more faithful to both Christian tradition and the facts of what the genuinely awakened actually experienced.

The diary that Brainerd kept furnished Edwards much of his material, and although Edwards edited Brainerd's entries in some places, on the whole he was faithful to what Brainerd himself had written. From earliest years, it appears, Brainerd both longed for God and thought of himself as abject and vile. This fit the Puritan model of the ideal soul. On occasion Brainerd certainly experienced sweetness, joy, and peace, but he always accounted himself vile, because not wholly dedicated to God. Diary entries for two days—August 20 and 21, 1742—show a pattern of up and down moods that was typical of Brainerd's interior life: "Friday, August 20. I appeared so vile to myself that I hardly dared to think of being seen, especially on account of spiritual pride. However, tonight I enjoyed a sweet hour alone with God. . . . I was lifted above the frowns and flatteries of this lower world, had a sweet relish of heavenly joys, and my soul did as it were get into the eternal world and really taste of heaven. I had a sweet season of intercession for dear friends in Christ; and God helped me to cry fervently for Zion. Blessed be God for this season.

"Saturday, August 21. Was much perplexed in the morning. Towards noon enjoyed more of God in secret, was enabled to see that it was best to throw myself into the hands of God, to be disposed of according to his pleasure, and rejoiced in such thoughts. In the afternoon, rode to New Haven; was much confused all the way. Just at night, underwent such a dreadful conflict as I have scarce ever felt. I saw myself exceedingly vile and unworthy; so that I was guilty, and ashamed that anybody should bestow any favor on me or show me any respect."[14]

As his pastoral exertions grew, Brainerd tended to run himself down physically, and Edwards criticized him for taking on more than his physical strength had allowed him to bear. The journeys that Brainerd had to take to meet the Indians he was serving could be dangerous. On one occasion his horse broke a leg and he had to shoot it and spend the night in the woods. The interpreter through whom Brainerd had to work was a burden, in that often not even he seemed to get Brainerd's message or feel the need for conversion that Brainerd hoped his preaching would stir. All in all, both his missionary labors and his spiritual searches gave Brainerd much reason for feeling burdened; and as the confessions in his diary mount up day after day, his perseverance in both work and prayer becomes impressive.

Brainerd was most gratified when those with whom he was working felt moved to confess their need of Christ and themselves persevered in efforts to obtain God's favor. No doubt this was one of the aspects of his faith that Edwards most admired. Edwards was most comfortable with a faith that took fully seriously the wickedness of human nature, and the grandeur of God, to the end that people lived simply, in considerable self-denial, blessing God and triumphing over whatever adversities it pleased God to send them. That Brainerd died a very painful death, and kept his faith to the end, probably pleased Edwards—not because he thought pain a good thing, but because it showed that even *in extremis* faith could keep a person clinging to God in hope.

In the sermon that he preached for Brainerd's funeral, Edwards seized on Brainerd as a witness against enthusiasm and Antinomianism: "He detested enthusiasm in all its forms and operations, and abhorred whatever in opinion or experience seemed to verge towards Antinomianism: as, the experiences of those whose first faith consists in believing that Christ died for them in particular; and their first love, in loving God, because they supposed they were the objects of his love; and their assurance of their good estate from some immediate testimony or suggestion, either with or without texts of Scripture, that their sins are forgiven, that God loves them, etc."[15] Clearly, Edwards wanted no gospel of cheap grace, was leery of emotion and feeling (which often did not last), and saw in the endurance of David Brainerd, who largely agreed with Edwards intellectually, a fine confutation of the errors to which the Great Awakening was prone.

The Great Awakening

We turn now to Edwards's book on the Great Awakening and an estimate of what that dramatic event meant to the Puritan view of human nature. Just as Edwards used David Brainerd to exemplify his interpretations, so he used his wife Sarah's experiences (without disclosing her identity) to justify his first impression that God was doing great things in New England. These experiences of Sarah Pierrepont Edwards, who was still a young woman in her mid-twenties when Edwards wrote *The Great Awakening: A Faithful Narrative* (1737), also figured in the signs that he developed for recognizing the religious affections that the grace of God bestows.

Edwards begins his description of the evidence provided by Sarah as follows: "I have been particularly acquainted with many persons that have been the subjects of the high and extraordinary transports of the present day; and in the highest transports of any of the instances that I have been acquainted with, and where the affections of admiration, love and joy, so far as another could judge, have been raised to a higher pitch than in any other instances I have observed or have been informed of, the following things have been united: viz. a very frequent dwelling, for some considerable time together, in such views of the glory of the divine perfections, and Christ's excellencies, that the soul in the meantime has been as it were perfectly overwhelmed, and swallowed up with light and love and a sweet solace, rest and joy of soul, that was altogether unspeakable; and more than once continuing for five or six hours together, without any interruption, in that clear and lively view or sense of the infinite beauty and amiableness of Christ's person, and the heavenly sweetness of his excellent and transcendent love; so that (to use the person's own expressions) the soul remained in a kind of heavenly Elysium, and did as it were swim in the rays of Christ's love, like a little mote swimming in the beams of the sun, or streams of his light that come in at a window; and the heart was swallowed up in a kind of glow of Christ's love, coming down from Christ's heart in heaven, as a constant stream of sweet light, at the same time the soul all flowing out in love to him; so that there seemed to be a constant flowing and reflowing from heart to heart."[16]

If Edwards used David Brainerd to specify his objections to an enthusiasm that would place the core of religion in emotion, he used his wife Sarah's experience to specify the kind of religious affections that he found beyond reproach. The spirituality of this experience, the way that the person was elevated to a pure love of God and taste for godly things, struck Edwards as a fine example of the divine benevolence. From the time he first admired Sarah, when she was only thirteen, he had been taken with her sweetness and spirituality. He had married her when she was seventeen, and she bore him eleven children. So the spirituality that he stressed was not a saintliness without flesh and blood anchors. In many ways Sarah exemplifed the Reformation ideal of a worldly holiness. She had been raised to communion with God not in the removed setting of the cloister but in the setting of a busy household. She had been sharing the burdens of Edwards's ministerial labors, and she would later know such sorrows as their expulsion from Northampton and the death of their daughter from tuberculosis. But her religious purity was such that Edwards could not deny the goodness of either the experiences she had received or the movement that had precipitated them. The Awakening, whatever its faults, had to be in goodly measure a work of God, if only because Edwards knew at first hand a saintly person who had been nourished by it.

In both his religious psychology and his speculative theology, Edwards showed himself to be a child of the Enlightenment as well as of Puritanism. Although he drew his convictions about the depravity of human nature and the need for close scrutiny of one's spiritual life from Calvinistic Puritanism, he drew from the Enlightenment his sense that nature (including human nature) could be examined empirically with great profit, and that philosophy and the other intellectual endeavors were proper exercises of human talent. The psychology of John Locke appealed to Edwards and helped him to scrutinize the phenomena of the Great Awakening. The stress of the Enlightenment thinkers on the power and rights of human reason encouraged Edwards to criticize those who concentrated on the emotional aspects of the Awakening. But neither Puritan fears about the depravity of human nature nor Enlightenment worries about emotionalism could gainsay what Edwards knew intimately from Sarah's religious exaltation. God had moved some people to an intense love of divine things. This had to be a good result, pure and simple, because in both its occurrence and its aftermath it produced only virtue and praise of God.

In later days, when many of those whom Edwards had encouraged during the days of Awakening had turned against him and contributed to his removal from Northampton, he tended to be more suspicious of religious affections than he was when the bloom was on Sarah's experiences. This did not mean that he renounced his earlier approval of and gratitude for the signs of grace, but it did mean that his assessment of the Great Awakening was ongoing. For more than twenty years Edwards wrestled with the implications of that momentous time, seeking after the nature of true, trustworthy religious feeling, and in the process bequeathing to his successor Puritans and religious thinkers a highly nuanced, sophisticated view of religious experience. In a preface to a friend's book written in 1750, when the wounds he had suffered from Northampton were still raw, Edwards was concerned with the power of false religion. False religion "has been the chief thing that has obscured, obstructed and brought to a stand all remarkable revivals of religion, which have been since the beginning of the Reformation; the very chief reason why the most hopeful and promising beginnings have never come to any more than beginnings; being nipped in the bud, and soon followed with a great increase of stupidity, corrupt principles, a profane and atheistical spirit, and the triumph of the open enemies of religion."[17]

The Great Awakening, with which Edwards will forever be associated, produced some of the best (most saintly) and the worst (most emotional) religion that this great thinker could conceive. So it both magnified the grandeur of God and showed the corruption of human nature, both lifted people beyond their ordinary station, into close intimacy with God, and led them to excesses and finally acts of pride that made their last state worse than their first. In many ways, of course, the Great Awakening simply wrote in large letters the ups and downs of human experience everywhere. However, under the pressure of the intense common conviction of the New England communities, exaltations were apt to be especially high and, at least to a sensitive person such as Edwards, later derelictions from faith were apt to be especially low.

From the Great Awakening the United States received what has proven to be a permanent license both to celebrate and to criticize evangelical fervor. People can rightly claim Jonathan Edwards as both the patron and the foe of ecstatic, revivalist religion. The problem posed by revivalist religion, as Edwards saw with uncommon clarity, is to discern the true fruits from the false. In the same meeting, one person may be converted by the Spirit of God to a life of greater spirituality and another may sow the seeds of pride and self-delusion. Perhaps the lesson most taken to heart by students of Jonathan Edwards has been that religious experience is instructively concrete. One has to proceed case by case, looking to the lasting effects in a person's life, if one is to judge whether a given claim to awakening is solid or spurious. On the whole, however, the Awakening and Jonathan Edwards convinced the Puritan sensibility of the United States that one was wisest when most suspicious.

Puritanism in American Culture

Moving now from Jonathan Edwards to a broader view of Puritanism, we shift from the part to the whole. Certainly Edwards has been considered the most luminous hero of the Puritan achievement in America, but the impact of Puritanism went much further than Edwards's theological and psychological contributions might imply.

For example, Puritanism contributed significantly to the American option for a democratic form of government. In England, before it emigrated to form colonies in America, the movement fought for limiting the royal government. Just as the Puritans resisted the monarchical impulse in church affairs, claiming as the heritage of the Protestant Reformation the right to let individual conscience (and the Bible) be the supreme authority, so they resisted a civil government that they had not elected and could not subordinate to what they considered the patterns desired by God. Along with other Calvinists, the Puritans tended to identify with the rising middle classes. Throughout Europe, monarchs tended to regard these classes as insubordinate, and so to disapprove of their religious and philosophical underpinnings.

In America, the Puritans distinguished but did not separate the religious and the civil realms. They were a literate and contract-minded people, tending to want written agreements to dominate their civil life. Thus the Plymouth community that arrived in 1620 immediately fashioned a "compact" to regulate its common life, and the other New England communities sought to gather a group consensus that could be committed to writing. By 1634, four years after its founding, the Massachusetts Bay Colony had formed a General Court composed of deputies elected from each town. This became a legislative body and all freemen (adult male church members) could stand for election to it. Although the New England Puritans sought consent, which in the beginning they believed to be a matter of coming to an agreement about the divine will, they also supported individualism. Each man had the right, indeed the duty, to form his own conscience. Women had lesser rights, due to their subjection to their husbands, but frequently Puritan women grew up to be literate and independent.

The distinction that the early Puritans made between church and state was only a limited one, but their recognition that the religious and civil realms did not completely overlap paved the way for the fuller separation established in the American Constitution. A pluralistic sense of citizenship, in both its religious and political aspects, also developed only slowly, but the establishment of a colony at Providence to welcome those unsuited for what the Bay Colony considered orthodoxy was a significant opening to pluralism. The Puritans themselves were loath to license a variety of religious opinions, but in time they were forced to recognize the conscientious claims of those who disagreed with them, because their own principles placed such weight on freedom of conscience (especially the freedom to worship as one thought best).

Because they were great Bible-readers and stood in the quite learned Calvinistic tradition, the Puritans always took a great interest in the schooling of their children. They wanted a literate, well-informed community and, above all, a learned clergy. The first institutions for higher education in New England arose to educate the clergy. First Harvard, and then Yale, set the standard for academic excellence for later eras. Princeton University arose to train Presbyterian clergy, while William and Mary in Virginia had Anglican ties. Virtually everywhere the roots of higher education in the colonies were religious, tied to the church or religious tradition strongest in a given area, but the Puritans had set the pattern. This was also true for what we now call secondary education. In 1647 Massachusetts enacted the first program for free public schools, and from this initiative developed such venerable institutions as the Boston, Cambridge, and Roxbury Latin Schools. Such private preparatory schools as Phillips Andover (1778) in Massachusetts and Phillips Exeter in New Hampshire (1781) set the standard for private education after the Revolution.

In addition to Harvard and Yale, Dartmouth (1769), Williams (1785), Bowdoin (1794), Middlebury (1800), and Amherst (1821) all stemmed from Congregationalist groups (the successors of the Puritans). As Easterners moved west, they continued their interest in higher education. Oberlin, Antioch, Western Reserve, Beloit, Grinnell, Carleton, Colorado College, and Pomona all had ties to former New Englanders. In most cases, these educational enterprises carried the aura of a holy mission. The Puritan sense of vocation frequently cast teaching as a sacred work, and usually the notion was that higher education included moral as well as intellectual training. One was preparing young people to be solid churchgoers and citizens, as well as bright scientists, musicians, educators, or businessmen.

In speculating about Puritan intellectual life, Daniel Walker Howe has discerned three durable philosophical traditions and found Jonathan Edwards to be a seminal influence on all three.[18] First, there has been a Platonic tradition, traceable to British thinkers at Cambridge, that has often expressed itself as an ethical rationalism—a concern to make reason the standard for moral behavior. Second, there has been a pietistic concern with religious experience. One may place Ralph Waldo Emerson and William James in this second stream, inasmuch as they were greatly interested in states of soul. Third, and perhaps most directly indebted to Jonathan Edwards (and Yale), has been an effort to keep a balance between the head and the heart—reason and the emotions. As we noted, this was Edwards's position regarding the Great Awakening, and frequently American philosophical thought has seemed to be groping after the balance that Edwards achieved.

The Puritans were sometimes leery of scientific findings, but more characteristically they welcomed new discoveries about nature, thinking that such discoveries told them more about nature's God. This was the case with Edwards, who maintained a lifelong interest in natural science. American literature has close ties with the propensity of the Puritans to write down their experiences and analyze on paper their states of soul. Thus not only a theological giant such as Edwards but even an ordinary minister such as David Brainerd wrote assiduously. New Englanders wrote thousands of sermons and lectures, but also histories and poems. The careful analyses of motivation that one finds in the novels of Nathaniel Hawthorne bespeak a Puritan background, while the broodings about the depravity of human nature that characterize Melville's novels owe much to the Calvinism that the Puritans espoused. Some analysts count the Puritans a direct influence on Thoreau and Emerson, while others view such writers as Poe, Irving, Santayana, and Mark Twain as self-consciously opposing Puritan views. The grim view of human nature that one finds in such Southern writers as Faulkner, Penn Warren, and Tennessee Williams seems a descendant of the Puritan suspicions, while many commentators consider Puritanism the background necessary to understand the poetry of the New Englanders Robert Frost and Robert Lowell.

In economic and civil matters, perhaps the greatest legacy of the Puritans was their commitment to hard work and public service. Until the 1960s, these virtues, combined with a sense that America had a divinely assigned providential role to create a commonwealth of singular virtue, lay at the wellsprings of American motivation. Many Americans attributed their success in business to a Puritan sense of industry and thrift, while the majority of the citizenry agreed that self-indulgence was improper, because human beings were given life so that they might make a good return to the Master who had given them their talents. Thus, many of the traits regularly accounted typically American have roots in the Puritan mind which Jonathan Edwards brought to full flower.

The Puritan God

We have glimpsed the sovereign majesty of the divinity that held center stage in the world of Jonathan Edwards, but perhaps we have not credited as fully as we should have the savagery that some later Americans have found in that divinity. Edwards himself certainly found the Christian religion uplifting, and one can argue that much of the reason was the beauty of God that he found reflected in nature.[19] However, Edwards found little contradiction in discoursing graphically on the torments that those who rejected God, or whom God had predestined to hell, would have to endure. Victorians such as Oliver Wendell Holmes could not stomach the deity that Edwards revered, and no longer was it effective to charge them with a heretical Arminianism. The temper of the times had shifted away from Calvinist terror and flint.

Nowadays, even scholars sympathetic to Jonathan Edwards are apt to deliver themselves of broadsides against his notion of God. Thus Herbert F. May, keynoting a conference on recent interpretations of Edwards, notes the opinion of Holmes and wades in alongside him: "It is not difficult to sympathize with these outraged Victorians. I agree with Holmes. To modify his statement slightly, if we can read the imprecatory sermons without horror, it is because of a failure of the imagination. Consistent Calvinism is admired in recent times chiefly by people to whom it has never occurred that its doctrines might really describe the true state of affairs. If one is seriously to follow Edwards, recent scholarship has made clear, one must accept his doctrine of Hell not as a minor blemish on his intellectual system, but as essential to it. One must accept as true his masterly descriptions of intolerable and interminable suffering. Still more difficult, to be a real Edwardsian one must come to terms with his insistence that God hates sinners and holds them in the utmost contempt. Once a human being has had his chance, and has not been able to accept it, God will never feel the slightest pity for him. If a person is saved, part of his duty will be to love all aspects of God forever, including his vindictive justice. Thus he will have to learn to rejoice in the rightness and beauty of eternal suffering for others. To be a real follower of Edwards, one must moreover come to terms with little Phoebe Bartlett, four years old, sure of her own salvation, sorry for her sisters, predicting their death, weeping over the sin of stealing plums but blaming her sister for talking her into it, and expressing plummy love for her minister, Mr. Edwards."[20]

Whether one has to come to terms with a four-year-old, no matter how unattractive, is questionable, though certainly one has to come to grips with the culture in which she was growing up. Inasmuch as the Puritan God haunted the dreams of many little children, and served others as a reason to feel superior and cold, it would seem to have done a disservice to the Christian gospel and its Master, who preached about the lilies of the field and the prodigal son. It is a commonplace that cultures tend to picture divinity in terms of their own psychic needs. Apparently the Puritans, and the Calvinists before them, felt most comfortable with an uncomfortable, frightening divinity. They would have rejected such a characterization, claiming that the God they worshiped was patent in the pages of the Bible, but it doesn't take a great deal of reading to realize that the pages of the Bible yield several different pictures of God. If the Puritans and Edwards chose the God of wrath, rather than the God of love, that was because of decisions they made regarding the Old Testament as much as the New Testament.

What is understandable in the Puritan choice of a God who could consign sinners to hell with no remorse? First, a reminder that God's ways can be different from the ways of human beings. To be sure, every generation has been read this lesson, since every generation has experienced or heard about storms, floods, earthquakes, fires, and other natural disasters; about cancer, idiocy, crime, war, rape, pillage, and injustice in high places. God has chosen the universe in which these things occur. Therefore, God must be different from human beings, must not be the easy benevolence that human beings want God to be. Regardless of how one's final efforts at theodicy (the attempt to justify the ways of God) turn out, as soon as one confronts the actual world that God has created it becomes clear that God is not the captive of our human sense of how the universe ought to run.

Second, the Puritan sense of God asks us to study holiness, which we are somewhat loath to do. Holiness is not a matter of merely smiling at children and helping the elderly, though many saints did both. Holiness is a matter of God's very being. For the Puritans, and many other traditional people, God was the first instance of being, the only fully real possessor of existence. Moreover, God possessed existence purely—without limit or defect. In the order of being, God was a fullness of power. In the order of intelligibility, God was a fullness of light. In the moral order, God was a fullness of goodness. The three orders were one for God, who was simple and perfect—without parts, and without any need to grow or achieve. Nor were these attributes of God simply vague ideas. They purported to describe what one would experience, were one to come close to God or be seized by God. God was a refining fire. For any creature to see God's "face" would be for that creature to die.

In these and dozens of other figures, the Puritans found the Bible to exalt God and deflate human pretensions. The Psalms, the Prophets, Job, and many passages of the Pentateuch drove home the message that God had a goodness and power dangerous to human beings, who manifestly were weak and often were not good. It was not simply that God had to be the opposite of human imperfection, the projection of the ideal that human imagination thought ought to be dwelling in heaven. It was also that religious experience, like that behind the Bible, reported that one ought to take off one's shoes when approaching the precincts of God, because even the ground close to God was holy. The cherubs surrounding the throne of God were fierce guardians, because their Lord was an awesome sanctity.

If one combines these notions of the otherness of God and the holiness of God, one gets much of the Puritan portrait. What is missing, though, is the distinctive description of God and approach to God that the New Testament ascribes to Jesus. Curiously, the Puritans seem to have avoided or neglected Jesus's own speech. In calling God his Father ("Abba"), Jesus had claimed an intimacy with the divinity that was astounding. Perhaps it was too astounding for the Puritans to accept. Or, perhaps the Puritan acceptance of the traditional Christian faith in the divinity of Jesus made theologians consider the intimacy that characterized Jesus's relations with God fitting only for him. To draw such a conclusion runs counter to the way that Jesus himself taught his followers to pray (see, for example, Lk 11:2) and urged them to deal with God, but if their greater need were for a conviction that God is primarily an awesome divine majesty sending human beings crashing to their knees, the Puritans might have committed such an infidelity.

In the next section, we reflect on such a need to feel abashed and humiliated, which says a great deal about the Puritan conception of human nature. Here it remains only to observe that the same sense of the transcendent holiness of God that can free people from the prison of worldliness or secularity can throw people into a new prison: terror at the otherness of God. Jonathan Edwards wrote some blood-curdling descriptions of hell and sinfulness, but he seems to have avoided such terrors. Does that mean that he himself took his descriptions, and the biblical texts on which they were based, with a grain of salt, at least implicitly agreeing with the biblical Christ that if human beings, evil as they were, knew how to give their children good things, the heavenly Father could not be an ogre? Perhaps so. Perhaps the Puritans who kept their psychic balance had tacit theological assumptions that balanced the awesome holiness of God with a divine mercy that made God slow to anger and abounding in steadfast love, as the Old Testament had claimed.

The Puritan View of Human Nature

What was the reason for, and what were the implications of, the Puritan view that human nature is depraved? The reason, in the Puritans' view, was the testimony of Scripture, as interpreted by Augustine, Luther, and above all Calvin. Both the account of the sin of Adam and Eve in Genesis and the interpretation of it in Paul's Epistle to the Romans spoke as though human beings inherited a fallen nature. Inasmuch as Augustine used the Vulgate mistranslation of Romans 5:12 to make the sinful Adam one "in whom" all human beings sinned, the notion arose that human beings had a solidarity in sin that tainted all of their humanity. Whereas other interpretations of original sin, both prior to Augustine and since his writing, have stressed the warped social conditions that generations of sinning produce, the Reformers tended to locate original sin in the core of human nature. Indeed, their theology of redemption opposed the Eastern Orthodox and Catholic theologies in making grace something extrinsic to the redeemed person and merely imputed to his or her credit because of the merits of Christ. Catholic and Orthodox theology, on the contrary, spoke of a substantial effect of grace, to the extent that grace brought divinization: a true sharing in the divine nature. Puritan theology never was comfortable with such divinization, worrying that it infringed upon the transcendence of God and might be idolatrous. After all, how could a creature (and a very sinful one at that) ever become divine—truly at one with God?

So sin remained even after regeneration, and one could never speak of human nature except as depraved. In heaven the saints would escape the effects of such depravity, but apart from the election by God that brought human beings to heaven, there was no health in the human person. Many times this view was more psychological than strictly theological. Many times the intent was more to combat pride and bring about what was considered a salutary humiliation than to dwell on the nature of the sinful human being. But, as we have seen so regularly in the case of Jonathan Edwards, psychology and theology tended to go hand in hand. Their beliefs drove the Puritans to experience human nature as depraved, and their experience confirmed their beliefs.

It is possible, of course, to experience the evil of human affairs, and the disorder of one's own desires, as a great proof for the thesis of human depravity. When one considers the history of human brutality, the regular injustice of states, the constant failure of the churches to be winning signs of God's goodness, and the selfishness mottling one's own actions, the human spirit can indeed seem to be sick unto death. The more that one places this perception in counterpoint with a perception of the divine splendor, the sharper the contrast becomes. That is why the saints, in all traditions, have regularly considered themselves to be great sinners. That is why the Lord's Prayer, asking for forgiveness of trespasses, has seemed suitable for every season. But a matter of emphasis remains. Orthodox and Catholics have never denied human sinfulness, just as sensible secular people have never denied human evil and folly. In none of these cases, though, has the doctrine of human depravity won favor. In none has it seemed either more accurate or more profitable to stress the wickedness of people. Why did the Puritans find such satisfaction in doing so?

Perhaps because it fit with the marginal status that they themselves had suffered in England. Perhaps because it justified a constant scrutiny of motives, both their own and those of their neighbors. There is some comfort in thinking that one's persecution stems from the wickedness of the powerful. There is some exaltation in joining oneself to the biblical prophets and Jesus and casting woes upon a wicked time. And there can be a sense of self-importance accompanying a regular scrutiny of one's motives and interior states, as the best advocates of a regular examination of conscience point out when they come to listing the dangers. Even as people scrape their souls and lament their sins they can be strengthening their egocentricity. Then bad news is good news that may finally be more bad news: I'm evil, but it's good to confess it, but in confessing it I may be focusing more on myself than on God. The spiritual life is full of perils, some simple and some complex. The Puritans, as a group, were sufficiently spiritually-minded to know this, but they did not always hack through the jungle to reach the clearing, where their own sins and self-concerns would have been relativized, because placed in the much greater context of the divine goodness.

The implications of this Puritan conviction of the depravity of human nature are significant. In the American case, much of what we call the "balance of powers" at the core of the Constitution and in our traditional political institutions comes from a suspicion of human nature. James Madison, the principal framer of the Constitution, was educated at Princeton in Calvinist theology, and that tradition's pessimism about human nature left its mark. Even though both Madison and Jefferson might have considered the Enlightenment the greatest influence on their thought, both men judged it prudent to restrain the ability of any one group to gain great power. The abuses of power that Americans had experienced at the hands of English kings were only part of the evidence for the necessity of suspicion that Madison and Jefferson could have adduced. Human nature was not to be trusted, even though the Enlightenment thinkers were right to free the human intellect from the fetters of religious dogma and encourage natural science. When it came to politics, where self-interest was more central, wisdom counseled suspicion, if not cynicism.

Abigail Adams, the wife of John Adams, the second U.S. president, kept faith with the dark Puritan view of human nature in a letter to her husband on the eve of the American Revolution. In thinking about the rights of women, Abigail Adams hoped for laws that would restrain the natural tendency of men to abuse them: "I long to hear that you have declared an independency—and by the way in the new Code of Laws which I suppose it will be necessary for you to make I desire you would Remember the Ladies, and be more generous and favourable to them than your ancestors. Do not put such unlimited power into the hands of the Husbands. Remember all Men would be tyrants if they could. If peculiar care and attention is not paid to the Ladies we are determined to foment a Rebelion, and will not hold ourselves bound by any Laws in which we have no voice, or Representation. That your sex are Naturally Tyranical is a Truth so thoroughly established as to admit of no dispute, but such of you as wish to be happy willingly give up the harsh title of Master for the more tender and endearing one of Friend. Why, then, not put it out of the power of the vicious and the Lawless to use us with cruelty and indignity with impunity. Men of sense in all Ages abhor those customs which treat us only as the vassals of your Sex. Regard us then as Being placed by providence under your protection and in immitation of the Supreem Being make use of that power only for our happiness."[21]

One could continue down the list of thoughtful Americans, politicians or artists, who have throughout our history regarded law as the restraint necessary to keep a corrupt human nature from breaking out into acts of violence or injustice. Politicians expressing fear of Communists, or totalitarian leaders, or people on welfare, have all taken refuge in the notion that if not checked, any group is likely to grasp for advantage. How this dark view of human nature has squared with an often romantic sense of America's destiny is hard to say. Perhaps the best explanation is the illogic attending most popular cultures. People sense that several judgments are true simultaneously, but they think it more important to acknowledge each such judgment than to work out how the judgments correlate.

NOTES

1. See Baird Tipson, "Calvinist Heritage," and "New England Heritage," in *Encyclopedia of the American Religious Experience*, ed. Charles H. Lippy and Peter W. Williams (New York: Scribner's, 1988), vol. 2, pp. 451–466 and 467–480.

2. The biography of Edwards that sparked a renewal of Edwards studies was Perry Miller's *Jonathan Edwards* (New York, 1949), which portrayed him as a modern. For a good indication of more recent views of Edwards (and of criticisms of Miller), see Nathan O. Hatch and Harry S. Stout, eds., *Jonathan Edwards and the American Experience* (New York: Oxford, 1988).

3. Quoted in Clyde A. Holbrook, "Editor's Introduction," in Jonathan Edwards, *Original Sin,* ed. Clyde A. Holbrook (New Haven: Yale University Press, 1970), pp. 19–20.

4. Ibid., pp. 112–113.

5. Paul Ramsey, "Editor's Introduction," in Jonathan Edwards, *Freedom of the Will*, ed. Paul Ramsey (New Haven: Yale University Press, 1957), p. 7.

6. Ibid., p. 239.

7. Ibid., p. 374.

8. Ibid., p. 407.

9. In a letter dated July 25, 1757, Edwards makes clear his view that the moral necessity he finds in human actions is not inconsistent with the liberty of any creature as a free and responsible moral agent. Whether he shows how this view of human agency squares with the omniscience of God and the necessity that God's will triumph is another question. See ibid., p. 464.

10. John E. Smith, "Editor's Introduction," in Jonathan Edwards, *Religious Affections* (New Haven: Yale University Press, 1959), pp. 3–4.

11. Ibid., pp. 253–254.

12. Ibid., p. 311.

13. Norman Pettit, "Editor's Introduction," in Jonathan Edwards, *The Life of David Brainerd,* ed. Norman Pettit (New Haven: Yale University Press, 1985), p. 3.

14. Ibid., p. 177.

15. Ibid., p. 547.

16. Jonathan Edwards, *The Great Awakening,* ed. C.C. Goen (New Haven: Yale University Press, 1972), pp. 331–332.

17. Ibid., p. 89.

18. See Daniel Walker Howe, "The Impact of Puritanism on American Culture," in *Encyclopedia of the American Religious Experience,* vol. 2, pp. 1064–1065.

19. See William A. Clebsch, *American Religious Thought: A History* (Chicago: University of Chicago Press, 1973), pp. 11–56.

20. Herbert F. May, "Jonathan Edwards and America," in *Jonathan Edwards and the American Experience,* p. 24.

21. Alice S. Rossi, ed., *The Feminist Papers* (New York: Columbia University Press, 1973), pp. 10–11.

Chapter 3

On Human Nature:
Responses from the Margins

Jewish Americans

In 1654 twenty-three Jewish refugees from Portuguese Brazil brought Judaism to New Amsterdam. They were seeking a haven from the discrimination rampant in Iberian cultures, and their Judaism was the Sephardic orthodoxy that had known a golden era in Portugal and Spain prior to the expulsion of the Jews by Ferdinand and Isabella in 1492. By the end of the colonial period, in 1776, Jews had established congregations in Newport, Rhode Island; New York City; Philadelphia; Lancaster, Pennsylvania; Richmond, Virginia; Charleston, South Carolina; and Savannah, Georgia. Prior to the arrival in the eighteenth century of Jewish immigrants shaped by the impact of the Enlightenment on European Jewry, all Jewish congregations aspired to have traditionally trained religious leaders, traditional liturgical celebrations, kosher food, and the other principal features of what they considered a traditional religious life.

However, even though emancipation had given some European Jews a taste of legal equality with Gentiles, the colonies and then the United States were remarkable for the freedom they offered. Religious prejudice certainly remained, especially during the first century or so of Jewish existence in America, when the colonial ideal was still an established religion, usually a Protestant version of Christianity, but the de facto pluralism of Americans, combined with the demands of establishing a new commonwealth, lessened the practical effects of such religious prejudice. By 1761 Jews in New York had produced an English translation of part of the liturgy for the High Holy Days—a sign of the adaptation to America that has characterized Jewish immigrants down to the present day. The desire to be accepted as Americans, and to take advantage of the freedoms offered in America, determined that American Judaism would be different from any Judaism that had preceded it. Because the original settlers often had to make do without rabbis, the tradition developed that the rabbi would serve the overall needs of the already established community that hired him. American rabbis tended to deal less with specifically religious questions than their traditional European counterparts had, and more with the general cultural life of their community, helping to coordinate the assimilation of Jews into American institutions.

The biblical and talmudic traditions of European Jewry offered a wealth of sources for developing a view of human nature.[1] Although their ideal would have been to develop a community life based on solid education in these traditions, for the first century of their residence in America the majority of American Jews did not have the luxury of leisurely study, nor the resources (books, teachers) for it. The arrival of Ashkenazic Jews (those of German and Eastern European origins) in the first half of the eighteenth century brought tensions, because the Ashkenazim did many things differently than the Sephardim. Thus in 1738 Jews in Savannah were frustrated because the two groups could not agree sufficiently to cooperate in the construction of a common synagogue. In almost all cases Jewish communities were relatively small (one estimate is that until 1800 the total American Jewish population was less than two thousand; by 1850 it had reached fifty thousand[2]), so such divisions were painful and frustrating. Until the arrival of Ashkenazic Jews influenced by the Enlightenment, however, virtually all American Jews instinctively looked to the Bible and the Talmud for instruction on matters such as the goodness or evil of human nature.

Naturally, neither the Bible nor the rabbis whose commentaries on the Bible and Jewish traditions were collected into the Talmud spoke about human nature with a single voice. Still, it seems clear that few would have agreed with the Calvinist view that human nature is depraved. Judaism never developed a doctrine of original sin like that of Christianity. For Jews the refrain of Genesis that when God saw his creation he found it very good remained a call to love the earth—be fruitful, multiply, and fill it with people. Judaism honored family life and held celibacy suspect. It tended to picture divine blessings as having a solid material component and to think that wealth, despite all its spiritual dangers, is a gift of God. In many periods Jews downplayed the notion of an afterlife, and this tended to increase the value of children and living well. Certainly, great numbers of Jews, in both Europe and the United States, suffered poverty and ill health, as well as persecution and contempt. But the instinct inculcated by the Jewish reading of the Bible and by Jewish family life was to consider life good. For such an instinct, human nature could not be depraved. People might be weak, liable to temptation, able to do one another great harm, but in the measure that people harkened to the Master of the Universe, they could become decent human beings, willing and able to render justice to one another. Those who had prospered would count it right, natural, a privilege as well as a duty to help the less fortunate. Few Jews meditated on the plight of sinners cast into hell, and while many Jews considered God a strict judge, few were dominated by fear of God's anger, let alone by thoughts that God is repulsed by a human nature rotten to the core. God might despise sin, and even more the suffering that it brought in its wake, but God could not despise the work of his hands. The problem was that human beings would not honor the potential, the divine image, that God had placed in them. They would not embrace the Torah (Instruction) God had given them and walk the pathway to life. There was nothing unworkable about either basic human nature or God's Torah. The problem was human weakness, human forgetfulness. Certainly, the prophets had developed a classic critique of injustice, idolatry, and hardness of heart. But the very sting of the prophets' lash was the assumption that human beings were free to act differently. The Puritan counsels about predestination would not have received a favorable hearing in the typical American synagogue. One could not blame God for human sin, and one could not blame human beings unless they were free to do otherwise.

The "reformed" Judaism that stemmed from the reconsideration of the human condition and Jewish tradition spawned by the Enlightenment was even more optimistic about human nature. The sixth and seventh articles of the Pittsburgh Platform, a formulation of principles agreed upon by a Reformed assembly in 1885, suggests the sympathy that Reform Judaism felt for Enlightenment ideas about human goodness and potential for progress: "We recognize in Judaism a progressive religion, ever striving to be in accord with the postulates of reason. We are convinced of the utmost necessity of preserving the historical identity of our great past. Christianity and Islam being daughter religions of Judaism, we appreciate their providential mission to aid in the spreading of monotheistic and moral truth. We acknowledge that the spirit of broad humanity of our age is our ally in the fulfillment of our mission, and therefore, we extend the hand of fellowship to all who operate with us in the establishment of the reign of truth and righteousness among men. We reassert the doctrine of Judaism, that the soul of man is immortal, grounding this belief on the divine nature of the human spirit, which forever finds bliss in righteousness and misery in wickedness. We reject as ideas not rooted in Judaism the beliefs both in bodily resurrection and in Gehenna and Eden [Hell and Paradise] as abodes for everlasting punishment or reward."[3]

There are many further things that one would have to study, including both the implications of traditional Judaism's desire to separate Jews from other peoples so as to avoid uncleanliness and the many Gentile portions of American culture that also rejected a Puritan sense of depravity, but for the moment it suffices to make the suggestion that Jewish Americans have seldom been possessed by a instinctive suspicion of human nature. Guilt, worries about human motivation, keen awareness of the ability of human beings to become bigots and hurt one another—these certainly have been part and parcel of American Jewish culture. But doubting the core goodness of the human nature that the Creator had made, and thinking of it as fit only for hellfire, have not been typically Jewish positions.[4]

Roman Catholics

Roman Catholic missionaries accompanied the Spanish explorers who roamed throughout the Americas in the sixteenth century. They also played a significant role in the French explorations and settlements of the seventeenth and eighteenth centuries. In the English colonies that were to become the backbone of the United States, Catholics were always a small minority. Frequently they suffered discrimination, through the extension of English anti-papist statutes that forbade them to hold full citizenship (voting rights, the right to hold political office) and to have a full ministry of their priests. Lord Baltimore, who founded Maryland, was a Catholic, and in its early years Maryland welcomed Catholic settlers. But Maryland was not a Catholic colony. At best it sponsored a tolerance that protected the legal and religious rights of all its members. At worst it imposed the prejudices of an Anglican majority and denied equal rights to religious minorities. The Catholicism of the Maryland colonists therefore was restrained. Their priests tended to support themselves as landholding gentlemen, their religious lives centered in the home, and they sought to avoid confrontations with the Protestant majority.

The first mass in the colonies was held on March 25, 1634, when English Jesuit missionaries, having sailed up the Potomac, disembarked on one of the islands, celebrated "the sacrifice" and erected a cross as a trophy to Christ. In the English colonies the Jesuits were the most prominent Catholic priests and the city of Baltimore became the center of Catholicism. John Carroll, the first superior of Catholic priests in the United States, came from a prominent family, one member of which signed the Declaration of Independence. The Jesuits were suppressed in 1773, but many former Jesuits continued to function as secular priests. John Carroll had been a Jesuit and served as the first archbishop of Baltimore. In his early career Carroll defended liberal American ways to Roman authorities who were fearful of them, including the significant influence that lay people had in the American church. By the end of his career, however, Carroll had retracted his enthusiasm for lay power. Still, Roman authorities have traditionally feared the impact of American democratic notions on American Catholics. The bishops who followed in the wake of Carroll tended to be autocratic, breaking the back of lay influence, but when they represented the American church to Rome, they often argued that the competitive atmosphere in the United States, where no church was established or had a legal advantage, suited Catholicism well.

When it came to a theological stance regarding human nature, the premier authority to which Catholics of the seventeenth and eighteenth centuries would have looked was the Council of Trent (1545–63). At this council the Catholic authorities had worked out their response to the Protestant Reformers, especially to the positions of Martin Luther. Luther anticipated the pessimistic reading of human nature that Calvin developed, so in dealing with original sin Trent had to grapple with the issue of where the fall of Adam and Eve had left human beings. As part of a decree on original sin issued after its fifth session (1546), Trent taught that "if anyone deny that the guilt of original sin is remitted by the grace of our Lord Jesus Christ conferred in baptism or assert that everything that has the true and proper nature of sin is not taken away but is erased or not reckoned—*anathema sit* [let him or her be anathema]. For God hates nothing in those who are reborn . . . The Holy Council, however, knows and confesses that there remains in those who have been baptized concupiscence or the inclination to sin. But since this is left for us to wrestle with, it cannot harm those who do not consent to but manfully resist it by the grace of Jesus Christ. . . . Of this concupiscence which the Apostle [Paul] occasionally calls 'sin' . . . this Holy Council declares that the Catholic Church has never understood its being called sin in the sense of real and actual sin in those who have been regenerated, but only as coming from sin and inclining towards sin. If anyone think to the contrary, *anathema sit.* "[5]

The Reformers' teachings about the corruption of human nature, which dovetailed with their stress on salvation through faith rather than works, inevitably focused the question of human nature on original sin. Prior to this focus, however, Catholic teaching had tended to treat questions of human nature in the context of creation. Thus the Council of Florence (1442) taught that the Church "most firmly believes, professes, and preaches that the one true God, Father, Son and Holy Spirit is the Creator of all things visible and invisible. Who, when he so wished, out of his bounty created all creatures, spiritual as well as corporeal. They are good, since they were created by the highest God, but mutable, because they were created out of nothing. She [the Church] affirms that evil has no nature, for all nature, as nature, is good."[6] Human nature, it followed, is good. Granted, through original sin humanity lost such gifts as immortality, but nothing essential to human nature was lost. Human nature was not twisted or rendered wicked. It remains good, though weak and subject to concupiscence (the inclination to sin, which creates the need to develop virtue [moral strength]).

These interpretations of Scripture and Christian tradition separated Catholic theology and piety from that of Protestants. Frequently the theological difference was slight, and appreciated only by experts. Frequently Catholic piety was rather gloomy, as it was during the late middle ages, the matrix from which the piety of the early Reformers arose. But in the background of Catholicism lay centuries during which the notion of Christendom had evolved. Christendom sought the permeation of culture by Christian ideals, so that art, science, politics, economics, family life, and everything else would be animated by faith and grace. The Catholic assumption in this enterprise was that creation itself is good, so everything that surrounds human beings can become the occasion or vehicle for praising God. The sins of human beings do not vitiate this assumption, though they do cast a pall over human existence and remind people of their need for divine help. Overall, creation and the human situation remain things to celebrate, because God made them good and Christ resecured their goodness by his death and resurrection.

On the precise question of human freedom, the Jesuits who helped set the character of American Catholic faith had a tradition of generosity. Indeed, in disputes with the Jansenists during the seventeenth century the Jesuits had been satirized by Blaise Pascal, the Jansenist genius, as far too optimistic about human nature, far too clever and lax. Whether in fact this was true is debatable, but what is beyond dispute is that the Jesuits, and many other Catholics, believed that people are responsible for their salvation and can respond well to offers of divine grace. The situation in which human beings find themselves may be challenging, and the first step on the road to pleasing God (and appropriating true human freedom) is to repent of one's sins, but the sacraments so prominent in Catholic church life are powerful helps in this regard.

In addition to the two sacraments (baptism and the Lord's Supper) approved by the Reformers, Catholics have offered five others (Confirmation, Penance, Matrimony, Holy Orders, and Last Anointing). The Catholic saints have been further resources for help, especially Mary, the Mother of Jesus. So in Roman Catholic estimation the human condition is cause for celebration. Though the majority of the race, who have been poor and burdened, have had to suffer, the crux of their situation as creatures of the holy God and objects of Christ's redeeming love has remained good beyond compare. From this goodness came the Catholic license to eat, drink, celebrate, and indulge high spirits that brought frowns to the faces of puritanical Protestants and compounded the problems of Catholic assimilation during the nineteenth century. Many of the Irish and Italians and Poles were not as serious and industrious as their Protestant bosses and landlords wanted them to be. They could not regard life or their neighbors so pessimistically. For they had been taught a different view of human nature, one that could not agree that human nature was depraved or that sobriety was godliness.

Women

American women have obviously been present in all the varieties of American religion and irreligion. Much in what American women have thought and taught about human nature therefore has depended on the religious or ethnic group to which they have belonged. On the whole American women, like women the world over, have lagged behind men in their access to education. Thus women frequently gained their impressions of human nature more from sermons and daily living than from sustained theological study. The Puritan women who listened to the early Bay Colony ministers, or to Jonathan Edwards, learned that original sin was virulent and human freedom was limited by the predestination of God. Nonetheless, because the Bible that was the center of their Puritan culture contained a variety of viewpoints, colonial women in New England such as Anne Hutchinson used passages such as Galatians 3:28, where Paul says that in Christ there are no distinctions between Jew and Gentile, slave and free, male and female, to throw over the subordinate status accorded women and speak out boldly. Anne Hutchinson was banished because she challenged the ministerial powers of her day, but also because her outspokenness was deemed unsuitable for a woman. There is no reason to think that she disagreed with the Calvinist assessment of human nature ruling in the Bay Colony, but her willingness to follow her own inner light suggests that in practice she did not distrust her own instincts.

Rosemary Skinner Keller has generalized about the experience of American women, proposing that those who lived in a religious or ethnic subculture tended to subordinate their aspirations as women to the assimilation or progress of their minority community. In other words, their first concern was that their families and neighborhoods gain acceptance and get ahead in American society, and they tended to view their religious affiliation as a means to that end. That does not mean they were not honestly committed to praising God in the fashion that their religious group chose, but it does mean that until their families had advanced, they tended to neglect what we now consider the feminist agenda of working for the rights of women precisely as women. Thus the early American feminists came from the Protestant mainstream, while Roman Catholic, Jewish, and African-American women only joined the feminist movement, and focused on sexist biases within their own traditions, once some measure of acceptance in the American mainstream had been achieved. Native-American women still focus more on their problems as Native Americans, rather than their problems as women, because their people have yet to achieve anything like full acceptance or progress.[7]

We shall see in later sections that both African-American and Native-American women had in their traditions powerful antidotes to the Puritan theses about human depravity. Even for Protestant women, however, the development of the cultural images of women in the United States worked significant variations on the going sense of human nature. As a result of the revivalism and evangelism that arose in the late seventeenth and early eighteenth centuries, the image of women shifted from the association with carnality that medieval Christianity had postulated to an association with spirituality and moral superiority. In concert with a privatization of religion, and a shift of the focus of religion from culture at large to the domestic sphere, women became the more religious sex, the sex naturally more suited for virtue and piety.

This was a two-edged sword, of course, inasmuch as it reinforced movements to sequester women from public affairs. But it meant a new way of thinking about human nature, one in which sex served to mark a person as naturally more or less godly. For Jewish women, this shift directly contradicted Orthodox tradition, according to which men were the sex naturally suited for study of Torah (the prime religious duty) and women were the sex suited for the practical tasks of running the home and even making the living. For Roman Catholic women, and also Protestant women, this shift seemed a contradiction of their churches' steadfast policy against ordaining women to the ministry. Nonetheless, the feminization of religion meant a certain sanctioning of supposedly feminine characteristics as proper to the religious (that is, the good) personality. Gentleness, meek-ness, sensitivity, concern for the weak, an inclination to spiritual things (prayer, Bible reading, hymn singing, works of charity) became nearly synonymous with human excellence.

Some women rode this wave to found new religious groups (for exam-ple, Mary Baker Eddy), while others began to preach and gradually won acceptance as religious leaders (first in evangelical, revivalist groups, later in more mainstream Protestant denominations). The Shakers founded by Mother Ann Lee had anticipated some of these implications—they had placed a female component in the godhead, coupled Mother Ann with Jesus, and developed a celibate community life in which men and women were strict equals. In their case, as in several other cases, the spiritualization of religion and ideal human nature associated with the new prominence of feminine virtues called the goodness of the body, and more specifically of sexuality, seriously into question, making the Shakers appear somewhat like the early Christian deviants who decried sex, marriage, eating, drink-ing, and other fleshly exercises and propounded a strict asceticism.

This tendency never became the dominant characteristic of American religious women, but during the Victorian period the feminization of religion certainly was a factor in an overall repression of sexual expression (and its consequent going underground). One can understand the attrac-tion that celibate communities had for American women seeking greater equality than what the culture at large offered, but whether the view of human nature implicit in a venture such as Shakerism promotes a full-bodied feminism is another question.[8] Equally, what the feminization of religion meant for men and the spheres of life allocated to them is another question. On the whole it may well have strengthened the notion that the world (business, politics, practical affairs) is a dirty place (dominated by the injustice one would expect human depravity to produce). If so, it contrib-uted to a dualism reminiscent of the early Christian sects (for example, the

Gnostics) and should have run afoul, at least conceptually, of the incarnationalism at the center of Christianity (the Word became flesh) and the earthiness characteristic of Judaism, where history has always been the main arena of divine revelation.

Roman Catholic nuns, along with Protestant women who were social reformers, disputed the tendency of nineteenth-century American religion to limit women to the domestic sphere. The activist orders that played a large role in the survival and acculturation of the masses of Catholic immigrants made education and nursing signal religious enterprises. Although the nuns did not petition for ordination, their celibate, ascetic lifestyles, combined with their practical services, meant that to many Catholic newcomers, and many Protestants as well, they were prime representatives of the Catholic church. Indeed, they became special targets for anti-Catholic sentiment, and some of their public services, such as nursing the wounded of the Civil War, seem to have been undertaken for the sake of public relations, as well as for their intrinsic merit.

Protestant women who became social activists, whether in the fight against slavery, or against alcoholism, or for women's suffrage, or simply to improve the lot of the poor, tended to begin their work from religious motives and to become more secular as they discovered the political and economic roots and ramifications of the problems they were addressing. Even secularized, however, their views on vice tended to reenforce the Protestant sense that human nature naturally tended toward unsavory activities and the nineteenth century's notion that women had the special vocation to elevate society above its baser instincts. Jewish women who became socially active sometimes aligned themselves with the labor movement and the socialist thinking prevalent in Europe, including Marxism. By the time the women's movement became organized in the middle of the twentieth century a consensus about the philosophy and tactics of social reform, greatly influenced by the African-American experience, led the majority of its leaders, who tended to be Protestant but also numbered among them many Jews and Catholics, to equate whatever religious idealism they had (the women's movement has been more secular than religious) with social action. Had they been inclined to translate their rationale into Christian terms, these leaders might have drawn on the Social Gospel movement, the principles of which were outlined by Walter Rauschenbusch early in the twentieth century: the crux of Christian virtue lay in work to establish the Kingdom of God, which for Rauschenbusch meant in significant measure social and economic justice. Behind this view, and the analogous view of the feminists, lay the notion that human nature is perfectible—an optimism challenging any view of human nature that understood original sin or depravity to make significant change problematic.

African Americans

The early history of African-American religion in the United States was dominated by a dividedness in the minds of the white slaveowners. Most slaveholders were Christians, so on occasion they practiced the ministry to slaves that Christianity required of them. The New Testament was ambiguous about slavery. In his short letter to his convert Philemon, Paul had not required him to free Onesimus, one of his slaves who had run away. Onesimus had also become a Christian, so the question was how the brotherhood created by their common faith affected the relationship between slaveowner and slave, all the more so when Onesimus (the property of Philemon) had run away (stolen something belonging to Philemon). Paul's preference for love and freedom is clear, but he does not challenge the institution of slavery, as it flourished in the Greco-Roman world, so he could be cited by slaveowners as considering slavery acceptable.

In 1701 the issue of whether Christians should try to bring slaves to Christian faith, and what consequences baptism would imply, became sharper, because the Church of England formed a Society for the Propagation of the Gospel in Foreign Parts. But while members of this Society urged as a Christian duty evangelizing slaves, they hastened to assure slaveowners that Christian faith ought to create better slaves—more docile and hardworking ones. By the 1770s colonial legislators had settled the juridical aspects of the issue, declaring that baptism did not alter the legal status of slaves. On the emotional side, many whites opposed trying to convert the slaves because they disagreed with the Society and thought that Christianity would spoil the slaves, making them think too well of themselves.

African-American slaves only became Christians in significant numbers from the time of the Great Awakening (1740s), and in general their enthusiasm for Christianity was a function of the attractions offered by a revivalist faith. Most slaves were illiterate (in many areas teaching them to read and write was a crime), and native African traditions had stressed singing, dancing, being filled by spirits, and other activities that we might call ecstatic. The spare, literary faith sponsored by the Puritans and the Anglicans did not serve African-American needs, but the rousing sermons of the revivalists, and their inclination to sing, shout, and confess their inner needs, had great appeal.

Even when they had become Christian converts, however, African Americans tended to suffer serious hindrances to the exercise of their faith. Prior to emancipation, when their fate lay in the hands of their masters, they often had to sneak away at night to "hush harbors" where they would try to pray, sing, dance, and externalize their pains quietly enough to avoid detection and so suppression. The main appeal of the Christian story to African Americans lay in its symbols of liberation. Whether they focused on the account of the exodus of the Hebrews from slavery in Egypt, or on the sufferings through which Jesus had redeemed the world from sin and given humanity a new future, African Americans understandably stressed the stories and teachings that spoke to their own sufferings. The majority probably interpreted the Bible in spiritual terms, seeking an interior strength based on the biblical confirmation that slavery was a sin against God and the biblical promise of a heavenly vindication. However, some African Americans focused more on the reforms of current social arrangements that the Israelite prophets and Jesus himself called for, and the slave rebellions of the first third of the nineteenth century tended to claim religious justifications. Thus Nat Turner, leader of the bloodiest of these rebellions, claimed that God had instructed him to rise up against whites.

It is instructive that African Americans regularly refused the interpretation of Christianity being preached to them by white ministers and slaveowners, instead interpreting the Bible to place God on their side as victims of oppression. After the Civil War, they tended to find the experience of attending racially mixed churches unsatisfying, either because of racist prejudice they encountered or because their desire for a vibrant, emotionally satisfying faith was not being met. African Americans both formed their own churches within established church lines (Methodist, Baptist, Episcopalian, Presbyterian) and created new groups. The forty-year period from 1877 to 1917 has been described as the nadir of African-American history, as Reconstruction ended and racism became virulent. The exodus of African Americans from the countryside to the cities, and from south to north, that occurred around the turn of the century was due mainly to an agricultural depression, but it created immense social problems for the dislocated and became another incentive to fashion all-African-American churches in which people might find both practical and emotional support.

From the earliest converted slaves coming together for prayer in hush harbors to recent liberation theologians, pondering the implications of slavery and racism has been at the center of African-American religion. With such a focus, this religion was bound to stress the sinfulness of what human beings tend to do, if not of what human beings by nature are. Protestant theology tended to impart some version, weak or strong, of the traditional Reformation teachings about the depravity of human nature, yet the African traditions at the roots of this culture jarred with such teachings. Without neglecting the reality of evil, such African traditions stressed the goodness of the body, of nature, of human time, and especially of spiritual experiences such as communicating with one's ancestors through dreams or visions. The African traditions on which most African Americans drew were holistic, fighting any tendency to overspiritualize religion or to distinguish religion as a feminine sphere. In the United States, African-American women did predominate over men in church membership, even though most congregations were slow to grant women ordination; and African-American women did see their churches as centers of support for their families more often than men did. But these churches served many men as vehicles for leadership and service, just as they served the entire community as the place that nurtured music (for example, spirituals), art, education, and social services. So the African-Americans' view of human nature, though certainly as rich and complicated as that of any other American group, has tended to identify sin and depravity more with the behavior, and so the character, of their oppressors than with human nature as such. African Americans did not deny that they could be inhuman to one another, but the massive evils in their lives flowed from white abuse of them as slaves and ongoing white racism. It made sense to ascribe the breakdown of the African-American family and community, through the flight of its fathers, crime, alcoholism, drugs, prostitution, and the like, to the unemployment and dim prospects that sapped pride and a sense of self-worth, rather than to anything inherent in human nature. It made even more sense to use religion to clarify this situation, help people muster the discipline and faith to fight back, and place their hopes in a reality beyond the corruptions of human nature: the liberating God depicted in the Bible.[9]

Native Americans

Although Native Americans have not had a large impact on white American culture, they have always been present to the American psyche as a mysterious "other." From the first European contacts with Native Americans, whites have tended either to romanticize them as noble savages, or denigrate them as primitive peoples. Understandably, neither character-ization is accurate, since Native Americans have been as human, and so as good and evil, as whites.

Moreover, the more that scholars have learned about Native-American peoples, the more they have been impressed by the diversity of languages, material cultures, and religious complexes the different tribes manifest. There is no such thing as a uniform Native-American religious culture, though in recent years, as a result of a growing realization of common suffering under white rule, some Native Americans have promoted pan-tribalism and spoken of such overarching themes as reverence for a Great Spirit.

As they developed historically, however, the different tribes varied widely in their sense of the forces running the world, the way that the world had arisen, what practices would most enhance a person's spiritual life, the rightful roles of women, and many other matters. All the tribal cultures were oral, in the sense of having no writing, and while they all certainly had histories (pasts containing steady change) and most of them assigned custody of oral traditions to certain tribal leaders, they were not historical in our modern Western sense. They could not document what had happened to them in the past, and they had no written texts around which to construct a doctrinal orthodoxy. Thus scholars such as Sam Gill suggest that the key to understanding Native-American religious cultures is penetrating their ceremonies.[10]

These ceremonies usually have amounted to a dramatic enactment of a rich system of symbols. The typical tribe has tended to represent its sense of how the world was organized, so that those participating in the ceremo-nies could be reconnected with objective reality. Even in ceremonies with pragmatic ends, such as healings, the desire to reaffirm the basic order of the world has been as important as the desire to cure the particular sickness. For what has always been at stake is the basic meaningfulness of human existence, and even when a curing ceremony did not avert death it could occasion an experience of the essential goodness of the world that com-forted patient and onlooker alike.

With the exception of the tribes, such as the Navaho, that thought of the world as housing truly malign spirits and feared the activation of such spirits by witches, Native Americans have tended to think that the land, the animals, and the spiritual influences that one could almost sense when one practiced quiet and solitude were good. Human beings could go wrong, and they had to purify their hearts, but there was no reason to castigate human nature as depraved. Human beings are as human beings behave: some are good and others are evil. Moreover, one could improve one's mind, heart, and soul. If one accepted the traditional disciplines, listened to the elders, and entered into the rituals generously, the wisdom of one's people's way might become manifest. Many Native Americans have undertaken vision quests and gained spirits (in the form of birds or animals) to help them attune themselves to the holy powers running the world. Many others have experienced the purification that suffering can bring. So, because of the possibility of gaining a conviction that their time was eminently meaningful, and of the beauty that they found in the natural world, most Native Americans did not doubt the goodness of their existence.

The devastations that white culture worked on Native-American cultures were probably the worst challenge to this optimism that Native Americans had ever faced. Much like African Americans, who found whites the source of their major burdens, Native Americans met something new and virulent in Europeans. The desire to conquer the land, fence it about, and own it that possessed whites baffled Native Americans. The use of treaties to avoid keeping one's word seemed an incredible perversion. Some Native Americans found the white religion attractive, but many more did not understand its moral code and suspected it would abet the destruction of Native culture. The greatest challenge to the Native-American convictions about the goodness of human nature therefore has been the behavior of white Christians, who could seem to exemplify the doctrine of original sin.

A good example of a traditional Native-American ritualistic system that assumed the goodness of the human condition is that of the Lakota. As reported by Black Elk, a Lakota who had been influenced by Christianity, the various rites given to the Lakota in mythological times by the Buffalo Maiden all could bring them into a fulfilling harmony with nature and the holy forces controlling it. The details of the Lakota rituals stress such matters as involving all the directions of the compass in the person's prayers and using natural elements (grass, tobacco, water) as vehicles of religious meaning. The sky above and the earth below served the person as holy parents. The rituals brim with the joy and satisfaction of honoring these parents and drawing closer to them. In the rite for purifying oneself in the sweat-lodge, the steam is a medium for communicating with holy powers. In the rite for smoking the sacred pipe, the smoke serves the same function. The underlying conviction is that the human spirit can gain union with the divine spirit. But in all of the Lakota rituals the human spirit never despises the body in which it is housed. Even when the rituals urge people to put baser thoughts out of their mind and concentrate on things that purify, there is no denigration of the body.

Native-American asceticism, as exemplified in the Lakota ritual known as the Sun Dance, might seem to contradict this assertion, but in fact it does not. The sacrifices that the dancers make, the pain that they suffer, constitute an effort to free the spirit and make over to the holy powers a worthy sacrifice. The pain involved is not good in its own right but only as a token of the person's willingness to suffer for the sake of the tribe and to honor the holy powers. The dancers are not mortifying a flesh that has been warped from the beginning by sin against God, let alone a flesh that has been tainted by the sexual transmission of life (as Augustine taught).

Perhaps the Lakota ritual for a ball game (similar to lacrosse) best expresses the conviction many Native Americans have had that human beings are citizens of an amazing natural world for which they ought always to give thanks. The ball game symbolizes the key features and functions of the universe, as the Lakota traditionally understood it. To play in that universe, trying to advance toward the success that would make one pleasing to the holy powers, was the main reason one had been given life. So in cooperating to score goals the players on a given team reminded themselves how they ought to help one another mature. Meanwhile, the opposition of the other team, which was trying to keep them from scoring, stood for the opposition that any person would face in trying to live a holy life. But the entire contest could be joyous, because the nature involved was beautiful.[11]

Asian Traditions: Buddhism

On the margins of American religious culture have lived hundreds of thousands of Asian Americans, who have been rooted in such ancient traditions as Buddhism, Hinduism, Confucianism, Taoism, Shinto, and Islam. As space provides, we shall consider representatives of this Asian-American contingent. For our consideration of human nature, Buddhism makes a good representative.

In the 1840s Buddhism came to the United States in the form of Chinese immigrants, whose numbers dramatically increased when the gold rush began. By the mid-1850s Chinese temples had appeared in San Francisco. Usually the religion practiced in them was a mixture of Buddhist,

Taoist, and Confucian traditions. Japanese immigration proceeded more slowly than Chinese, and until the end of the nineteenth century the Japanese-American population was small.

At the World Parliament of Religions held in conjunction with the World's Fair in Chicago in 1893 oriental religions made a great impact. Among the more impressive representatives were a Buddhist from the Rinzai Zen tradition and a Buddhist representing the Ceylonese Theravada tradition. Zen has been the most influential Buddhist sect in the United States, and it traces its lineage to Mahayana Buddhism, one of the two major divisions that had become well formed during the period from the death of the Buddha (483 B.C.E.) to around 200 B.C.E. Zen had begun in China in the sixth century C.E. The monk Bodhidharma is traditionally credited with founding the Zen lineage, and his great interest was meditation. Zen makes meditation the pivotal point at which all the major concerns of Buddhism converge. Several schools of Zen have been influential in both China and Japan, and both the Rinzai and the Soto sects have won American followers (Caucasian as well as Oriental). D.T. Suzuki, the figure who led the way in introducing Zen to the United States, came from the Rinzai lineage, while Shunryu Suzuki (no relation), who founded the Zen Center in San Francisco, came from the Soto lineage. Rinzai urges people to strive hard to gain enlightenment, while Soto teaches that people should practice calmly, letting the enlightenment intrinsic to the human being manifest itself.

In this latter attitude we find a trenchant expression of the Buddhist sense of human nature. The Buddha (563–483 B.C.E.) had been born into a princely family and lived a protected life. In his late twenties, however, he began to wrestle with the problem of suffering: disease, old age, death. The solution he found was an insight into both the cause of suffering and the moderate religious practice that can overcome it. The cause of suffering is desire. The way to remove desire is through Buddhist practice, which is an eightfold path that one may summarize in terms of wisdom, meditation, and morality. These three aspects of Buddhist practice reinforce one another. Wisdom teaches one the cause of suffering and the configuration of reality. Meditation helps one actualize this teaching, so that its light floods one's entire being with understanding and freedom. Morality keeps one living in accord with wisdom, most basically by preventing one from killing, stealing, lying, taking intoxicants, or acting unchastely. Buddhism has always considered the monastic setting the ideal place in which to practice all three aspects of the eightfold path, but Mahayana Buddhism developed several modifications of monastic life to suit laity. On the one hand, it promoted devotions to the Buddha and many Bodhisattvas (Buddhas-to-be, saints). On the other hand, it reasoned that nirvana (the extinction of desire) occurs in the midst of samsara (the world of suffering, in which people must endure a cycle of death and rebirth). As the Buddhist philosophers and meditation masters pondered this notion that nirvana occurs in the midst of samsara, they sharpened the instinct, implicit in the Buddha's experience of enlightenment (a Buddha is an Enlightened One), that human nature itself is full of knowledge. When one removes the desire that clouds the human mind and weakens the human will, the intrinsic clarity of the human person can burst forth. So one may say that enlightenment is simply the revelation of what has always been so: the world and the human person alike have always been intrinsically good and full of truth.

Buddhism is not always clear or persuasive when it comes to explaining how desire entered the world or why it has such a hold on human beings. Sensibly enough, many meditation masters have taught their disciples that all would become clear once their meditation had brought them to enlightenment. In this they have been reminiscent of Christian masters, who have said regularly that one must believe in order to understand. But the overall effect of Zen teaching has been to foster an approach to the arts and work that tries to carry into practice the conviction that one's inner nature has only to flower for painting, poetry, swordsmanship, archery, the tea ceremony, or even industrial production to advance toward excellence. The combination of discipline and optimism in Japanese Buddhism has contributed greatly to Japan's impressive culture.

The Theravada tradition, representing the second branch in the early split among the Buddha's disciples, has also stressed meditation. And even though Theravada masters have not been so bold as the Mahayanists in equating nirvana with samsara or developing Bodhisattvas to hear people's prayers, they certainly have encouraged the notion that if one can remove desire one can liberate the forces of creativity, wisdom, and happiness latent in the human personality. Theravada masters have often become very sophisticated psychologists, analyzing the different thoughts, images, and desires that travel on the stream of consciousness. Regularly, though, they have assumed and taught that in itself that stream is intended to be full of light. Theravada has flourished in Sri Lanka, Burma, and Thailand. Because there have been fewer immigrants from those lands than from China, Japan, Vietnam, and Korea, where Mahayana traditions have flourished, Theravada has not made as great an impression as Mahayana in the United States.

A third branch of Buddhism, known as Vajrayana, has developed tantric traditions that lay deep in the religious history of India. Tantra has sponsored exercises to draw the imagination and libidinal energies into the work of rooting out desire and achieving enlightenment. Tantric traditions gained their fullest flowering in Tibet, where the use of mandalas and mantras (special shapes and sounds) to mobilize the imagination and libidinal energies became highly skillful. In the background of Tibetan Buddhist practice lies the Mahayana philosophy locating nirvana in the midst of samsara and the Mahayana confidence about the intrinsic purity or lightsomeness of the human personality. Several of the Tibetan lineages have established centers in the United States. Perhaps the most influential has been the Naropa Institute in Boulder, Colorado. The Dalai Lama, honored with the Nobel Prize for Peace in 1989, has been the symbolic leader of the Tibetan Buddhist community, dramatizing the sufferings and exile that Tibetans have undergone since the Communist Chinese takeover of their country in 1959.

Whereas all of the Buddhist traditions that have taken root in the United States (and we have neglected several important ones, such as the Nichiren sect, which stresses devotion to the Lotus Sutra, an influential Mahayana scripture, and promises this-worldly prosperity) have served Asian Americans, most have also exercised a mild proselytism towards non-Asians. Non-Asian Americans have been most attracted to Zen, but Tibetan centers have also drawn numerous adherents. For these non-Asian Americans, the discipline and self-help prominent in Buddhism have been the great attractions. Nontheistic, Buddhism tells people that their fate is in their own hands. If they wish, they can come to understand where their sufferings come from and how to eliminate them. Obviously, this advice is very different from the Puritan counsel that, because of human depravity, one can do nothing saving without the grace of God.[12]

Sectarians: Latter Day Saints

By "sectarians" we mean groups whose roots lay in the Protestant mainstream but who separated themselves, becoming in the eyes of that mainstream both heterodox and marginal. The Latter Day Saints (Mormons), a group that began in western New York in 1830, are in many ways representative of American sectarianism. Joseph Smith (1805–1844), the sect's founder, was born in Vermont but moved with his family, who were poor farmers, to western New York. That area was a hotbed of both revivalism and spiritualism (concern with occult practices). At the age of fourteen, Smith experienced what he claimed was a revelation of God and Jesus. At the age of twenty-two, he claimed that an angel told him where to find golden plates describing the history of Native Americans and tracing them to the biblical Hebrews. Smith translated these plates and published in 1830 the resultant *Book of Mormon*. In the same year he started a church in Fayette, New York, that he claimed would restore primitive Christianity. Until he was murdered by a mob in Carthage, Illinois, in 1844, he led an increasing Mormon community from New York to Ohio, Missouri, and Illinois. At his death the town he headed in Illinois, Nauvoo, numbered about twenty thousand Mormons. Dissent within the Mormon community, and antagonism from outside, centered on rumors that Smith was advocating polygamy. Orthodox Christians were offended by Smith's claims to have received a new revelation, to supplement the Old and New Testaments, while the growing political strength of Mormons frightened other outsiders. In February, 1844, Smith had announced his intention to run for president. The opposition crystallized and violence threatened. Smith and his brother Hyrum were imprisoned in Carthage, near Nauvoo, and murdered by a mob of armed men with blackened faces. He became a martyr in Mormon eyes, sealing the power of his prophecy.

At Smith's death, the Mormons split into two factions. In 1847 the majority followed Brigham Young on a trek to the Great Salt Lake in Utah. Those who rejected Young's leadership splintered, only becoming organized in 1860 when Joseph Smith's son, Joseph III, was old enough to take charge of a Reorganized Church of Jesus Christ of Latter Days Saints. Today only about five percent of the six million or so Mormons belong to this group. In the 1840s, prior to Smith's death, there were perhaps 30,000 Mormons. By 1850 those loyal to Brigham Young numbered about 60,000, and by Young's death in 1877 the Mormons in Utah totaled about 150,000. The major source of such growth was the large number of children that Mormons produced, but they also drew significant numbers of converts. Young created a complex organization for his group, the Church of Jesus Christ of Latter Day Saints. The church has evolved, due to its understanding that the prophet who heads it can continue to receive revelations. Alongside the traditional Bible Mormons place *The Book of Mormon* and several collections of revelations that Joseph Smith received, considering all to be Scripture. Smith's revelations drew on Jewish notions and themes as much as Christian ones, blurring the question of whether the Mormon church should be considered a Christian group.

Virtually all Mormon men enter the priesthood at the age of twelve.

The opportunity for Mormon women to hold church offices is severely limited. In Utah the Mormon practice of polygamy, said to have been revealed to Joseph Smith prior to 1843, aroused hostility, as did Mormon clannishness. For their part, Mormons recalled vividly the murder of their founding prophet, and they tended to interpret the hostility of outsiders as a confirmation of their election and special mission.[13] They rejected the doctrine of original sin, preached that the atonement of Christ made salvation available to all willing to accept him in faith, and considered Joseph Smith the source of the revelation that completed the Bible. Because the successors to Joseph Smith have been prophets, able to receive further revelation, the Mormons constitute the only legitimate Christian church. They also claim to have restored the Old Testament priesthoods of Aaron and Melchizedek. The dispensation or order revealed in *The Book of Mormon* is that foretold by the angel in Revelation 14:6, and this dispensation will last until the second coming of Christ, which is near. From 1833 Joseph Smith had decreed no consumption of alcohol, coffee, tea, or tobacco, and this became a prominent feature of Mormon life after 1890. Between 1849 and 1887 the Mormons in Utah applied for statehood six times, but Utah was only admitted to the union in 1896, when the Mormons were willing to renounce polygamy and the People's Party that they had formed. Tithing has become a requirement, as has "temple work" in which Mormons perform such services as baptism to save deceased relatives who had not become Mormons. This temple work has stimulated a great interest in genealogy, in order to trace ancestors who still need such help. Until the 1960s Mormonism was mainly concerned with consolidating its doctrines and elaborating its organization, but since the 1960s it has placed great stress on missionary activity. The result has been phenomenal growth, as well as the presence of Mormons all around the globe.[14]

When one reflects on the implications of Mormon history and doctrine for our question of human nature, several features stand out. First, Joseph Smith's first revelations came at a time when evangelical fervor ran high in western New York (and many other areas). The assumption was that people desperately needed the experience of being saved, if they were to avoid hellfire and triumph over their depravity. The story that Mormons found in the *The Book of Mormon* was like that found in the historical books of the Old Testament (Judges, Kings, Chronicles), in that virtue brought blessings but backsliding brought sufferings and conflicts. In other words, human beings were good in the measure that they followed the divine laws. Apart from those laws, they were wicked and benighted. The Mormon rejection of original sin suggests that the sense of human depravity being promoted in evangelical religion (the Second Great Awakening so influential in the early years of the nineteenth century) disturbed the first Mormons. They were convinced that they had a new, hopeful message to proclaim and in their understanding original sin was a doctrine that would have dampened the impact of their message. On the other hand, the prohibition against alcohol, tea, coffee, and tobacco expressed a desire to purify the body. Like Seventh Day Adventists and other sectarian groups, the early Latter Day Saints considered themselves to be living in the final days, before the return of Christ, when purity was especially appropriate. The doctrine of polygamy represented a desire to return to the usages of the Old Testament, and perhaps also to free sexuality. Later Mormon teaching has emphasized a solid family life, making the home a religious center and decrying the drift of secular culture toward divorce. Mormon teaching also decries drug abuse and promotes secondary education. Higher education is desirable but raises questions about consonance with church teachings. Prospering in business is a sign of divine favor.

Overall, then, Mormonism seems a good example of the drive toward purification that flourishes among many sectarians. By withdrawing from the mainstream, one has a better chance of living in ways that please God. By disciplining the body, through dietary restrictions, one prepares a better vessel for the divine Spirit. The implication is that society at large is dangerous, and that human nature needs considerable discipline if it is to be kept under control. So Mormon psychology seems more like than unlike that of the New England Puritans, despite the vast differences in the theological teachings of the two groups. Puritans often were not dogmatic about alcohol and tobacco, and they had no strictures against tea and coffee. They would have rejected as most offensive the notion of a new revelation to supplant the Bible and considered Joseph Smith deluded. Polygamy would have deeply offended them. But they would have understood the Mormon praise of discipline and self-control, arguing that their own views of original sin and human depravity gave such discipline and self-control a much firmer foundation.

Protestant Reflections

If one considers the history and theology of such mainstream Protestant groups as the Presbyterians and Methodists, what are the sorts of reflections that they would be likely to make at this point? How would the quite varied reactions of Jews and Catholics, Buddhists and Mormons, to the issue of human nature strike such mainstream Protestants? Naturally, Presbyterians and Methodists would never speak with a single voice, and there are significant differences between these two church bodies. Naturally, many other sizable American Protestant churches (Congregationalists, Baptists, Lutherans) have helped to shape the vague mainstream consensus about the depravity of human nature and could as well be summoned for a hearing. Indeed, most of these churches contributed to the American devotion to liberty of individual conscience, agreeing with the strain of the Enlightenment that made this a key political and religious demand. In counterpoint to their struggles to fashion creeds and orthodoxies, then, most American Protestant groups that one would place in the mainstream have honored the right of individuals to speak out their dissent. Still, despite all the variety and qualification these observations introduce, it remains interesting to consider the mainstream response, as groups such as the Presbyterians and Methodists might represent it.

The Presbyterians have collected people of various ethnic backgrounds, but certainly English, Scots, and Scotch-Irish have predominated. Presbyterians first gained strength in the mid-Atlantic colonies, where they established a church polity as indebted to the Calvinist heritage as that of the New England Puritans (whom we may consider Congregationalists) but stressing the authority of elders. Presbyterians looked to the Westminster Confession, the product of an assembly convened by Parliament in 1643 to reform the English church, as an authoritative expression of their faith. This document revised the thirty-nine articles of the Church of England and expounded all the leading doctrines of Christian faith. Among its distinctive features was a crisp exposition of the Calvinist doctrine of election. In the United States the Second Great Awakening owed much to Presbyterian ministers, and one effect of such evangelism was to soften Calvinist teachings about predestination. As well, those Presbyterians drawn to evangelical work drew criticism from Presbyterians who wanted a soberer church order and the traditional stress on the rational side of Christian faith.

Presbyterians have contributed greatly to the intellectual life of the United States by founding numerous institutions of higher education, and they have been leaders in many areas of theological scholarship. Thus biblical scholarship and the influential neoorthodoxy that dominated Protestant theology in the middle third of this century have both flourished in Presbyterian circles. At the end of the nineteenth century a conservative group at Princeton took the lead in opposing liberal theological trends, proposing a refocusing on the Christian "fundamentals." This was a prod to American fundamentalism, the key feature of which has been a literal reading of the Bible as God's inerrant word.

Methodists trace their origins to John and Charles Wesley, Anglican priests who worked in Georgia in the 1730s. They returned to England and developed a reform movement within the Anglican church. After the American Revolution, they sent preachers schooled in their evangelistic disciplines to the United States, where Methodism flourished. Francis Asbury (1745–1816), one such English preacher, became one of the first bishops of the American Methodist church and is revered as the American founder. In 1784 John Wesley agreed to the separation of the American Methodists from their Anglican ties, in recognition of the strains existing between the United States and England after the Revolution. Wesley established an ordination procedure for the American Methodists and supplied them their original materials for both worship and governance. The church structure in effect is episcopal. In the United States Methodism has been greatly involved in evangelical movements, starting with the Second Great Awakening, and it flourished along the western frontier, due to a system of circuit riders and a stress on plain, emotional preaching. Along with Baptists, Methodists became leaders in evangelism and the most populous group. Nowadays there are about thirteen million Methodists (as opposed to just over three million Presbyterians).[15]

Methodists and Presbyterians differ in their perspective on the question of human nature, because Methodists do not share the Calvinist convictions so important to Presbyterians. The Anglican roots of the Wesleys determined that a Catholic influence would offset the influence of the Reformers. Methodist preachers certainly called people to repent of their sins, and across the evangelical board it was obligatory to stress the importance of a conversion experience. Presbyterian evangelists shared this attitude, but in their case the doctrines of depravity, predestination, and election bulked larger. Methodists have tended to stress the positive side of the work of the Holy Spirit in encouraging people to find their fulfillment in God. Both churches worked against the consumption of alcohol, though Methodists were more prominent and stipulated that their clergy were not to consume it. Methodists also adopted the use of grape juice, rather than wine, in the celebration of the Lord's Supper. Presbyterians were more prominent in the fight to hallow the Sabbath, supporting "blue laws" that would prohibit business and recreational activities on Sunday.

From both groups came solid contributions to the moral earnestness characteristic of the American religious mainstream. Virtue, social activism, and church fellowship have been major concerns of most Presbyterian and Methodist groups (each tradition has historically numbered several separated collections of churches). Whether such moral earnestness appeared simply as the healthy overflow of a sincere faith, or as a lack of relaxation and trust in God, it set its stamp on American politics and culture. In general, the Protestant ideal became a firm commitment to elevating the moral tone of the nation and sponsoring civil, polite interactions among all citizens. Indirection tended to prevail over direct confrontation. The bawdy and raucous were considered inappropriate, if not un-Christian.

So the reaction of mainstream Protestant groups such as the Presbyterians and the Methodists to Jewish or Catholic earthiness tended to be negative, probably more as a matter of custom or taste than as a direct effect of theological differences, though theological differences played a significant role in the background. Buddhists and Mormons were different cases, standing farther outside the stream of revelation that mainstream Protestantism honored. Mormons might seem familiar in their earnestness, but their view of revelation, determined by the visions of Joseph Smith and *The Book of Mormon,* seemed bizarre. Buddhists were pagans who might have rich native cultures but needed the gospel to fulfill their full human potential. (Catholics agreed. Jews, however, had a more sophisticated notion of the different covenants that God established with people, including the Noachite covenant with humanity at large.)

The political or civic result of mainstream Protestant earnestness, rooted in its stress on appropriating the Bible as the means to save and sanctify a dubious human nature, was great energy expended on making democracy and American industry flourish. The government and business that developed in the first half of the twentieth century to make the United States the most powerful Western nation both came from Protestant energy and convictions (and also from the labor of many marginal groups). As it allowed others into American prosperity (or could not keep them out), the Protestant mainstream extended its convictions about industriousness and propriety, never completely winning over those on the margins but sometimes moving them toward greater sobriety.

Sophistication and Naiveté

When one considers the question of the probity or bentness of human nature, in the context of American religious experience, the dozens of qualifications and distinctions that are necessary produce a certain sophistication. It is clear that American Christians, let alone the full sweep of American religious groups, have had no exact consensus about human nature. It is clear that mainstream Protestant doubts have been influential in shaping a general culture honoring hard work and political suspicion, but that such doubts have not quenched a confidence that hard work and sobriety could make a great country. And if some preachers were naive about what warm feelings in the breast could produce, others were clear that conversion and regeneration were ongoing processes, never completed once and for all. The Americans who thought of their country as God's chosen agent for renewing the earth were naive, but not completely so. Compared to the centuries-old antagonisms and corruptions afflicting the European nations, the American venture could indeed seem like a chance to make a truly godly nation and so show the world how to live. Compared to European class-consciousness, American democracy, though far from perfect, could seem a breath of fresh air. Immigrants picked up this theme of new possibilities, and flocked to the United States in record numbers. The beneficiaries of American generosity during the two world wars of the first half of the twentieth century had to be impressed.

But a closer look at American history gave reason to pause. First, there was the competition among British, French, and Spanish in the colonial era, which reminded students of American history that the nation had inherited Europe's antagonisms. Second, there was the treatment of Native Americans and African Americans, which from the beginning was more destructive than helpful and constitutes the sorriest feature of American history. Third, there was the Civil War, in which the dreams of a nation that would stand like a beacon on a hill, illuminating for the world how Christian godliness could set new standards of prosperity and civility, turned into a nightmare. Fourth, there was the exploitation of the working classes that accompanied the industrialization of America. And fifth, only becoming fully evident in recent years, there was the pollution of the natural environment, due to a long-standing policy of leaving land-use up to the individual. When one adds the inevitable amounts of political corruption, crime, addiction, and folly in international relations, any naiveté about the American venture, or the newness of the humanity developing on American soil, comes crashing down to earth.

Still, this is not the whole story, because one has to calculate the influence of pessimistic views of human nature through American history. Inasmuch as their Puritan heritage counseled Americans to be wary of their instincts and expect expressions of sinfulness, Americans should have been well guarded against naiveté. Why is it that frequently they were not? Why is it that neoorthodox theologians, rising in the generation between the two world wars, had to preach a gospel of self-criticism, above all when it came to estimating the nation's own motivations? Perhaps it is because those holding power and setting the political agenda thought that their sensitivity to suspect human nature had produced a nation relatively impervious to fraud or self-deception. Perhaps it is because the best and brightest came from families and universities that had profited so handsomely from the industry and government to which Puritan industriousness had led that they found it hard to think they could be deceived. The trauma that the best and brightest experienced in the era of the Vietnam War was a strange sort of awakening to self-knowledge. In its very intensity, it suggested that, despite their schooling in the depravity of human nature, the Protestant elite found it hard to think that their own power might be corrupt.

Certainly American Protestants have had no monopoly on such blindness. Probably every originally hardworking, altruistic group has been amazed to discover that, gradually, its motives have shifted toward self-preservation. After such a discovery, there is no period of history that is not subject to review, no individual biography that cannot be examined for biases and blind spots. Interestingly, that is the very lesson that the Calvinist view of human nature wanted to inculcate, so perhaps the complementary lesson is that only when one's pride has made a mess of things can the orthodoxies one thought one was honoring be seen in their true, more radical light.

Another possibility, intriguing to the sophisticated and instructive for those wanting to become sophisticated, is that a wrong emphasis on human depravity does more harm than good. Unless people can feel that their basic instincts are healthy, they are likely to become filled with doubt, even self-hatred. This contributes to social disorder. The first movement in good social relations is one of trust and positive expectations. I have to grant you a fund of good will, if I am to negotiate with you, do business, or collaborate successfully. If you and I cannot establish this fund of good will, our social prospects are dim. Virtually any human action can be interpreted negatively. All one need do is assign a selfish motive or a will to deceive. This in turn leads to complex motives and tactics on the part of the other party, and soon the entire relationship is Byzantine. Writers of spy novels featuring the CIA and the KGB specialize in the absurdities to which the radically suspicious imagination leads, but one need not turn to fiction. Any large institution is likely to harbor influential leaders who think it imprudent to tell the truth, deal with people warmly and sympathetically, apologize quickly for their mistakes, and generally operate with a hopeful view of human nature, their own as well as other people's. What is hopeful and what is naive, where one must in justice begin to apply sanctions for poor performance or mistakes—these are everpresent management problems. But the American history of operating from a background conviction that human nature is depraved suggests that true sophistication, or wisdom, means offering good will and expecting good performance without being surprised at stupidity, sloth, corruption, or even evil.

It is difficult, perhaps impossible, not to be surprised at evil. The most sophisticated analyses of the evils generated in the human mind and heart lead to a mystery: people can choose or be bedazzled by non-being, what does not truly exist. Evil is disorder, irrationality, moral pain. When one is intending order, what is reasonable, what brings fulfillment and joy, one is not intending evil. So to intend evil, something one knows is wrong and probably destructive, all but the most corrupt human beings have to blind themselves. They have to say that their actions are necessitated by considerations of American national security, or by the corruption of their opponents, or by their responsibilities to the firm, or by the needs of their family, or by the rightness of avenging themselves on people who did them wrongs in the past. These motives are disordered, of course—precisely what a human nature weak, concupiscent, in need of a religious perspective could be expected to succumb to. Whether that makes human nature depraved is an interesting additional question. So is the matter of how best to manage a human nature that regularly sins, colluding with deception, agreeing to what it knows is not right. Does one best educate people to goodness, and true knowledge about the human condition, by making them suspect themselves and fear the wrath of their God, or by showing them causes, above all the beauty of their God, that make pettiness and disorder seem unthinkable, hardly worth their while? It is attractive to think that human beings want to do what is right, follow the light, find a beauty and goodness justifying their time, worthy of their complete self-donation, but making such a thought practical seems to involve defining the human vocation as a call to mysticism—union with the one Being who alone might be real enough, powerful enough, beautiful enough to offset human selfishness. As we shall see, the American mainstream has not been comfortable with such an understanding of either human nature or the proper functions of religion, though the strong dose of revivalism running through American history suggests a naive effort to articulate a mystical view of the human condition.

Human Nature: American Wisdom

The revivalists who played a prominent role in American religion beginning in the middle third of the eighteenth century numbered many de facto Arminians. To move their hearers to change their lives, the preachers assumed and inculcated the view that people had a say in their salvation. People could amend their conduct, revive the fires of religious devotion, consecrate themselves again to high moral standards. George Whitefield, Peter Cartwright, Billy Sunday, Dwight Moody, Billy Graham, and numerous others in the revivalist tradition challenged the doctrine of predestination, at least implicitly. God offered salvation, and the end result of a person's life rested in his or her hands: would the offer be accepted or rejected? This optimism about human freedom did not entail an optimism about human nature as such, though logically it should have raised questions about a doctrine of depravity. Most of the revivalists continued to beat the drum of human sinfulness, human need to turn to God and accept the divine grace. But the requirements of building a new nation pressured the most popular preachers to develop a religion in which human initiative and diligence made a difference. Revivalists such as C.G. Finney and Dwight Moody became quite systematic about the business of bringing people to God, promising that if their methods were followed carefully, conviction of sin and return to God were virtually certain to result. This view of human perfectibility put into religious terms the sort of optimism later couched in secular terms by positivistic sociologists. It was a far cry from the resignation (or surrender to divine providence) that the older Orthodox, Catholic, and Calvinist theologies had finally counseled. In that older theology, at the end of one's human efforts one had to surrender one's spirit into God's hands, as Christ had on the cross. Otherwise one had failed to honor the most basic precept of the Lord's Prayer: "Thy will be done."

The American wisdom about human nature has been to admit the obscurity of the issue and let the diverse elements of the population follow their own lights. In part, this American wisdom has been a concomitant of the decision, practical as well as ideological, that the best religion is not established by the state, not a marital partner of the civil culture, but a personal (though social) practice of what people's own consciences dictate. In other words, the American wisdom about human nature has run in tandem with the American conviction that religious liberty is the most precious of human freedoms.

We shall consider this thesis at some length in the next part, where the focus is the influence of the Enlightenment. Here we may conclude our ruminations about human nature by making explicit the implications of the American choice of religious pluralism. On the face of it, this choice implies only that people ought to hold and practice what religious beliefs they themselves think best, including what beliefs about human nature they find most satisfying. Below the surface, however, there is a conviction that human nature is such that freedom is better than compulsion, and that the common good is better served by allowing a variety of judgments about ultimate matters, including the character of human nature, than by enthroning any one or several of them through official sanction. In its depths, the American choice implies that the matter of beliefs, ultimate verities, and the character of human nature is mysterious—not resolvable, sure to be a matter of controversy, and best left for the Judgment Day, when divinity itself will make things plain.

This last implication is the most interesting. For what does it say about human affairs, politics and culture, if the most basic or ultimate questions are judged unanswerable? What happens to human affairs if the most realistic assessment of the human condition makes mystery the milieu in which all people live, move, and have their most significant being? On the one hand, it says the obvious: human affairs continue to go on; the majority of human beings distract themselves from the mysteriousness of their condition and narrow their sights to survival. Only the very few are so driven that they either despair, calling all judgments and actions ultimately meaningless, or consecrate themselves to living as though the mysteriousness ought to absorb all their energy. On the other hand, it is apparent, at least to the thoughtful, that the mysteriousness of the human situation is a great blessing, because it means that no human judgments are ever definitive and that the past, as well as the future, is always redeemable. If the fact of the matter, the most brute fact, is that no one—king, president, pope, professor, Nobel Laureate—ever knows as a matter of empirical fact the origin of the human situation, or its final destiny, or the treasure on which to set the human heart, or the exact character of human nature, then all human beings are free, and condemned, to make up their own minds, live out their own experiments. This freedom is not something that a government can grant. It is prior to any Constitution or Bible or Creed (though these can make it known, perhaps for the first time, and so seem to be creating it). And it is inalienable, as Jefferson and those who approved his Declaration of Independence saw. One cannot give to others one's right and responsibility to decide how the world is constructed, what God requires, how the human being is designed in its moral makeup, or any of the other key decisions that logically shape practical, everyday life. Much as human sociability mediates and forms such decisions, human beings remain free to accept or reject any given mediation or formation. They can change churches, or synagogues, or mosques. They can outgrow, or repudiate, or reassert in their own name the education they received. They can seem to agree, to go along, but in fact be bracketing their allegiance, waiting for a word, an inner conviction, that will make clear what they themselves really think.

The Puritans did not think this way about religious citizenship or the makeup of the human personality, but they did probe the foundations of human freedom and divine grace sufficiently to set in motion the processes that resulted in the de facto American choice of religious liberty. In the Puritan scheme of things, orthodoxy was the safeguard of social order and individual morality. But orthodoxy proved impossible to establish, as the Puritans' own history of dissent from Anglican orthodoxy should have warned them it would be. True, Americans have not always been as wise about what they have lost by judging such theses as the Calvinist doctrine of the depravity of human nature to be unverifiable and unfalsifiable, as about what they have gained. They have not always appreciated the beauty and depth of a culture whose people have managed to attain a significant unanimity or concord about God and worship, family life and love, the reason we are born and the significance of our dying. In their pursuit of religious liberty, they have often forgotten the cry of Deuteronomy to hear about the Oneness of the Lord, or the prayer of the Johannine Jesus to his Father that all of his followers be one. It has not suited the American temper to be reined in by these reminders that human beings are not sovereign over their own consciences, if they claim to be convenanted to a transcendent, holy God. It has often escaped American notice that the individual freedoms they cherish can become the enemy of the common good, can create an individualism as destructive as the tyranny of monarchs or of authoritarian churches.[16] So the wisdom emerging from American religious experience may stand in need of further lessons, the nature of which may appear more clearly as we consider the relations of church and state and the pros and cons of pragmatism.

NOTES

1. See "Man, the Nature of," in *Encyclopedia Judaica* (Jerusalem: Keter, 1972), vol. 11, pp. 842–850.

2. See Abraham J. Karp, "The Emergence of an American Judaism," in *Encyclopedia of the American Religious Experience*, ed. Charles H. Lippy and Peter W. Williams (New York: Scribner's, 1988), vol. 1, p. 279.

3. "Pittsburgh Platform," in *Encyclopedia Judaica*, vol. 13, p. 571.

4. For talmudic views on topics relating to an estimate of human nature, see A. Cohen, *Everyman's Talmud* (New York: Schocken, 1975).

5. Josef Neuner and Heinrich Roos, *The Teaching of the Catholic Church As Contained in Her Documents* (Staten Island, N.Y.: Alba House, 1967), pp. 139–140.

6. Ibid., p. 110. On the history of American Catholicism, see James Hennessey, *American Catholics* (New York: Oxford University Press, 1981) and Jay P. Dolan, *The American Catholic Experience* (Garden City, N.Y.: Doubleday, 1985).

7. See Rosemary Skinner Keller, "Women and Religion," in *Encyclopedia of the American Religious Experience*, vol. 3, p. 1557.

8. See Sally L. Kitch, *Chaste Liberation: Celibacy and Female Cultural Status* (Urbana: University of Illinois Press, 1989).

9. See two studies by Albert J. Raboteau: "Afro-American Religions: An Overview," in *The Encyclopedia of Religion*, ed. Mircea Eliade (New York: Macmillan, 1987), vol. 1, pp. 96–100; and "Black Christianity in North America," in *Encyclopedia of the American Religious Experience*, vol. 1, pp. 635–648.

10. See Sam D. Gill, "Native American Religions," ibid, p. 141.

11. See Black Elk, *The Sacred Pipe*, ed. Joseph Epes Brown (Baltimore: Penguin, 1973).

12. On American Buddhism, see Charles S. Prebish, "Buddhism," in *Encyclopedia of the American Religious Experience*, vol. 2, pp. 669–682.

13. See R. Laurence Moore, *Religious Outsiders and the Making of Americans* (New York: Oxford University Press, 1986), pp. 25–47.

14. See Jan Shipps, "The Latter-Day Saints," in *Encyclopedia of the American Religious Experience*, vol. 1, pp. 649–665.

15. For statistics on the approximate membership of the main religious bodies in the United States, see *Yearbook of American and Canadian Churches*, ed. Constance H. Jacquet, Jr. (Nashville: Abingdon, 1986) and *Handbook of Denominations in the United States*, ed. Frank S. Mead and Samuel S. Hill (Nashville: Abingdon, 1985).

16. On this theme see *Individualism & Commitment in American Life*, ed. Robert N. Bellah *et al.* (New York: Harper & Row, 1987).

Part Two

THE
ENLIGHTENMENT
FOUNDATIONS

Chapter 4

Thomas Jefferson and Disestablishment

The Enlightenment Background

The Enlightenment did not spring forth from nothingness. Like all historical and cultural events, it had predecessors that prepared its way. Among
such predecessors one can mention the medieval scholastics and scientists,
who used the Aristotelianism made available by Arab scholarship to encourage close reasoning. It took some time for modern science to emerge,
so for centuries the relations between empirical evidence and close reasoning were not clear. People knew about induction and deduction, but they
did not yet grant empirical data the crucial scientific role, as both stimulus
to disciplined investigation and the main source by which to verify the
fruitfulness of such investigation. In the seventeenth century, Descartes
and Newton, the two greatest natural philosophers, differed significantly
in their approaches to thinking about reality, but they agreed in relying on
reason rather than revelation. Both looked to what the human mind and
community could discover, even when it was a question of the reality and
operations of God. Michael Buckley has shown how the theologians fell
in with Descartes and Newton, virtually abandoning faith and Christology
as sources for the discussion of God's existence, attributes, and significance
that gripped the late seventeenth and early eighteenth century.[1]

The Enlightenment influences that were greatest in the American
colonies came from England and France. The writings of John Locke and

David Hume, along with the thought of Voltaire and the Encyclopedists, amounted to a new humanism. Whereas the humanism of the Renaissance had looked back to classical Greece and Rome for its inspiration, the new humanism looked to natural philosophy and science. In both cases, the result was a stress on what human beings have the capacity, the right, and the obligation to do. No longer were human beings to live heteronomously, letting others dictate the laws by which they conducted their lives and thought about the world. Neither the church nor the monarchy ought to have control of people's thought or behavior. Mature people would think and act autonomously, out of the conviction that what they were doing was rational, accorded with the laws of nature, and served the common good. Reason was showing itself so fertile and powerful (in the works of the physicists and astronomers) that developing and following reason seemed the moral thing to do. Religion had produced so much superstition, bigotry, repression, and bloodshed (recall the wars between Protestants and Catholics) that religion seemed best left behind or to the side. The only sort of religion that boded well for the future was one that squared with reason. Thus before long divine revelation, the privileged status of the Bible, the divinity of Christ, the miracles of Christ, and the notions of hell and heaven all came under attack. Among the intelligentsia influenced by the leading Enlightenment thinkers, the goal was a self-sufficiency and maturity that would deal with traditional religious convictions lightly, considering them the products of humanity's adolescence and appreciating their value in guiding the common people to decent morality, but no longer granting them primary authority.

Jefferson, Madison, Franklin, Washington, and many of the other founding fathers of the new American nation had imbibed Enlightenment thought and applied it to both the question of revolution and the question of what sort of political entity the union of the former colonies ought to create. Epistemologically, these men wavered between a skepticism influenced by Locke and Hume and a common sense buoyed by the successes of natural science. In general, they thought that if one disciplined a good intelligence to observe closely and reason well, one would negotiate dealings with nature and dealings with human beings quite well. Politically, the founding fathers were impressed by the rights of human beings that the Enlightenment was spotlighting, to the detriment of authoritarian forms of government, above all of monarchies. Human beings, as rational and possessed of individual rights, ought to form their political associations freely, making contracts and spelling out the consent of the governed to the power exercised by those they chose to govern them. The old theory of the divine right of kings was passing from the scene. In its place came such notions as the illegitimacy of taxation without representation, and the need for participatory democracy.

Religiously, the most popular position among the founding fathers was what came to be known as Deism. For reasons of conviction, as well as reasons of expediency, these men did not want to do away with the notion of a supreme Being. Their sense of the universe was such that it required a governing intelligence to oversee its passage from beginning to consummation. Their sense of human nature was that the majority needed the pressure and guidance of a moral code invested with the sanctions of divinity, if they were to live together justly and peacefully. But when they could have their way (when they were not constrained by public occasions and the sentiments of the masses), the founding fathers had little use for traditional Christian liturgy, theology, and church life. It was too mythological and emotional, too reminiscent of the days when priests dominated people's consciences and fear meant more than reason.

It is a measure of his uniqueness, and of the complexity of intellectual history as it actually unfolds, that so prominent a figure in the Great Awakening as Jonathan Edwards should have been a child of the Enlightenment as well as of New England's Puritan origins. Edwards loved to study nature, and he thought highly of Locke's psychology. Yet he also loved the Bible and thought in categories bequeathed to him by Calvinist theology. Indeed, he was forced by personal experience and observation to grant the power and goodness of revivalist fervor, when it stayed in touch with reason and theological orthodoxy. So his notion of the fully developed human being was not that of the Enlightenment, even though he loved the Enlightenment's stress on science and reasoning. Edwards gave more weight to the actions of God on human affections, and at the center of this anthropology, as we have seen, was a profound conviction that human nature, on its own, is depraved. The actions of God on human affections are the prime way that grace overcomes such depravity, and while the entire process of regeneration is wrapped in the mystery of God's predestining counsels, what indications one can glean of the usual dealings of God with human beings, as both Scripture and the observation of revivalist renewals clarify them, suggest that only when the person has become convicted of personal sin and swept away by the beauty of God does true fulfillment flower.

Most of this was foreign, if not repugnant, to the founding fathers we have mentioned. Their reading of the Enlightenment made predestination, depravity, religious affections, and the like suspect, even abominable. They were willing to grant that the Bible was a great source of moral counsel, and that Jesus was an exemplary human being. But they were not impressed by the evangelical fervor that kept springing up in the colonies throughout the eighteenth and early nineteenth centuries. It hardly seemed the basis for the laws, politics, and business that the new nation would need, were it to fulfill its promise.

One can argue that though this Enlightenment strand was crucial for the formation of the new nation, and though it entered the brick and mortar of the Constitution, it never was as popular—as powerful with the ordinary citizenry—as the revivalist view of things. Certainly, many ordinary citizens (often the majority) were unchurched and probably sighed with relief that the revivalists were not in charge politically. But it is unlikely that the majority of ordinary citizens in the new nation agreed with the rationalism and Deism of the founders. What drew them was the founders' persuasive rationale for liberation from England and federating the colonies into an independent nation. The work of Madison, Hamilton, Jay and others in convincing the general populace to accept the Constitution designed to order the new nation is astounding. When one considers the sophistication of the arguments they made, one realizes that in early national history citizenship called forth the best in many of their hearers, and that the importance Jefferson placed on having a citizenry well educated in the traditions and reasons of democracy was supported by the response the nation's first generations gave him and the other founding fathers.[2]

The Life of Jefferson

In July of 1778, when the American Revolution was well under way, Thomas Jefferson wrote to David Rittenhouse, an astronomer from Philadelphia, applauding Rittenhouse's service of his country but stressing more the superiority of his work as a scientist to any political offices he might fulfill. The letter shows the temper of Jefferson's mind, which always remained convinced that the noblest thing one could do was study the natural world. Note the Enlightenment strains in Jefferson's praise of Rittenhouse's scientific vocation: "Though I have been aware of the authority our cause [Independence] would acquire with the world from its being known that yourself and Dr. [Benjamin] Franklin were zealous friends to it, and am myself duly impressed with a sense of the arduousness of government, and the obligation those are under who are able to conduct it, yet I am also satisfied there is an order of geniuses above that obligation, and therefore exempted from it. Nobody can conceive that nature ever intended to throw away a Newton upon the occupations of a crown. It would have been a prodigality for which even the conduct of Providence might have been arraigned, had he been by birth annexed to what was so far below him. Cooperating with nature in her ordinary economy, we should dispose of and employ the geniuses of men according to their several orders and degrees . . . Are those powers then, which being intended for the erudition of the world are, like air and light, the world's common property, to be taken from their proper pursuit to do the commonplace drudgery of governing a single state, a work which may be executed by men of an ordinary stature, such as are always and everywhere to be found? Without having ascended Mount Sinai for inspiration, I can pronounce that the precept, in the decalogue of the vulgar, that they shall not make to themselves 'the likeness of anything that is in the heavens above' is reversed for you [Rittenhouse had created a splendid representation of the solar system], and that you will fulfill the highest purposes of your creation by employing yourself in the perpetual breach of that inhibition."[3]

Before we sketch the biography of the man who wrote those lines (when he was 35), let us comment briefly on several instructive usages. First, notice the lofty status accorded Newton, who stands for genius *par excellence.* Second, notice the passing reference to Providence—an indication of the remnants of traditional Christian theology in Jefferson's thought. Third, it is instructive that human beings might arraign Providence (drag God before a court of judgment), were Providence to violate what human reason found fitting. Fourth, the Enlightenment ideal was to cooperate with the natural order that geniuses such as Newton had disclosed, substituting such a cooperation for the older religious notion of obeying the will of God. Fifth, Enlightenment thought was implicitly universal, as physical science increasingly came to be, caring less for national boundaries than for the common property of humankind, above all its fund of knowledge. Last, the ironic reference to Mount Sinai and the Law of Moses (the ten commandments for the "vulgar"—the common people) shows both Jefferson's acquaintance with the biblical culture in which the mainstream of his time still lived and his willingness to downplay it. The notion that astronomy might be a breach of God's commands is playful, yet it seems quite clear that Jefferson rates the rights of reason to investigate the natural world far higher than any traditional morality that might limit them.

Thomas Jefferson (1743–1826) was born and died in Virginia. Family holdings made him a wealthy planter, and he began his political career in the Virginia House of Burgesses in 1769. His father had died in 1757, but had provided for Thomas's solid education. After studying the classics, he had enrolled in William and Mary College in 1760, and after two years left to study law, being admitted to the bar in 1767. In 1775 he went to Philadelphia as a Virginia delegate to the Second Continental Congress. Recognizing his fine mind, the delegates assigned him the task of drafting the Declaration of Independence in 1776.

Jefferson instituted democratic reforms in Virginia's laws and served as the state's governor from 1779 to 1781. He returned to the Continental Congress in 1782 and was in Europe on diplomatic missions from 1784 to 1789, when he observed the rise of the forces producing the French Revolution. He served in Washington's presidency as secretary of state. Within Washington's cabinet Jefferson found himself opposing Alexander Hamilton, the secretary of the treasury, on the grounds that Hamilton was exceeding the powers delegated to the executive branch by the Congress, was undemocratic, and was wrongly preferring British to French friendship. From the philosophical differences between the two men came the two-party political system, Jefferson symbolizing what became the Democratic-Republican party and Hamilton the Federalist. Jefferson and Madison fought against Hamilton and John Adams, the former men favoring individual liberties and the latter favoring more conservative policies geared to national development. Jefferson was elected president in 1800, engineered the Louisiana Purchase, and tried to keep the United States from becoming entangled in the Napoleonic wars. In 1809 he retired to his Virginia plantation, Monticello, and for the next decade worked to establish the University of Virginia. After that he continued with his interests in farming and his studies. Both he and John Adams died on July 4, 1826, precisely the fiftieth anniversary of American independence.

Jefferson stood out among his colleagues not only for his height (6 feet 2 inches), and (originally) for his youth, but also for the power of his mind. He loved languages (Latin, Greek, French, Spanish, Italian, and Anglo-Saxon), the sciences, and the classics. We shall consider his study of Jesus and the New Testament. He conducted a voluminous correspondence with the leading figures of his day, both American and foreign, and his *Notes on Virginia*, written after the completion of his term as governor of Virginia in 1782, is one of the classic studies of its kind, describing and analyzing the land that he loved.

Jefferson had been frustrated politically during his term as governor, and he was worried about the health of his wife, so the *Notes* show him less guarded than he was normally. Contemporary accounts remark on his equanimity and privacy, suggesting that his passionate defense of individual rights was rooted in his desire always to control his own destiny. His marriage appears to have been unusually happy. He opposed slavery in principle but presided over a band of 150 slaves who worked his Virginia lands, where he was greatly interested in the scientific aspects of farming. Although his fellow Virginians had to be coaxed and bullied into supporting higher education as he thought it should be, he remained a great advocate of learning as a necessity for democratic government as well as national progress.

Among the reforms of Virginia law that had occupied Jefferson from his first service in the Virginia legislature and through his term as governor was enacting a statute guaranteeing religious liberty. As noted, Jefferson considered this achievement, along with the Declaration of Independence and the establishment of the University of Virginia, one of the principle glories of his life. All three bore on freedom (religious, political, educational), and Jefferson's pride in them, rather than in his political offices, suggests that the analysis he made for Rittenhouse applied in his own life: matters of the mind and spirit, intellectual achievements that might benefit all people, rated higher than any political work, however necessary. The latter was a duty that Jefferson the good citizen shouldered willingly. The former was where his heart lay: in advancing the liberation of humanity, as the Enlightenment had conceived it.[4]

The Declaration of Independence

In offering several "prolegomena" to a reading of the Declaration of Independence, Garry Wills has tried to situate the document in both its time and the personality of Jefferson, its principle author: "[Jefferson] was addressing mankind, out of a decent respect for its opinions, explaining the step [separation of the colonies from England] already taken. It was an expression *of* the American mind *to* mankind's candor, in terms that unite the two. From this very function of the Declaration, some men have argued to a necessary vagueness in it. Jefferson was writing war propaganda, with all the license that gives men who are locked in a life-and-death battle. But Jefferson himself did not limit its application. He recurred to it as equally relevant, sometimes as more relevant, long after the war had been decided. He urged the document's celebration and use in later struggles, foreign and domestic. It is given prominent, disproportionate, space in his autobiography. When he ordered it placed first on his monument, he was making a very conscious choice, based on a firm belief that it was his most important contribution to America—not to its war with England, not even to its subsequent history but to history *tout court.* To History. Men of his time did not choose their epitaphs lightly, but with posterity in mind."[5]

First, then, we should have no doubt that Jefferson was proud of the Declaration and considered it a work that rose above the needs of the original moment when it was composed and stood apart as a piece of permanent value. Second, if we consider what Jefferson says about the Declaration in his autobiography, we realize that to the end of his life he regretted the changes that the Continental Congress had made in his draft. The majority of such changes were deletions, which are usually regarded as having tightened the text and made it more forceful. Some changes, however, are striking, in view of the later history of the United States. For example, the Congress deleted a sizable paragraph in which Jefferson excoriated the practice of slavery and laid it at the door of the British King: "He has waged cruel war against human nature itself, violating its most sacred rights of life and liberty in the persons of a distant people who have never offended him, captivating and carrying them into slavery in another hemisphere, or to incur miserable death in their transportation thither. This piratical warfare, the opprobrium of infidel powers, is the warfare of the Christian king of Great Britain. Determined to keep open a market where men should be bought and sold, he has prostituted his negative for suppressing every legislative attempt to prohibit or to restrain this execrable commerce. And that this assemblage of horrors might want not fact of distinguished die, he is now exciting those very people to rise in arms among us, and to purchase that liberty of which he has deprived them, by murdering the people on whom he also obtruded them: thus paying off former crimes committed against the liberties of one people, with crimes which he urges them to commit against the lives of another."[6]

One can see how readers of Jefferson's draft might have judged him excessively rhetorical in this passage, yet the general report of those who observed him during his life and have studied his writings closely is that he was usually most exact in speech. So we may take it that Jefferson himself thought that among the many crimes and misdeeds of the tyrannical king the slavery in the colonies was signal.

The delegates also changed the conclusion of the Declaration that Jefferson originally wrote. In this case they added two references to divinity lacking in Jefferson's draft. Jefferson had no "appealing to the supreme

judge of the world for the rectitude of our intentions" or "with a firm
reliance on the protection of divine providence." For him the "authority
of the good people of these states" was enough. One suspects, then, that
the assembly as a whole either was more religious, in a rather Deistic sense,
than Jefferson himself, or that they judged a public reliance on the approba-
tion of divinity useful politically.

Still, Jefferson's own words, the most famous of which occur at the
beginning of the Declaration, retain a sense that what the delegates were
approving in separating from Britain was a matter of conscience, worked
out under the watchful eye of God their creator: "When in the course of
human events it becomes necessary for one people to dissolve the political
bonds that have connected them with another, and to assume among the
powers of the earth the separate and equal station to which the laws of
nature and of nature's God entitle them, a decent respect to the opinions
of mankind requires that they should declare the causes which impel them
to their separation. We hold these truths to be self-evident, that all men are
created equal, that they are endowed by their Creator with certain inalienable rights, that among these are life, liberty, and the pursuit of happiness.
That, to secure these rights, governments are instituted among men, deriving their just powers from the consent of the governed."[7] In these opening
lines the only changes the delegates made in Jefferson's draft were the
introduction of the word "certain" and the omission of the words "inherent and" before "inalienable." The "certain" is not significant. The "inherent" perhaps is, in that for Jefferson the rights to be enumerated were part
of human nature—part of the basic makeup of the singular species called
mankind.

We have seen some of the features of the Enlightenment thought that
meant so much to Jefferson. He was the brilliant debtor of this movement
when he overthrew centuries of prior thinking to situate the legitimacy of
a government in the consent of those it governed. Certainly, he had a
tradition of English common law on which to draw—a tradition that from
the time of the Magna Carta had been trying to gain leverage against the
powers of monarchs. But prior to the American and French revolutions
democracy as Jefferson was expounding its foundations was not predomi-
nant. One might say that the American and French revolutions both were
grievance movements in search of a rationale, but that would be to underes-
timate the interaction between experience and theory, especially in the case
of the French. Even for the Americans, Enlightenment principles were
leading to the notion that nothing outside the free consciences of people
like those in the British colonies could compel them morally to submit to

monarchical authority. Unless their submission agreed with their judgment that the authority to which they were submitting was legitimate and just, they had the right, perhaps even the duty, to revolt. Behind this right or duty lay the divinity that reason honored, the God who had fashioned the human being and finally justified its autonomies.

Taking up the question of how honestly Jefferson himself thought that the truths the Declaration enumerated were self-evident, Garry Wills has commented further: "No one ever aimed to be more accurate, more 'correct,' in manner, in word, in deed; in his drawings and plans; in his beliefs, so meticulously dissected through letter after letter of his correspondence. A man with these standards would hardly commend to posterity, as his main claim upon it, an effusion of enthusiasm. When he used words like inalienable, or self-evident, or happiness, he drew on meanings sharpened by debate in his day, though dulled by use in ours. To understand him we have to re-enter those debates—the debates over common sense, over alienable property, over the pain-pleasure calculus—the debates he took part in, along with his friends."[8] No doubt we should regard the phrase "nature's God" as something Jefferson meant similarly exactly.

The Statute on Religious Liberty

As noted, Thomas Jefferson was proud of his authorship of the Virginia statute of religious freedom. In fact, in the directions for his epitaph Jefferson wrote: ". . . On the faces of the obelisk the following inscription, and not a word more, 'Here was buried Thomas Jefferson, author of the Declaration of American Independence, of the statute of Virginia for religious freedom, and father of the University of Virginia,' because by these, as testimonials that I have lived, I wish most to be remembered."[9]

The Virginia statute of religious freedom did not come easily, but it did have far-reaching effects. In 1776 Virginia had passed a "Declaration of Rights" that had affirmed the principle of religious liberty. Only in 1779 was the Anglican church disestablished, however. Even then, many Virginians thought that tax monies should support all religious denominations. Jefferson drafted the statute of religious freedom in 1779, but the Virginia legislature would not pass it. In 1785 James Madison, Jefferson's great ally in this matter, wrote an influential "Remonstrance Against Religious Assessments," which swung public opinion against using taxes to support religious institutions. By passing Jefferson's bill in 1786, the legislature provided freedom of religious opinion (one could think and publish one's opinions about religion as one wished). It also prohibited using tax money to support any church or other religious institution. By separating church and state in this way, the Virginia statute provided the model for the First Amendment to the United States Constitution, engineered by Madison. So what Jefferson and Madison accomplished in Virginia became the law of the entire nation, breaking with long-standing tradition in both Europe and the colonies to disestablish religion and separate church and state.

As is true of the Declaration of Independence, Jefferson's beginning lines in the statute are the most memorable: "Whereas Almighty God has created the mind free, so that all attempts to influence it by temporal punishments or burdens, or by civil incapacitations, tend only to beget habits of hypocrisy and meanness, and are a departure from the plan of the Holy Author of our religion, who, being Lord both of body and mind, yet chose not to propagate it by coercions on either, as was in His almighty power to do; that the impious presumption of legislators and rulers, civil as well as ecclesiastical, who, being themselves but fallible and uninspired men, have assumed dominion over the faith of others, setting up their own opinions and modes of thinking as the only true and infallible, and as such endeavoring to impose them on others, has established and maintained false religions over the greatest part of the world, and through all time; . . ."[10]

The first two arguments, then, are a dazzling combination of the positive and the negative. Respectful people presumably wish to imitate their God, and for this question of religious liberty the most significant fact about God's dealings with human beings is that God has left human beings free. He (Jefferson's time was patriarchal, simply assuming the masculinity of God) does not force people to worship him nor determine the forms they must follow if they choose to worship him. He places no coercion on either their bodies or their minds. Jefferson the rationalist finds the freedom of the human mind the most religious feature of the human condition, and perhaps the most remarkable, admirable feature of divinity. Here one finds the mediate influence of the Protestant Reformation, which made freedom to interpret the Bible its linchpin. The Protestant Reformers were quicker to demand religious liberty than to grant it to their own followers, but they inserted the decisive wedge in the assumption of Christendom that citizens could be compelled to orthodox thinking and practice. The divisions among the different colonial Protestant groups had made establishing a single church for even a limited area such as Virginia problematic, but in principle the majority of colonists right down to Jefferson's day assumed that church and state ought to go hand in glove.

It was the Jeffersons and Madisons who radicalized the implications of the Reformation, joining the Enlightenment's praise of reason (as the most significant human endowment) with the Reformers' insights into the sanctity of the human conscience. How pious Jefferson in fact was about this matter is hard to determine, but if he did have genuine religious feelings— awe before the work of the Creator—they welled up much as they had for the premier Enlightenment philosopher Immanuel Kant (1724–1804): when he contemplated either the natural world (Kant's "starry heavens above") or the human mind (Kant's "moral law within").

Complementing this conviction about the character of the divinity that decent people would want to imitate is Jefferson's second argument for religious freedom, which is negative. It is a blasphemy that, throughout history, mere mortals have arrogated to themselves the right to dictate others' beliefs and compel certain kinds of religious behavior. This has resulted in false religion the world over (Jefferson no doubt thought that only Christianity, preferably in the Deistic mode, was fully desirable), and in great hypocrisy, as many people have conformed outwardly to what in their hearts they judged untrue. Here Jefferson is drawing on the prejudices of the majority of his fellow citizens, for whom an authoritarian religion conjured up images of foul popery. The Enlightenment looked upon the medieval era as a time of darkness and backwardness. The medievals were priest-ridden, and the subjugation of their minds had been the main reason they had lived so shabbily. Much of this was myth, of course, since the medieval period had glories quite competitive with those of the 18th century. But it was a powerful myth, mixed into the very foundations of colonial America, which looked upon itself as a place of refuge from religious oppression. Even though the proximate religious oppression from which the New England Puritans had fled was not Roman Catholic but Anglican, and even though the Virginia colonists had been moved more by the chance for economic gain than by the need for religious freedom, it fit the story of American origins that was developing to make the colonial venture an exercise in moving from darkness to light, from oppression to freedom, from an old culture (European) to a brave new world where human potential might finally be realized. Jefferson's negative argument therefore rang bells both familiar and well tuned. In disestablishing religion and supporting religious freedom, Virginians would be heeding their own better selves and honoring the logic of their colonial spirit. The context of the independence declared in 1776 made it fitting, even imperative, that the states of the new American nation set its character as admirably as possible.

The statute of religious freedom would accomplish a giant piece of that work.

When it came to the practical significance of the statute, Jefferson toned down his rhetoric and became utterly plain: "No man shall be compelled to frequent or support any religious worship, place, or ministry whatsoever, nor shall he be enforced, restrained, molested, or burdened in his body or goods, nor shall otherwise suffer on account of his religious opinions or belief, but that all men shall be free to profess, and by argument to maintain, their opinion in matters of religion, and that the same shall in no wise diminish, enlarge, or affect their civil capacities."[11]

The stress on noncompulsion reminds us that in established churches people were often forced to attend worship services, as well as to support religious institutions by their taxes. The implication of Jefferson's statute is that one's religious opinions are one's own business. One may publish them abroad, but they should have no effect on one's civil capacities—one's political rights. Atheists should have all the civil rights of theists. Jews and Orientals should fare no better or worse than Christians. All of this was implied in the statute, and made explicit (somewhat) in Madison's "Remonstrance." While it may seem commonplace to Americans of the late twentieth century, it was a bombshell in 1779. Enlightened as they might consider themselves to be, the majority of Virginians, or other citizens of the new nation, had not appreciated the implications of seeing all people as equal under the law, as equally endowed by their Creator with certain inalienable rights, and so as having the freedom to worship or not worship as they saw fit. At a stroke, the religious pluralism that has characterized the United States swung so firmly into place that ever after it seemed inevitable.

The University of Virginia

From the end of his term as president to the end of his life, a period of over seventeen years, the main passion of Jefferson's days was the development of the University of Virginia. Though some described him as "the hermit of Monticello," Jefferson in fact took a lively interest in the world of political affairs, as well as in the details of his home and farmlands. But the development of the University of Virginia nearby, in what is now Charlottesville, was his great passion. A "Report of the Commissioners for the University of Virginia" dated August 18, 1818, deals in part with the scope that Jefferson foresaw for the university. He assumed that primary education would provide the basic skills necessary for citizens' private and civic lives: reading, writing, knowledge of their basic rights and duties, arithmetic, geography, and history. The higher education for which the public was being asked to found universities such as that of Virginia built on this foundation, but targeted different goals. Among those were: "To form the statesmen, legislators and judges, on whom public prosperity and individual happiness are so much to depend; to expound the principles and structure of government, the laws which regulate the intercourse of nations, those formed municipally for our own government, and a sound spirit of legislation, which, banishing all arbitrary and unnecessary restraint on individual action, shall leave us free to do whatever does not violate the equal rights of another. To harmonize and promote the interests of agriculture, manufactures, and commerce, and by well informed views of political economy to give a free scope to the public industry; to develop the reasoning faculties of our youth, enlarge their minds, cultivate their morals, and instill into them the precepts of virtue and order; to enlighten them with mathematical and physical sciences, which advance the arts, and administer to the health, the subsistence, and comforts of human life; and, generally, to form them to habits of reflection and correct action, rendering them examples of virtue to others, and of happiness within themselves."[13]

A report from the University's Board of Visitors covering the period 1822–25 reviewed the place of religion among the subjects to be studied and drew out some of the principal tensions attending this topic. First, it had been determined that, following the neutrality of the Constitution of the United States regarding religion, there should be no professorship of divinity. The idea was that establishing such a professorship would interfere with full liberty of religion, presumably because the professor would have to advocate religion, perhaps even a particular denominational theology. It was judged better to leave to each religious group provision for the higher education of its members in religion. On the other hand, this was not to mean no study of the phenomenon of religion, simply that it ought not to be done under public auspices. Religion itself was most significant: "The relations which exist between man and his maker, and the duties resulting from those relations, are the most interesting and important to every human being, and the most incumbent on his study and investigation. The want of instruction in the various creeds of religious faith existing among our citizens presents, therefore, a chasm in a general institution of the useful sciences."[14] However, that chasm would have to be filled outside the university's own curriculum of instruction. One way to do that would be to attract denominational schools to associate themselves with the university and offer instruction that, while private, would supplement the university's public offerings.

In leading the University of Virginia as its rector, Jefferson oversaw all the details of construction and daily order, as well as the basic philosophy of the enterprise. The Board of Visitors, in effect, rubber-stamped his designs. One biography of Jefferson sees the University of Virginia as his last effort to forward the liberty and democracy at the heart of his political philosophy: "The University of Virginia afforded Jefferson his last great opportunity to work for the principles of liberty and republican democracy. His behavior still displayed a characteristic element of paradox. In the name of liberty he had been willing to disobey the law of 1798 when the Congress was enacting laws curtailing the freedom of speech and press, and in 1803 he had unconstitutionally extended the empire of liberty by purchasing Louisiana. So now he did not hesitate to ignore academic freedom to make sure that the new university would spread the doctrines of freedom. He was not much concerned about the political opinions of the professors of languages or the sciences, or even of moral philosophy, but he wanted to make sure that the professor of law was an unswerving Republican who could be counted on to train up a generation of 'Whig' lawyers to man the legislature."[15]

The paradox may not be so acute as it seems at first blush. For Jefferson, at age eighty-two, the cause of freedom must have seemed more precarious than it might to those who had less experience of the assaults to which it was liable. Just as he had to pressure the legislature year after year for the budget of the university, so Jefferson had spent years battling the recalcitrance of his fellow citizens to embrace the means necessary to develop the United States as a nation where freedom could work well. No doubt Jefferson had considerable ego and was not above thinking that his way was correct, even if a majority opposed him. But his way of thinking about democracy and political freedom never overlooked the tendency of human beings to work against their own truly best interests. What people thought were their best interests tended to be products of the short view, not wise estimates based on detachment and the long view. So it was not a violation of his understanding of freedom to shape the selection of the professor of law, who Jefferson expected would have a special influence on the next generation of Virginia legislators. It was simply joining a passion for liberty (to be achieved by good laws) to common sense, as that common sense had been sharpened by practical experience.

At this point we may also be meeting the aspects of Jefferson's philosophy that come closest to Edwards's convictions about the depravity of human nature. On the whole, Jefferson espoused the Enlightenment's view of human potential. But that did not mean assuming that ordinary people would usually think and act aright. Experience showed that self-interest, in the low sense, warped many an endeavor, and Jefferson had been in politics too long not to know how impure a business it was. He had agreed with Madison about the need for a balance of powers, and his sense of freedom was mixed with a conviction that those who gained political power had to use it fearlessly in the prosecution of what they considered to be the right ends. If this meant an elitist view of who in fact understood freedom and best deserved to wield power, so be it. When the day came that the nation abounded in talented, selfless, wise people able to discern what served the common good, embrace it, and persuade others to follow suit, there might be no need for willful acts on the part of the few holding substantial power. But that day might well be the end of history. Jefferson seems not to have doubted his own intelligence or virtue. His share in the Puritans' pessimism was less than his share in the Enlightenment's optimism. But he did doubt the success of many of his ventures, with the result that he was willing to cut through opposition and obstacles whenever he had the opportunity, perhaps thinking that this was the prerogative of those not only gifted for political leadership but pressed into it by their fellow citizens.

Jefferson's Jesus

It is another revealing quirk of Jefferson's protean personality that although he believed firmly in the disestablishment of religion, and although he despised much of what institutional Christianity had done throughout history, and although he worried constantly about the potential of religions to infect people with superstition, nonetheless he admired Jesus as the greatest of moral teachers. Indeed, he produced his own version of the story of Jesus, working his way through the New Testament to winnow the grain from the chaff. The "Thomas Jefferson Bible" that resulted is a slim life of Christ, "prepared by arranging chronologically all of the verses from the four gospels that pertain to the career of our Lord, omitting, however, 'every verse or paragraph that to his mind was ambiguous or controversial, and every statement of fact that would not have been admitted as evidence in a court of justice.' "[16]

The Jefferson Bible is interested in Jesus the moral teacher. It has no interest in what it considers superstition or mystical theology, and Jefferson believed that Jesus had been badly served by his editors (a bunch of "groveling authors" responsible for the vulgarity, ignorance, fanaticism, and fabrications that one finds in the gospels, alongside the pure gems of moral wisdom that are so far above the rest that they could only have come from an inspired source, the genius of Jesus himself). Jefferson deliberately passed over the question of the divinity of Jesus, no doubt because if he were to declare his own views they would amount to a denial of the traditional teaching that Jesus was God as well as man. He had a low view of the Judaism in the midst of which Jesus was working, and he saw Jesus's task as a reformer to have been perilous. He had to walk a narrow path between reason and religion, between the parts of the Jewish heritage that urged an antisocial spirit (toward Gentiles) and the parts that preached philanthropy and a universal charity. His great enemies were superstitious priests, cruel and remorseless, who were out to snare him by fair means or foul. So Jesus had to express himself obliquely, and manage carefully the tradition of divine inspiration, strong among his people but susceptible to "the fumes of the most disordered imaginations."[17]

Thus Jefferson pruned the gospels radically, obtaining an account of Jesus that gave only the bare bones of his life and concentrated on his ethical teachings. For example, in inserting John 9 into his narrative, Jefferson included only the first three verses: "And as Jesus passed by, he saw a man which was blind from his birth. And his disciples asked him, saying, Master, who did sin, this man, or his parents, that he was born blind? Jesus answered, Neither hath this man sinned, nor his parents: but that the works of God should be made manifest in him."[18] The verses that follow in John illustrate the kind of material that did not suit Jefferson's purposes or taste: "We must work the works of him who sent me, while it is day; night comes, when no one can work. As long as I am in the world, I am the light of the world" (John 9:4–5). After this comes the miracle of Jesus's giving the blind man his sight, and then the wonderful dialogue between the blind man and the Pharisees, which is a prime example of the irony running throughout this gospel (the one born blind is the only one who sees who Jesus really is). What Jefferson made of Jesus's relationship with his Father, who sent him; of the work that Jesus's mission entailed; of Jesus's claim to be the light of the world; of the sign that Jesus gave in curing the blind man; and of the brilliant play on seeing and blindness, on openness and unbelief, that runs through the dialogue between the cured man and the Pharisees we do not know. Suffice it to say that he could not defend these in a court of law and so found no use for them. Whether in fact he was as blind to religious symbolism, poetry, and psychology as the omission suggests is hard to determine. It is safer to say that Jefferson the Enlightenment rationalist had a bias against the mythical, metaphorical, and mystical (a bias shared by many in his day and not really undermined until modern biblical studies showed the sophisticated meanings being conveyed through the plurivocal construction of the gospel narratives).

Taking Jefferson as an emblem of the world in which the new American nation arose, Daniel Boorstin has described some of the key features of Jeffersonian Christianity as follows: "When the Jeffersonian came to the traditional subject matter of religion, he showed a similar disposition to humanize his God into a beneficent being, and to make the primary quality of religion the exposition and inculcation of that benevolence . . . Since it was axiomatic that God's conduct must provide the example for man's morals, God could be neither unpredictable nor malevolent. His will and the precepts of His conduct must be benign and intelligible. Jefferson, for example, asserted that the apocalyptic books of the Bible could not be sacred or genuine: for it would have been blasphemy to impute to the Creator a revelation couched in terms which could never be understood by those to whom it was addressed. . . . Jefferson declared his moral theory to rest on his concept of God: 'He has formed us moral agents. Not that, in the perfection of His state, He can feel pain or pleasure in anything we may do; He is far above our power; but that we may promote the happiness of those with whom He has placed us in society, by acting honestly towards all, benevolently to those who fall within our way, respecting sacredly their rights, bodily and mental, and cherishing especially their freedom of conscience, as we value our own.' "[19]

This is the God of the Deists, remote and benign. His main concern is that the world run in an orderly fashion, and the ideal would be for human affairs to imitate the precision of the affairs of nature. Jefferson's concern with politics makes sense as an extension or execution of his convictions about the primary responsibilities that people receive from their Creator. If their main charge is to promote the happiness of those with whom God has placed them in society, then (assuming they have the talent) they can do few things more pleasing to God than to improve the laws and institutions having so great a say in people's happiness. Indeed, Jefferson was following this ethical calculus when he wrote to Rittenhouse about the special status of the scientific genius. The ultimate justification for a life lived apart from political burdens and given over to scientific research was the contribution such a life could make to the welfare of humankind, both speculative and practical. A Newton was a great philanthropist. One might consider him a gift of the Creator, raised up to benefit the whole race, and one might consider his scientific labors benefactions made at the cost of his own great toil. Against this background, Jesus had to be primarily a moral reformer and sage. The benefactions of Jesus boiled down to his offering his benighted Jewish contemporaries a way out of their ruinous religious culture and his offering subsequent generations the most sublime view the world has ever seen of how human beings ought to treat one another.

For those who thought as Jefferson did, "Jesus had been a great 'philosopher'—in the strict Jeffersonian sense. He was not a system builder, but a reformer. He had cleared away the fabrications of priests and metaphysicians, bringing men back to simple facts which all could and should have known for themselves. . . . Jesus' achievement was fourfold: he corrected some of the crude Jewish ideas of the attributes of God; he improved the moral doctrines of the ancients regarding kindred and friends, and went beyond these to a universal philanthropy; he 'pushed his scrutinies into the heart of man . . .'; 'he taught, emphatically, the doctrines of a future state. . . .' The result, according to Jefferson, was that of all the systems of morality, ancient and modern, none was so pure as that of Jesus."[20]

Reason and Religion

Erik Erikson, the father of modern studies of the life cycle, has published an interesting series of lectures on Jefferson that touch on his motives in editing the gospels to produce a life of Jesus: "In 1801, Jefferson had become president with an overwhelming mandate from the people, though not without being exposed to such slanderous reportage as was to become typical for American campaigns but which could only deeply offend a man who, on the one hand, was so jealous of his public image, and yet so ready to disavow ambition and to withdraw to Monticello. Furthermore, the attacks on him concerned those most sensitive and central aspects of a man's life which Jefferson never aired in public: his personality, his (very) private life, and his religion. As he once put it, 'I not only write nothing on religion, but rarely permit myself to speak of it, and never but in reasonable society.' And so, during his first presidential campaign, he had to tolerate with silence the most sinister insinuations concerning the devastating consequences for the whole country of an atheist administration. And, indeed, all his life Jefferson avoided public Christian display and loud sectarian controversies and shunned any contrivance with clerical power struggles: 'To the corruptions of Christianity I am, indeed, opposed; but not to the genuine precepts of Jesus himself. I am a Christian in the only sense in which he wished anyone to be; sincerely attached to his doctrine in preference to all others; ascribing to himself every *human* excellence; and believing that he never claimed any other.' "[21]

In Erikson's scenario, Jefferson could only make such a claim after he had scrutinized the teachings of Jesus. That he would spend the evenings of his first presidency poring over the New Testament (using Greek, Latin, French, and English versions) to sift out the sayings of Jesus he considered genuine must testify to the need he felt to settle the question of his own brand of Christianity. Behind this effort, in Erikson's view, is the task typically arising, at least for reflective people, in the second half of the life cycle: to relate oneself to eternity. We dread the possibility that at the end of our brief span of time we may find that "we have lived the wrong life or not really lived at all. This dread seems incomparably greater than that of death itself, after a fulfilled life—awful as the sudden cessation of life always is."[22]

For those open to a psychoanalytic interpretation, Erikson's should serve quite well. In clarifying his understanding of Jesus, Jefferson was working through the problems of identity presented him by the assaults on his character and the charges that he was an atheist. As well, he was affording himself the opportunity to come to grips with his own mortality and discern what it was he wanted his life to have accomplished. Prominent in Jefferson's interpretation of Jesus was the Sermon on the Mount, where the Matthean Jesus overturns what we might call worldly standards of judgment and suggests the new standards required by God. Erikson finds Jefferson's political strategies nonviolent in a way reminiscent of Mahatma Gandhi, and he implies that through the confrontation with ultimate questions occasioned by his study of Jesus, the new president was stabilizing himself, like a tree sending down deeper roots to stand fast against future storms.

Arguing for this interpretation is the serenity and conviction that one finds in the older Jefferson's pronouncements on both religion and political issues having moral import. In retirement Jefferson was concerned to make the University of Virginia a training ground for succeeding generations of political servants, imbuing them with ideas of republican democracy that would keep alive the vision of those who had declared independence and constituted the new nation so as to respect individual liberties above all else. Most of Jefferson's discussions of religious and moral questions occurred in private letters to trusted friends. In public statements he remained silent or prudent. On one occasion, however, he was drawn into a public matter. He was called to witness for a bookseller prevented by public authorities from offering a work on the creation of the world that challenged the account in Genesis (with findings from astronomy and geology). Jefferson's letter of April 19, 1814 makes plain his complete opposition to censorship on religious (or virtually any other) grounds: "I am really mortified to be told that, in the United States of America, a fact like this can become a subject of inquiry, and of criminal inquiry too, as an offense against religion; that a question about the sale of a book can be carried before the civil magistrate. Is this then our freedom of religion? And are we to have a censor whose imprimatur shall say what books may be sold and what we may buy? And who is thus to dogmatize religious opinions for our citizens? Whose boot is to be the measure to which ours are all to be cut or stretched? Is a priest to be our inquisitor, or shall a layman, simple as ourselves, set up his reason as the rule for what we are to read and what we must believe? It is an insult to our citizens to question whether they are rational beings or not, and blasphemy against religion to suppose it cannot stand the test of truth and reason. If M. de Becourt's book be false in its facts, disprove them; if false in its reasoning, refute it. But, for God's sake, let us freely hear both sides if we choose . . . I have just been reading the new constitution of Spain. One of its fundamental bases is expressed in these words: 'The Roman Catholic religion, the only true one is, and always shall be, that of the Spanish nation. The government protects it by wise and just laws, and prohibits the exercise of any other whatever.' Now I wish this presented to those who question what you may sell or we may buy, with a request to strike out the words 'Roman Catholic' and to insert the denominations of their own religion. This would ascertain the code of dogmas which each wishes should domineer over the opinions of all others."[23]

Just as Jefferson consigned what he considered superstitious aspects of the New Testament to the backwardness of the Judaism contemporary with Jesus, so he consigned what he considered outrageous censorship to the authoritarian view of religion promulgated by Roman Catholicism. In addition to firming up our impression of Jefferson as a son of the Enlightenment who insisted that religion cohere with reason and honor the freedoms of individual conscience, this quotation may also remind us that what we are calling "mainstream" American religious thought was very much a Protestant enterprise, and that in two senses. First, it owed its main debts to the Reformers who had broken with Roman Catholicism in the sixteenth century. Second, it took a dim view of Jews, Catholics, and others who did not adhere to the Protestant family of religious interpretation. The same

Jefferson who fought valiantly for religious freedom, and agreed that it should be extended to all citizens, Jews and Catholics as much as Anglicans and unbelievers, had several personal grievances with traditions outside the Protestant mainstream.

This sort of complexity occurs everywhere, of course, and we should not tax Jefferson with schizophrenia or hypocrisy. Indeed, we can note that the Protestant powers who were trying to engineer the prohibition of the book in question about creation fare no better in this letter than the Spanish Catholics. But we have to appreciate the difficulty with which any individual, least of all one occupying a privileged place among the mainstream powers, can be truly open or nonjudgmental about so potentially passionate a matter as religion. Jefferson and his like did extremely well in laying the foundations for a national culture that would be civil toward all religious groups because it established none. The uncivil character of much de facto interaction among believers of different allegiances is not the fault of Jefferson and his associates.[24] But even the most rational of people tend to have blind spots, exceptions to their reasonableness, including emphatically those whose great passion is rationality. This raises again the relevance of the Puritans' view of human nature and suggests that Jefferson might have profited from a study of the data and arguments that those opposing the Enlightenment's convictions about the perfectibility of human nature tended to bring forward.[25]

The Constitution

Before the Constitution of the United States had even been ratified, there was agitation for amendments to clarify and secure individual rights. Those opposed to the Federalist philosophy of the Constitution agitated most strongly, and the Federalists promised to honor their concerns. Accordingly, on September 9, 1789, James Madison led the House of Representatives to recommend to the states for their adoption twelve amendments that had originated in states' discussions of the Constitution. The ten amendments that were adopted became known as the Bill of Rights and were declared to be in force on December 15, 1791. Of these ten the very first deals with things Congress shall not do: "Congress shall make no law respecting an establishment of religion, or prohibiting the free exercise thereof; or abridging the freedom of speech, or of the press; or the right of the people peacefully to assemble, and to petition the Government for a redress of grievances."[26]

It is interesting that what has become the pillar of religious liberty in the United States does not stand apart from freedom of speech, of the press, of assembly, and of access to government. All four of these freedoms expressed the worries of the Anti-Federalists about the powers of a national government. In the case of religion, the principle that had emerged, not without considerable debate and dissent, was that there should be no single national religion. The atmosphere of the time determined that "religion" would first signify something denominational: Congregationalist or Presbyterian, Anglican or Quaker. Implicitly, however, the word implied "Protestant or Catholic, Christian or Jewish or Hindu." No group, Christian or non-Christian, was to gain the status of being the official religion of the nation. To be American was not to be Methodist or Protestant or Christian the way that to be Spanish was to be Roman Catholic. The further implication was that there was no single "true religion." The First Amendment denied the assumption of the Spanish Constitution.

Why did the young United States deny that assumption? Because of both American history and the American religious worldview.[27] From its earliest beginnings, colonial America had been pluralistic. The religion of Virginia was not the same as the religion of Massachusetts. Moreover, as the colonies grew they came to house more and more religious denominations. Certainly, it took some time for the former colonies to accept the provisions of the First Amendment and make their own state law equally nonestablishmentarian. As James H. Smylie reminds us, ". . . the liberal age showed vestigial remains of an illiberal past which caused dissenters to suffer civil disabilities for religious opinions. In only two out of thirteen original states were full rights of conscience conceded without legal qualifications. In Rhode Island such freedom had become a habit; in Virginia, it had recently been won. In contrast with this, five states, viz., New Hampshire, Massachusetts, Connecticut, Maryland, and South Carolina, maintained a religious establishment through a legalized and supposedly equal policy of assessment. Beyond this there were provisions in state constitutions supporting religious tests for holding office. Six states—New Hampshire, Connecticut, New Jersey, the two Carolinas, and Georgia— insisted on an acceptance of Protestantism. Delaware and Maryland widened this to Christianity as a whole. In Pennsylvania and South Carolina officials had to believe in one God, and in a heaven and hell, while Delaware demanded assent to the doctrine of the trinity. Three states—New York, Maryland, and South Carolina—excluded clergymen from holding civil office. Although in most areas vigorous forces opposed many of these provisions, the 'prevailing liberality' did not prevent the continuation of tests in state constitutions."[28]

The second half of the treatment of religion in the First Amendment balances the first half. If Congress was to make no law respecting the establishment of religion, it was also to make no law prohibiting the free exercise of religion. The second half is a negation of a possible negation. In denying Congress the right to legislate against the free exercise of religion, the framers of the First Amendment were saying that the nation should allow people to worship and otherwise express themselves on religious matters as people wished. Did this amount to encouraging religion? Probably Madison and Jefferson did not think so, since they favored a strict neutrality, such that unbelievers would suffer no civil liabilities for not going to church or agreeing with believers. But the veto on prohibiting the free exercise of religion did make it clear that the United States was not to be an antireligious realm, as revolutionary France first seemed to be and the Soviet Union later was. The neutrality or secularism of the civil government ought not to infringe upon the rights of citizens to be as religious, or irreligious, as they wished.

Furthermore, although it was inevitable that many Americans would draw the conclusion that religion, or irreligion, was a private matter, theoretically distinct from one's public life as a citizen, in fact it was equally inevitable that the social character of religion would challenge this conclusion. The free exercise of religion included the right to assemble with others who shared one's convictions, for worship, education, acts of charity, or whatever else came to mind. If people had any question that the First Amendment protected such a social exercise of religion, they had only to note that the amendment explicitly included the right of people peacefully to assemble. Similarly, were there any question about the right to publish religious opinions, they had only to note the amendment's words about freedom of speech and the press to make the case that the right to express religious views, whether those of individuals or those of groups, was part of the American Bill of Rights. So the First Amendment secured a broad avenue for the exercise of religion, and the subsequent interpretation of many citizens that theirs was a religious land had some legal as well as much empirical evidence. Though those convinced of the importance of the separation of church and state could point to the First Amendment, so could those who wanted American culture to be saturated with religious convictions. Both groups have had their way, which suggests there was a touch of genius in the First Amendment.

Among the groups responsible for this popular interpretation and acceptance of the First Amendment, the Protestant clergy stand out: "Most Protestant clergy accepted the Constitution of the United States as an attempt to deal with the problem of power about which they shared the same presuppositions. They accepted power, the dominion of some men over others, as essential to human society. They also believed that power is of an encroaching and corrupting nature. This is true of ecclesiastical as well as civil power. This is true especially of civil power sanctioned uncritically by ecclesiastical establishment, and of ecclesiastical power supported by civil coercion. Power, civil and ecclesiastical, has to be deflated, diffused, and properly related in order to keep it from becoming absolute, arbitrary, and abused. Therefore, the First Amendment with its no establishment and free exercise clauses may be seen as contributing to the proper equilibrium of power."[29]

Here is a clear expression of the suspicion of human nature that abetted the acceptance of the First Amendment. By not establishing any religion, the nation could avoid the tyranny of coercion. By not prohibiting the free exercise of religion, the nation could avoid the worse tyranny of irreligion. There was potential abuse on the left and potential abuse on the right. Only in the middle, when the two potentials were aligned so that they offset one another, might there emerge sufficient virtue to safeguard the nation's religious health.[30]

The Secular and the Religious

In recent years many students of American religion have discussed the concept of civil religion.[31] The discussion has focused on the many ways in which Americans have collapsed patriotism and piety, creating an ethos that has made being an American a matter of religious moment. Scholars could point to the religious imagery, language, and emotion running through such celebrations as Memorial Day, Fourth of July, and Thanksgiving. They could adduce the religious language found regularly in the addresses of presidents, which tended to give America a providential sacredness. Running across the boundaries of the particular religious denominations was a common reverence for such virtues as hard work, belief in God, willingness to sacrifice oneself for one's nation, and patriotism. Times of war understandably brought this civil religion into boldest relief, but it played itself out in the peacetime activities of the American Legion, the Veterans of Foreign Wars, the Daughters of the American Revolution, the Masons, the Elks, the Kiwanis, and numerous other civic groups. Even the American obsession with sports was susceptible of interpretation as having a religious dimension, inasmuch as sports symbolized American convictions about fair play and teamwork.

To be sure, critics have questioned everything about American civil religion, from the fact of its existence, to the modes of its exercise, to its desirability. The denominations centered in biblical theology have had a hard time with the concept, inasmuch as it could seem to be promoting an idolatrous nationalism. On the other hand, many evangelical groups saw in the activities associated with civil religion an affirmation of the Protestant cultural consensus they thought had made America great. For them, returning to traditional ideas about the family, the place of women, opposition to promiscuity, prostitution, alcoholism, the use of drugs, divorce, and a host of other evils might return America to its God-given destiny as the light to the other nations.

Most supporters of American religion, in practice and theory, have waxed eloquent about the sacredness of democracy. America has been the land where individual liberties flourished, tyranny had no legal or popular support, people might live as their consciences dictated, and free enterprise reigned. The great carrier of civil religion has been the public school system, which promoted saluting the flag, pledging allegiance, the idea that all people, regardless of religious or ethnic background, had the same rights as citizens, the possibility of becoming a great success through hard work and native talent, and so forth. In fact the moral profile promoted by the public school system in most times and places has been a version of Protestant idealism, but the promotion has been diffuse and tacit rather than explicitly Protestant. Indeed, most scholars agree that civil religion is nebulous both as concept and reality, because it has floated across and through virtually every institution in American life. Catholics and Jews have breathed its air and shaped their patriotism to its moods. Only the sectarians, such as the Amish and the Jehovah's Witnesses, who removed themselves from the mainstream of American culture out of convictions that religious fidelity required them to stand apart, have resisted civil religion clearly and named its likely conflict with a radical allegiance to the One God. For the rest, the great majority of Americans, an agreement that belief in God ought to be compatible with patriotism, and that belief in God ought to shape one's civil life, created a willingness to let the secular and the religious borders blur. Each has been permeable by the other. The churches and synagogues have displayed flags and boosted Americanism, while the funerals and speeches of presidents have been laced with religious symbols.

American civil religion therefore sums up the practical effect of the lively experiment with religious liberty and nonestablishment. Sidney E. Mead has stressed the roots of nonestablishment and religious liberty in the

Enlightenment,[32] but equally important has been the evangelical Protestantism that never accepted the radical implications of nonestablishment. If the majority of Protestants agreed that the government should not favor one denomination at the expense of others, because that one denomination might not be their own, they did not agree that America should be a secular, let alone an atheistic, nation. They assumed that Christian values and virtues would continue to provide the backbone of American culture, and they interpreted the democratic institutions that developed as excellent civic channels for the work of God. By enshrining freedom of religion, the Constitution had enabled all religious groups to proselytize, spreading the good news of Jesus Christ. Attenuated as that good news might sometimes be, it remained in the minds of the proselytizers the best hope for American prosperity.

The long-playing equation of virtue and success, once buttressed by Calvinist notions of election and later democratized into a divine blessing for hard work and patriotism, made cleanliness, godliness, and good citizenship interlocking desiderata. The sacredness of the individual conscience, clarified during the Protestant Reformation, was extended to include the sacredness of the individual's freely chosen enterprise. People ought to be able to work with as little governmental restriction as possible, because the genius that would flower in such economic and cultural freedom was finally an expression of God. A similar fervor appeared across the realms of religion, business, and sports: in the evangelical tents where preachers implored people to open themselves to conviction of sin; in the business meetings and locker-room assemblies where company presidents and football coaches exhorted their troops to give their best. The notion that sincerity and peak effort would produce both victory and something pleasing to God ran throughout American culture. Only with the radical challenge to assumptions about American godliness in the 1960s and 1970s did a significant portion of the general public join with traditional theologians in relativizing the sanctity of the American civil enterprise.

And whereas the traditional theologians merely brought forth the prophetic strand of biblical theology, where anything less than the mysterious God had always been feared as an idol, the popular skepticism came from the perception that the language of civil religion had become a way of obscuring crimes and misdemeanors. Although the war in Vietnam was the great breaking point, the civil rights movement had spotlighted the immense stain of American racism. Combined, the civil rights movement and the antiwar movement forced the country as a whole to reexamine its equation of patriotism and religion, suggesting that much had grown facile if not corrupt. The assaults on the veracity of Lyndon Johnson and Richard Nixon were the spearheads of this feeling, but the feeling targeted great portions of American public life, such as the law, the educational establishment, and the business world.

To be sure, mainstream America quickly retreated from radical prophecy, becoming sufficiently conservative to elect Ronald Reagan president and revivify the sanctity of business. But the relationship between the secular and the religious had changed, because it had become clearer that resistance to mainstream American culture might be a religious duty. The shades of Roger Williams, Anne Hutchinson, and other colonial witnesses to the primacy of religious conscience joined with such new witnesses as Martin Luther King, Jr., Robert Kennedy, and Cesar Chavez. Each argued that telling the truth, committing oneself to radical justice, rooting out destructive prejudice and privilege, and opposing violence was a political translation of a commitment to God. Each insisted that genuine religion takes to the streets, the workplace, the halls of congress, the fields and hospitals and schools, trying to incarnate its convictions so that it makes human existence better, removing the poverty, disease, and ignorance that blight creatures made in God's image. Collectively, they reassembled the pieces of the kaleidoscope, setting the issue of the secular and the religious into new configurations—often ones quite different from what the framers of the First Amendment probably had in mind.

American Religious Pluralism

The history of both colonial and republican America has carried so much ethnic and religious variety that pluralism has been inevitable. Not only did the original colonists come from different religious traditions, the many non-English immigrants quickly added new religious backgrounds. The First Amendment provided the legal framework to build a true religious pluralism, one in which people might respect, even prize, diversity. But the First Amendment could not dictate how people felt about the religious traditions of other citizens, so it did not settle the question of the acceptability of Jews and Catholics, Mormons and Chinese. Even when such people became citizens they could suffer considerable discrimination, some of it based on fears of their religious convictions.

For example, Josiah Strong, a prominent evangelical churchman, thought that Roman Catholic views of authority threatened the basic

American liberties, which Strong identified with Protestant and Anglo-Saxon traditions. Thus in a book published in 1891 Strong wrote: "We have made a brief comparison of some of the fundamental principles of Romanism with those of the Republic. And, 1. We have seen the supreme sovereignty of the Pope opposed to the sovereignty of the people. 2. We have seen that the commands of the Pope, instead of the constitution and laws of the land, demand the highest allegiance of Roman Catholics in the United States. 3. We have seen that the alien Romanist who seeks citizenship swears true obedience to the Pope instead of 'renouncing forever all allegiance to any foreign prince, potentate, state or sovereignty,' as required by our laws. 4. We have seen that Romanism teaches religious intolerance instead of religious liberty. 5. We have seen that Rome demands the censorship of ideas and of the press, instead of the freedom of the press and of speech. 6. We have seen that she approves the union of church and state instead of their entire separation. 7. We have seen that she is opposed to our public school system. Manifestly there is an irreconcilable difference between papal principles and the fundamental principles of our free institutions."[33]

Defenders of Catholicism, such as James Cardinal Gibbons, archbishop of Baltimore, pointed out that American law itself stated that no religious test should be required as a qualification for public office, that Catholics had shown themselves to be loyal citizens (for example, by serving in the military), that most of the logical difficulties that opponents found in professing a loyalty to the pope as well as to the United States vanished in practice, and that the American spirit of tolerance and fair play was badly served by antagonistic if not prejudiced attacks on the sincerity of American Catholic citizens.[34] In the long run the position of Gibbons prevailed, but that only became clear with the election of John Kennedy as President in 1960. During the 1928 presidential campaign, the Democratic candidate, Alfred E. Smith, a Catholic, was the subject of strongly anti-Catholic propaganda.

So de facto pluralism has not necessarily meant acceptance and liberality of spirit. In the case of Catholics, their church's traditional sense of the relations between the religious and the secular did warrant interest, if not concern, about how they would adapt to American traditions about the separation of church and state, but of course the truly relevant data should have been how Catholics actually were behaving. The same went for Jews, Mormons, and Chinese Buddhists. Since the United States boasted of religious liberty and liberty of intellectual opinion, the debate ought to have been focused less on how those outside the Protestant mainstream were thought to believe and more on how they actually fulfilled their duties as citizens.

Whatever its failures, however, the American experiment in religious pluralism has offered many less tolerant cultures a lesson in liberty. Repeatedly, Jews, Catholics, and others have come to the United States from countries where their religious rights were repressed and have quickly hailed their adopted country as a land of wonderful opportunities to prosper, spiritually as well as materially. In the midst of their negotiations with the mainstream, they have usually imbibed considerable amounts of civil religion, agreeing to solemnize public holidays and occasions as times when the providential aspects of American history rightly come to the fore.

The further question is whether civil religion of this sort can satisfy the needs of many human beings to worship God clearly and in the company of passionate fellow believers. The framers of the Constitution no doubt were aware of this further question and considered it less pressing than the need to assure harmony and religious liberty. The same intensity that attends denominational religion at its best can easily slip over into fanaticism and intolerance. Granted Europe's history of religious wars, the thinkers shaped by the Enlightenment feared intolerance more than tepidity. Their main goal was fashioning a nation where individual rights would predominate. If people used such rights to produce a pluralistic culture, sacrificing depth for variety, that was their privilege. God was sufficiently removed from the hurly-burly of daily affairs, most of the founding fathers thought, that the first order of business was political rather than theological.

From an explicitly Christian perspective, religious pluralism is equally ambiguous. On the one hand, the principle that people have to follow their own consciences, worshiping God and treating others as they feel is right, has good roots in Christian tradition. Jesus was willing to clash with the religious authorities of his day because of his convictions, and so were his disciples. God spoke to people by means of conscience, so conscience had the sanctity of a shrine, a place where the divinity made itself present. On the other hand, there was the prayer of Jesus (John 17) for the unity of his followers, and the longstanding conviction that unity is one of the four great marks of the true church of Christ (holiness, catholicity, and apostolicity are the others). The willingness of the Christian denominations to ignore the challenges to religious pluralism stemming from this second aspect of Christian faith is remarkable. Until the ecumenical movement that arose after World War I, both Protestants and Catholics paid the prayer of Jesus little heed. In the United States, the tradition of religious diversity was so strong, and the fears of abridging legal rights or the rights of conscience were so deeply rooted, that diversity, competition, and even antagonism were accepted as simply facts of life. The churches had come to define themselves in opposition to one another. Were they to give up their opposition to other groups, they might be hard pressed to explain their identity.

On the horizon at the present time is the pressure exerted by non-Christian religions. As more Muslims, Hindus, Buddhists, and others become American citizens, the American traditions of religious liberty penetrate to a new level and religious diversity widens. Whether this will bring Christians, or Jews, to lessen their internal differences is hard to predict. On the one hand, Orthodox, Conservative, and Reformed Jews all have sizable investments in their distinctiveness, as do Methodists and Baptists, Lutherans and Catholics. On the other hand, the presence of more dramatically different fellow citizens may incline some Jews or Christians to focus on what they hold in common with their fellow Jews or Christians. In the Protestant Christian case, more relevant to the mainstream of American history and culture, the question is whether organizations such as the National Council of Churches will in fact become super-churches. Presently, that does not seem likely. Denominational loyalties continue to be strong, and the growing influence of evangelical churches, previously marginal to the mainstream but now sufficient in number to constitute a powerful stream in their own right, seems to be a force for independence and diversity rather than for unification. Thus, it is likely that America's religious diversity will continue to grow, making the historic choice for nonestablishment more and more significant.

NOTES

1. See Michael J. Buckley, *At the Origins of Modern Atheism* (New Haven: Yale University Press, 1987).

2. See John Corrigan, "The Enlightenment," in *Encyclopedia of the American Religious Experience*, ed. Charles H. Lippy and Peter W. Williams (New York: Scribner's, 1988), vol. 2, pp. 1089–1102.

3. Thomas Jefferson, "On the Superiority of Science to Politics," in *The Annals of America* (Chicago: Encyclopaedia Britannica, 1976), vol. 2, p. 502.

4. See Henry Steele Commager, "Jefferson and the Enlightenment," in *Thomas Jefferson*, ed. Lally Weymouth (New York: Putnam, 1973), pp. 39–67.

5. Garry Wills, "Prolegomena to a Reading of the Declaration," *ibid.*, p. 79.

6. Thomas Jefferson, "Autobiography," in *Thomas Jefferson: Writings* (New York: Library of America, 1984), p. 22.

7. "The Declaration of Independence," in *The Annals of America*, vol. 2, p. 447.

8. Garry Wills, ibid.

9. Thomas Jefferson, "Virginia Statute of Religious Freedom," in *The Annals of America*, vol. 3, p. 53.

10. Ibid., pp. 53–54.

11. Ibid., p. 54.

12. See Charles B. Sanford, *The Religious Life of Thomas Jefferson* (Charlottesville: University Press of Virginia, 1984), pp. 23–34.

13. Thomas Jefferson, "Report of the Commissioners for the University of Virginia," in *Thomas Jefferson: Writings*, pp. 459–60.

14. Thomas Jefferson, "From the Minutes of the Board of Visitors, University of Virginia, 1822–1825," ibid., p. 477.

15. Stuart Jerry Brown, *Thomas Jefferson* (New York: Washington Square, 1966), p. 171.

16. Thomas Jefferson, *The Life & Morals of Jesus Christ of Nazareth* (New York: David McKay, 1946), pp. vii–viii.

17. Thomas Jefferson, "Letters: 1820," in *Thomas Jefferson: Writings*, p. 1438. See also pp. 1436–1439 and 1120–1126.

18. Thomas Jefferson, *The Life & Morals of Jesus Christ of Nazareth*, p. 75.

19. Daniel J. Boorstin, *The Lost World of Thomas Jefferson* (Chicago: University of Chicago Press, 1981), pp. 152–153. Boorstin's source is *The Writings of Thomas Jefferson*, ed. Albert Ellery Bergh (Washington, D.C.: Thomas Jefferson Memorial Association, 1907), vol. 1, p. 259.

20. Ibid., pp. 157–158.

21. Erik H. Erikson, *Dimensions of a New Identity* (New York: W. W. Norton, 1974), pp. 39–40.

22. Ibid., pp. 41–42.

23. Thomas Jefferson, "On the Censorship of Religious Books," in *The Annals of America*, vol. 4, pp. 348–349.

24. See Robert N. Bellah and Frederick E. Greenspahn, eds., *Uncivil Religion: Interreligious Hostility in America* (New York: Crossroad, 1987).

25. See Thomas Jefferson, "On Science and the Perfectibility of Man," in *The Annals of America*, vol. 4, pp. 113–115.

26. *The Encyclopedia of American History*, ed. Richard B. Morris (New York: Harper & Row, 1976), p. 575.

27. See Denise Lardner Carmody and John Tully Carmody, *Exploring American Religion* (Mountain View, CA: Mayfield, 1990).

28. James H. Smylie, "Protestant Clergy, The First Amendment and the Beginnings of a Constitutional Debate 1781–91," in *The Religion of the Republic*, ed. Elwyn A. Smith (Philadelphia: Fortress, 1971), p. 117.

29. Ibid., p. 153.

30. See Glenn Miller, "Church and State," in *Encyclopedia of the American Religious Experience,* vol. 3, pp. 1369–1391.

31. See Donald G. Jones, "Civil and Public Religion," ibid., pp. 1393–1408.

32. See Sidney E. Mead, *The Lively Experiment* (New York: Harper & Row, 1976).

33. See Josiah Strong, "Our Country," in *Religious Issues in American History,* ed. Edwin Scott Gaustad (New York: Harper & Row, 1968), p. 201.

34. See James Cardinal Gibbons, "The Church and the Republic," ibid., pp. 206–211.

Chapter 5

On Disestablishment: Responses from the Margins

Jewish Americans

The most salient feature of Jewish-American life has been the immigrant character of the American Jewish population. Because Jews did not come to America in sizable numbers until the nineteenth century, they usually had the task of adapting to the mainstream culture shaped by Protestantism. Deborah Dash Moore, writing a social history of American Judaism, has estimated the American Jewish population to be 1500 in 1790, 6000 in 1830, and 150,000 in 1860. In 1940, when Jews numbered about 4,770,000, the Jewish fraction of the American population reached its height: 3.61 percent. Regularly, therefore, Jews have been a small minority. The only qualification to this judgment comes from the tendency of Jews to cluster in urban centers and achieve a significant presence in such cities as New York, Chicago, Los Angeles, Philadelphia, and (recently) Miami. Thus, in 1955 there were over two million Jews in New York City, making the Jewish population a strong cultural and political force.[1]

Many of the Jewish immigrants who came to the United States in the nineteenth and twentieth centuries were fleeing from persecution. The first wave of immigrants consisted of mainly German Jews, among whom Reformed ideas prevailed. At the end of the nineteenth century persecutions in Eastern Europe precipitated a huge influx of Jewish immigrants (2.3 million between 1882 and 1924), the majority of whom spoke Yiddish

and were religiously Orthodox. The tension between the German Reformed Jews and the eastern-European Orthodox frequently was considerable, due to differences in education as well as religious instincts. But both
groups tended to agree that the United States offered Jews an opportunity
virtually unparalleled in history. Because of its democratic institutions and
nonestablishment of religion, the United States in principle did not dis-
criminate against any group. In practice, Jews did experience many forms
of discrimination, some subtle and some gross. Nonetheless, compared to
the violence and hatred they had experienced regularly in Europe, their
experience in the United States seemed benign.

Traditional Judaism, like traditional Christianity, Islam, and other religions, had assumed that religion and the other features of cultural life
would form a unified worldview. Although Jews had lived under foreign
rule since their dispersal from Jerusalem in 70 c.e., they had tended to form
communities in which their own teachers, rulers, and tradespeople dominated everyday life. The rabbi was the authority on all matters of religious
law and ritual, which permeated both the home and the community life.
Diet, social behavior, worship, business, and even music and art came
under the rabbi's sway, inasmuch as he was the main interpreter of *halakah*,
talmudic religious law. Traditional Judaism provided for the salvation and
significance of non-Jews, but its instinct was to segregate Jews from non-
Jews. For example, in strict interpretation, Jews were not to eat with
Gentiles, and to marry a Gentile was to court excommunication. Indeed,
if one married outside Judaism, one's parents were supposed to mourn as
though one had died.

The two obvious options facing immigrant American Jews were to try
to adapt their traditions to American culture or to try to sequester themselves in Jewish neighborhoods where they might live according to traditional norms. The German Jews who were the first wave of immigrants
tended toward the first option, while the Eastern European Jews who were
the second wave of immigrants tended toward the second option. However, following a pattern observable in other immigrant groups, even the
children of traditionally observant, Orthodox Jews tended to assimilate
themselves to American norms and try to blend into the mainstream.
Sometimes their children, the third generation, swung back to traditional
customs, in an effort to reclaim their roots, but usually by the end of the
third generation a compromise identity, Jewish-American, had emerged.

The major qualification to this pattern has been the rise of Zionist
consciousness, beginning late in the nineteenth century and escalating after
World War II. With the Holocaust, the extinction of six million Jews in

Nazi death camps during the war, and then with the creation of the modern state of Israel in 1948, American Jews experienced a resurgence of Jewish consciousness. Although the number of Americans who have emigrated to Israel is small, a great many have visited Israel and contributed financial support. Because of such help, along with the political pressure of Jewish Americans for American support of Israel, a strong axis between America and Israel has come to structure the self-conception of many American Jews. They remain fully American in their sense of identity, but they tend to think that without Israel they would not be as fully Jewish as they want to be.

Although Israel has tried to create a democracy in which religious allegiance will not determine civic status, it has been preoccupied with squabbles among different Jewish factions and has granted Orthodox Jews preponderant authority, alienating many Reformed Americans. It has not solved the problem of integrating its Palestinian population, Muslim or Christian, into the mainstream of its culture, and Palestinian hostility has made Israel a pariah in the Middle Eastern world dominated by Islam. American supporters of Israel have lauded it as a venture in democracy and an island in a sea of Soviet-influenced authoritarian regimes of Islamic cast. But one cannot call Israel a follower of the United States in the disestablishment of religion, due to the power given the Orthodox.

The Jewish experience in the United States has generally supported the wisdom of disestablishment. That is, the majority of American Jews have found that the religiously pluralistic American culture has provided them opportunities to prosper. If material prosperity has been more evident than spiritual, most Jewish observers would say this too reflects freedom of choice. Having had the legal right to establish their own schools and synagogues, they could be as spiritual as they wished. An exception to this positive judgment on American culture is offered by the extreme Orthodox, most of them Hasidim clustered in Brooklyn, who have resembled Christian sectarians such as the Amish in condemning modern culture as pagan and trying to live pure lives apart from the mainstream. Many of these Hasidim are also anti-Zionists, opposing the secularism of the state of Israel, as they see it. They may praise the United States for having offered them refuge from oppression, but they have yet to be convinced that the nonestablishment of religion and pluralistic culture one finds in America do not carry great debits. What sort of Jewish life is it, they ask, when one does not live out the prescriptions of the millennial Law with exact fidelity and enter into the great joy of Jewish identity? For what have the Jewish ancestors suffered and died—so that their grandchildren can drive big cars and feast on unclean food? The treasures of traditional faith, which centered on absorption in the holiness of the Lord, are beyond compare. To sacrifice them for material prosperity, or even religious freedom, is a poor bargain.

Most American Jews repudiate this line of thought, believing that modernity has radically changed the existential situation of all people and so required all people to adapt their religious ideas. For the majority, ethics has replaced theology proper as the central focus of religious life and ethnic identity, as the Reform leaders suggested it should. The climate of the United States certainly presents ethical challenges, lest so much freedom and prosperity be corrupting, but it also provides the indispensible condition for ethical maturity: liberty to follow one's conscience. In the labor movement, and more recently such movements as those for civil rights and women's liberation, many Jews have found secular causes on which to lavish their ethical energies. In the educational opportunities offered in the United States, many have also found the equivalent of the old dedication to study that focused on the Talmud. So American Jews, on the whole, have praised the disestablishment of religion and accepted its Enlightenment rationale, thinking that it is better to have legal protections against discrimination and take one's chances coping with materialism than to live sequestered in a ghetto.[2]

Roman Catholics

Despite the charges of Protestants such as Josiah Strong, American Catholics have partaken of a tradition supportive as well as critical of democracy. Alexis de Tocqueville's classic work, *Democracy in America*, noted how Catholics were prospering and argued that lay status in Roman Catholicism prepared one well for democracy (all except priests were equal). John Courtney Murray, the leading American Catholic theologian of the era prior to the Second Vatican Council (1962–65), studied the roots of Catholic theory about church-state relations and argued that the better Catholic tradition favored religious liberty. Murray received vigorous opposition from Roman authorities and fellow American Catholic theologians who stressed the singular truth of Catholic religion, which in their view entitled it to a privileged status in any country housing a Catholic majority. But Vatican II sided with Murray, producing a document on religious liberty that so stressed the sanctity of individual conscience that no religion could rightly be established in ways that infringed on religious liberty or made religious minorities second-class citizens.

American Catholics did suffer misunderstanding from Roman authorities, and they were the subject of a papal encyclical, Leo XIII's *Testem Benevolentiae* of 1899, that accused them of several deviations from traditional faith. But the accusations were vague, the defenders of American Catholicism found it easy to show that the accusations were ill founded, and the entire episode had little significant effect, except to make Catholic intellectuals wary of incurring Roman wrath. American Catholics also had internal problems, however, many of them related to the ethnic diversity of their population. The leadership of the immigrant church tended to be Irish bishops, whose ease with English gave them an advantage in the new country. The Irish and the Germans had been the first Catholics to immigrate in significant numbers, and the Irish had dominated the eastern cities that had more political clout. So the Germans fought to retain their ethnic heritage: language, religious piety, and political style, while the Irish tended to push, now more and now less tactfully, for a homogeneous adaptation to American customs.

At the end of the nineteenth century, when other ethnic groups (Italians, Poles, French-Canadians) immigrated, the question of unity and diversity repeated itself. Generally, the American Catholic church took a balanced position, for practical more than theoretical reasons. Ethnic parishes continued to be the rule until the middle of the twentieth century, and these parishes were primary agents in the assimilation of Catholic immigrants to American society. In recent decades, something of the same pattern has continued regarding Hispanic and Asian Catholic immigrants. Tensions remain, but the general stance of the church has been balanced: an effort to help immigrants retain their native identity, along with an effort to assist in their Americanization (learning English, preparing them for citizenship, preparing them to join the American work force).

Lecturing on the question of how American culture and Roman Catholicism have interacted in the case of American Catholics, Richard P. McBrien has noted both positive and negative effects. Making the judgment that American culture has influenced American Catholicism more than Catholicism has influenced American culture, McBrien has singled out the experience of democracy in America as a major reason American Catholic bishops have exercised considerable leadership in the worldwide renewal of Catholicism since Vatican II. On the other hand, he has found American individualism to have had a deleterious effect: "Although Catholicism is a strongly social and communal tradition, the impact of individualism is more pronounced now than before . . . Individualism is especially apparent in the upwardly-mobile Catholic population, where the 'free to choose' mentality, encapsuled in economist Milton Friedman's book of the same title, has taken hold. Recent voting behavior indicates that American Catholics are less sensitive than ever before in their history to the interests of the poor and the socially marginal. Their obvious lack of enthusiasm for the U.S. Catholic bishops' pastoral letter on the economy is a case-in-point. American Catholics, in increasingly large numbers, are rejecting, or at least choosing to ignore, some of the principal tenets of Catholic social doctrine. The American experience, as it has evolved and expressed itself in the politics of the 1980s, seems to be enticing many Catholics away from their own tradition and closer to Pelagianism ('God helps those who help themselves') and an extreme Calvinism ('Prosperity is a sign of God's favor; poverty is a sign of God's displeasure')."[3]

On the precise question of how Catholics have viewed living in a land where no religion has been established or privileged, the answer is relatively plain. The vast majority of Catholics have found American culture congenial. They have suffered some discrimination from the Protestant mainstream, but generation by generation they have gained greater access to economic, political, and even social power. The dramatic growth of the American Catholic population, which for several generations has made it the largest individual religious group and now numbers about fifty-two million (over 25 percent of the American population), has qualified the minority status of Catholics and also contributed considerable ideological diversity. One now finds evangelical and charismatic Catholics, as well as traditionalists who demand a return to the Latin Mass and the Catholicism of the Council of Trent. One also finds many Catholics who are disaffected, secularized, and "fallen away" from regular attendance at Mass and reception of the sacraments. Whether their fraction is greater than the corresponding fraction of disaffected that has long weakened European Catholic countries is debatable—probably not. But the decline in vocations to the priesthood and religious life has brought American Catholics to the brink of a situation in which a great many parishes have no priestly ministers, so the future may well see American Catholicism as again a missionary venture, due to the secularization of its younger generations and the intransigence of Rome regarding the celibacy of Catholic clergy and the ordination of women.

Historically, American Catholics have espoused the disestablishment of religion because it served to benefit them. If there had been an established

American religion, it would have been Protestant, and perhaps anti-Catholic. During the first centuries of their existence in America, Catholics did experience legal discrimination. Ironically, it was especially strong in Maryland, the only colony to have been founded by Catholics. When Protestants became a majority in Maryland, they reduced the legal status of papists. How seriously one ought to take pre-Vatican II Catholic theory to the effect that error has few rights and, as the only true faith, Roman Catholicism ought to be the religion of every country, especially those with a Catholic majority, is hard to say. If one looks at Catholic practice through the ages, instead of at isolated papal statements and the practice of countries such as Spain, one finds considerable variety.

The authoritarian mentality that stood out rightly gave democrats pause, but the free-spiritedness of many reformers, religious and lay alike, provided counterbalance. The great leap for modern Catholicism was to make an act of trust that divine truth is its own best witness and needs no heavy-handed protectors. In a related way, Catholics were only recovering their own theological anthropology and understanding of grace when they backed away from a view of human nature as so weak or bent that it needed censorship and outside direction. The American situation of religious freedom and competition stimulated Catholics to rethink just how divine grace works. In renewing their appreciation of the divine option for persuasion rather than compulsion, American Catholics could have thanked their new culture for bringing them back to the view of Aquinas and Paul that grace perfects nature and that where sin abounds grace abounds the more.

Women

Religious American women naturally tended to think about disestablishment in terms of their own tradition—Protestant, Catholic, or Jewish. What interested them precisely as women, however, was the effect that religion had on their various freedoms, spiritual and material. For most of American history, women could not vote and had fewer legal rights, regarding property and politics, than men. The feminist reformers who labored to change this state of affairs often came to consider the prevailing religious ideas and mores their greatest foes. As already noted, the feminization of religion in the nineteenth century had pushed both women and religion toward an exclusively domestic sphere. The worlds of politics, business, and changing history belonged to men. These were dirty or sullying, unfit for women. Women were the more spiritual sex, and much of their social function was to raise bestial masculinity into a fuller humanity. The feminist reformers who sought equality for women came to realize that this bifocal view of the sexes was no friend. Whether deliberately or not, it kept women out of the boardrooms and chambers of power, where social change was engineered. It was not enough for women to run admirable, spiritual homes, or to infuse education, medicine, and social work with intelligence, tact, compassion, practical help, and religious values. If they were to be truly free, fully human, and so capable of making the contribution that their nation required of them, women would have to challenge the limiting view of their potential that many found in the Bible.

Elizabeth Cady Stanton (1815–1902) became so convinced that the Bible was a huge obstacle to women's suffrage and entry into equality with men that she composed her own version of Scripture. Explaining her rationale, Stanton anticipated recent scholars who have inveighed against the "patriarchalism" of the Bible by exposing the sexist assumptions of the text and demonstrating its contribution to women's subjugation: "From the inauguration of the movement for women's emancipation the Bible has been used to hold her in the 'divinely ordained sphere,' prescribed in the Old and New Testaments. The canon and civil law; church and state; priests and legislators; all political parties and religious denominations have alike taught that woman was made after man, of man, and for man, an inferior being, subject to man. Creeds, codes, Scriptures and statutes are all based on this idea. The fashions, forms, ceremonies and customs of society, church ordinances and discipline all grow out of this idea. Of the old English common law, responsible for woman's civil and political status, Lord Brougham said, 'it is a disgrace to the civilization and Christianity of the Nineteenth Century.' Of canon law, which is responsible for woman's status in the church, Charles Kingsley said, 'this will never be a good world for women until the last remnant of canon law is swept from the face of the earth.' The Bible teaches that woman brought sin and death into the world, that she precipitated the fall of the race, that she was arraigned before the judgment seat of Heaven, tried, condemned and sentenced. Marriage for her was to be a condition of bondage, maternity a period of suffering and anguish, and in silence and subjection, she was to play the role of a dependent on man's bounty for all her material wants, and for all the information she might desire on the vital questions of the hour, she was commanded to ask her husband at home. Here is the Bible position of woman briefly summed up."[4]

Individual women, such as Stanton herself, might evade the restrictions implied by this biblical view of women as the subordinate sex, but the entire fabric of American culture was dyed by the negative or secondary view of women prominent in many biblical passages. Indeed, the particular question of women's suffrage, to which Stanton devoted much energy, only became settled in women's favor when persistent agitation brought home to the populace at large the discrimination involved in denying women the vote. In breaking through this discrimination, suffragettes and their supporters had to make a persuasive case against the literal message of those parts of the Bible that subordinated women to their fathers and husbands. They had to anticipate modern biblical criticism, which has disclosed the historical limitations of the textual authors and forced a more sophisticated view of revelation—one in which God is not the author of limitations or deficiencies, such as patriarchal or sexist views of women.

If any particular church had been established in the United States, women would have run the risk of being subjected to its view of their status and rights. Those working for the emancipation of women in the nineteenth and twentieth centuries have appreciated this situation, all the more so when they have run into opposition from conservative church groups trying to restrict women's rights. Implicitly, the First Amendment made it legitimate for women to work to change the view of the sexes espoused by any church or by the American public at large. No religious view had canonical status in the laws of the American people, and women had the right to publish their opinions about the proper understanding of Scripture or their own status. So the women who agitated for the vote, and for greater liberty in general, tended to become champions of the impartiality expressed in the First Amendment. If they wished, they could take the principles of the Enlightenment and of Jeffersonian democracy and extend them to their own sex. The basis for judging a person's worth ought to be what that person actually did. No religious or legal a priori views ought to prejudice the outcome. That was the way the early feminists reasoned, and their logic has prevailed, except in fundamentalist religious circles, where the Bible has been read as denying women's aspirations to strict equality with men.

The feminist reformers who slowly changed the condition of women in the United States tended to translate religious ideals into practical, ethical actions. Indeed, "for many women, reform became their religion, a position of faith as much as a cause espoused. In a biographical sketch of her friend and co-worker Susan B. Anthony, Elizabeth Cady Stanton described that stance and suggested that it was appropriate for the era in which they lived: 'Every energy of her soul is centred [sic] upon the needs of the world. To her work is worship. She has not stood aside shivering in the cold shadows of uncertainty; but has moved on with the whirling world, has done the good given her to do, and thus in the darkest hours has been sustained by an unfaltering faith in the final perfection of all things. Her belief is not Orthodox, but it is religious,—based on the high and severe moralities. In ancient Greece she would have been a Stoic; in the era of the Reformation, a Calvinist; in King Charles's time, a Puritan; but in this nineteenth century, by the very laws of her being, she is a Reformer.' Such a description might serve equally well for numerous women who, 'by the very laws of their being,' supported several reforms during their lifetimes. They believed, with Angelina Grimke, that 'moral reformations . . . are bound together in a circle like the sciences; they blend with each other like the colors of the rainbow; they are the parts only of our glorious whole and that whole is Christianity, pure *practical Christianity.* ' "5

Women like Stanton, Anthony, and Grimke claimed the right to reinterpret religion to suit their needs and the needs of the society they saw around them. They seized upon the American tradition of religious liberty to sanctify the causes that seemed to them obligations in conscience. They therefore owed a considerable debt to the disestablishment of religion and the American principle that each person should be sovereign over his or her own conscience. Unlike Anne Hutchinson, they enjoyed a situation in which their religious deviance could not justify their banishment. So they had to be supporters of the First Amendment, grateful to the Madisons and Jeffersons who established the principle that in America religious practice and speech had to be free.

African Americans

African Americans have been deeply affected by their experience of slavery and racism and so have had to struggle to avoid cynicism about religious freedom. Until the Civil War, they had at best a small share in the rights of free citizens, and after the Civil War they suffered such prejudicial treatment that their legal rights seemed irrelevant. Nonetheless, from a dual background of African traditions and Christian beliefs, many African Americans became deeply religious. The most consistent theme of their religion has been that God is not a supporter or sanctioner of the unjust status quo. In the sight of God, slavery, racism, and the other forms of injustice they have suffered are abominations. So God had either to change the current status quo, improving earthly conditions for African

Americans and other victims of injustice, or provide in heaven a full recompense for their suffering. African-American churchgoers regularly blended both possibilities, asking God (and themselves) to labor to improve conditions here and now, yet finally possessing their own souls in the patient faith that "bye and bye" things would finally be as they ought to be.

African traditions were holistic, encouraging people to love the earth, their bodies, and the potential of the human spirit. Some African tribes had myths amounting to exercises in theodicy, asking God to justify his creation of a human condition so full of suffering and death. But more tribes had rites of passage (for birth, puberty, marriage, and death) that implied that human time was a progressive initiation into wisdom. If one participated in the tribal traditions, one would slowly come to appreciate how the world was constructed and why things had to be as they were. Most traditional religion finally inculcates this lesson: human beings are brief, whereas nature and God are long-standing. The brief ought to adapt to the long-standing. If people are right to be impatient with human injustice, they are wrong to be impatient with God. They cannot fathom God, so they cannot pass judgment on the ultimate wisdom or folly of God's ways.

The Christian version of this traditional African wisdom was the cross of Christ. When they tried to fit their sufferings and longings for justice into Christian mythology (storied faith), African Americans were bound to be riveted by the sufferings of Jesus. Certainly, they loved the story of the Exodus, identifying with the Hebrew slaves who had escaped from Egypt and finally gained the promised land, flowing with milk and honey. But the specifically Christian exodus that buoyed the faith of African Americans was the passage of Christ from death to resurrection. If Jesus had been despised, rejected, a man of sorrows acquainted with grief, Jesus could understand African-American suffering. If Jesus had been raised to the right hand of the Father, his followers might one day find vindication, compensation, a just reward for their innocent sufferings.

The distinctive form in which African-American Christians cast their patience and their hope was their songs. The spirituals, and later, in more secular form, the blues, expressed their deepest hurts, giving them the opportunity to heal their spirits and renew their determination to keep going. White slaveholders, whether Christian or not, tended to fear African-American religion. On the one hand, it might serve as a safety valve for slave resentment, but on the other hand it might stir slaves to thoughts of liberation, even to thoughts of equality with whites in the human family of the one God. So slaves often had to develop their rituals, their songs, their exegeses of the Bible in secret. As well, they had to develop a dualistic mentality, according to which they interpreted the Bible in one sense while in the presence of whites and in another sense when on their own. This second sense, the one they really believed, made God a champion of suffering innocents and ridiculed the notion that God would support slavery. The slave revolts tended to draw on this second sense, along with biblical imagery of inspiration, to make rebellion a holy cause.

When African Americans did come into a measure of legal freedom, they found white churches racist or strange enough to make them want to form their own churches. These new churches tended to be Baptist or Methodist, and many rather explicitly sought to develop African dimensions, usually by contemplating missions to Christianize Africans. Despite its distortion by whites, Christianity seemed to many African Americans a religion of depth and liberation. So they hungered to share its good news with Africans as yet unevangelized. In sponsoring such missionary work, many black churches capitalized on the rights granted in the First Amendment, as they did when they formed their churches, or preached in the street, or published church newspapers and tracts.

The prophetic mission of Martin Luther King, Jr., in the 1960s spelled a great leap forward for African-American religious activism. Though King had many predecessors among African-American clergy who had been champions of progress toward greater civil rights, his leadership of the attack on segregation was the crystallization of the logic that had been simmering since emancipation nearly a century earlier. King used the legal freedoms guaranteed all Americans to force white America to face its own racism. Many whites turned aside, but many others listened and moved at least part of the way toward repentance and conversion. Toward the end of his life King had to face the challenge of the war in Vietnam, which he realized was siphoning away resources needed by America's own poor, African Americans most prominent among them. He also had to face the challenge of the movement for "black power," which criticized his advocacy of nonviolence and spoke in confrontational, even militaristic tones. The eloquence of Malcom X, along with his ridicule of Christianity and advocacy of Islam, complicated the task of African-American theologians. While the majority of them sought a way to remain hopeful about America, the African-American community as a whole felt the need to give vent to the outrage that centuries of degradation, combined with its present experience of poverty and frustration, had built up.

Commenting on the experience of blacks in America, Vincent Harding has summarized much of the result and posed the key questions for the future: "In a sense, though, we Blacks are professional amateurs at the recreation of America. Still, we must also recognize the many dangers built into our current situation as Blacks in America. There are profound internal problems within the Black community. On the bottom levels of its developing class structure there are men, women and children with too large an experience of being victims, too heavy a mentality of being victims and not being able to do anything for themselves. At the bottom layers of our class structure there are too many people who have been excluded from the processes of disciplined work and productivity and who do not know how to participate in or build their own society. . . . Still, in the face of these dangers, following the great and maddening tradition of Black religion, I dare to hope. I dare to hope that Black people will continue to provide leadership to the community of visionaries that I believe is persistently coming up out of America [and is] . . . another way of expressing the genius of Black religion, another way of saying, 'Nobody knows the troubles I've seen, Glory! Glory, hallelujah!' "[6]

African Americans have used what religious liberty their country allowed them to create a profound understanding of both suffering and hope. Whether their version of a theology of liberation will get the hearing it deserves is difficult to say. On the one hand, racism continues to marginalize black thought. On the other hand, slavery remains the greatest stain on the American conscience, and African Americans may be the best mediators between white America and the Third and Fourth Worlds. So any serious American effort either to exorcise past sins or to enter fully into the international community of the twenty-first century could spotlight black talent. In the process, either would be likely to further white appreciation of the depth and beauty of African-American religion.

Native Americans

Like traditional Africans, Native Americans created holistic cultures in which there was little separation between religion and daily life. The customs and rituals of the tribe were at one and the same time their religion and their self-expression as Lakota or Navaho, Algonquin or Inuit. It made no sense to speak of a separation between the religious and the secular, let alone between church and state. Native Americans did not have to face the question of pluralism. Because their tribal units remained relatively small, and they had most of their social intercourse with tribes of a background or from a cultural family similar to their own, they did not have to adjudicate competing religious claims or work out laws guaranteeing the rights of religious minorities.

Moreover, they did not have a history of persecution by religious authorities, and they were not moderns, captivated by the genius of the individual and intrigued by the antagonism between the individual and the group. The individual had to fit into the patterns customary in the group into which he or she had been born. The common good predominated over individual needs, and the necessity of cooperation tended to smooth away individual angularities. Tribes appreciated the singular talents of particular hunters or weavers, shamans or chiefs, but these talents were more important as resources for the whole group than as expressions of an individual's creative needs. Whether an individual who developed deviant ideas was tolerated depended on how disruptive those ideas were. When they threatened physical survival, the individual clearly had to go. When they disturbed traditional lore, conflicting with the myths and wisdoms long handed down, they made the individual suspect. Native-American cultures were conservative, because they sensed that traditional ways had kept the people surviving since time out of mind.

The encounter with whites was traumatic for Native Americans in dozens of ways. The most obvious were the deaths suffered in warfare and the loss of tribal lands. More subtle were the deleterious effects on native cultures. As whites multiplied across the continent and possessed more and more of the land, Native Americans became dispossessed of their millennial birthright. The disease and alcoholism that ravaged many tribes were outer expressions of the spiritual sufferings within. No longer was it clear what it meant to be a Hopi or a Lakota. No longer was it something of which to be proud. The material success of white culture dazzled some Native Americans, making them ashamed of their traditional ways. It disturbed other Native Americans, making them wonder why any people would sacrifice intimacy with a quiet, beautiful land for ugly "progress." Intimacy with the land, and the spiritual forces that gave it its beauty and vitality, was the heartbeat of Native-American culture. The tribe took its orientation from the sense of reality imparted to it by its given physical locale. Human beings did not stand apart from the ecological whole. They were brothers and sisters to the animals and plants of their area. The Great Spirits, such as the Father in the sky and the Mother in the earth, were the parents of all creatures, bears and birds as much as men and women. When they prayed, Native Americans tended to invite all of nature—the directions, the seasons, the winds, the sunshine, the rainfall, the grasses and stones and animals—to join with them. Indeed, they sometimes thought of their own prayer as joining the worship that all the other creatures offered more spontaneously.

After the devastation wreaked on their traditional cultures had sunk in, some Native Americans attempted revivals of the old ways. Whether these attempted revivals had militaristic overtones of trying to remove the whites from their lands or, more realistically, sought simply to renew their dignity and contentment by revivifying what had given their ancestors joy, Native Americans used such efforts to fight back against the destruction of their peoplehood. They did not want to be swept into white American culture and drowned. However quixotically, many tried to recreate what it meant to be a Navaho or Pueblo, not denying the realities of modern American life but still hoping to tap the wellsprings of their old spirituality.

It was a small consolation to the participants in such restoration movements to realize they had some rights under the American legal system. For example, the Native American Church, which used peyote in its rituals, found a defense for its practice in the First Amendment's guarantees of free exercise of religion, and Indian tribes could get a hearing if they claimed that development would desecrate native burial grounds.

These recent experiences represent some progress beyond the Native-American experiences of the mid-nineteenth century, when the Ghost Dance was the prototypical form of Native-American revival. Because the Ghost Dance had the ultimate aim of ousting the whites, it was bound to generate opposition, but in its more strictly religious aspects it might have qualified for protection under the First Amendment. Scholars debate the extent to which the Ghost Dance, and other native revivals, were fresh religious initiatives or responses to the socio-economic conditions in which Native Americans found themselves after generations of white dominance. Perhaps the two motivations blended, but the majority of anthropologists favor the view that the Ghost Dance movement stemmed from the expansion of white power over Native Americans' lives.

Reflecting this opinion, Ake Hultkrantz, a leading student of Native-American religions, has written: "The impetus for the Ghost Dance revivalism was the Indians' enforced contact with an expanding white civilization beginning in the 1860s. Because of growing white settlements, the white military takeover, and the introduction of white jurisdiction, there was no more room for the continuation of the old native existence, in particular for the hunters and gatherers of the West. Their independent cultures ceased rapidly, sometimes even abruptly, as on the Plains: the whole culture of the northern Plains tribes, built on hunting buffalo, collapsed when in 1883 the last herd of buffalo was exterminated. The Indians had to adjust to white man's culture and, in part, to his values, in order to survive. At the same time they drew on their past to mobilize a desperate spiritual resistance against the overwhelming white influence. In this reactive effort they combined Christian or Christian-derived elements with indigenous ideas and rituals to form a resistance ideology."[7]

The key idea behind the Ghost Dance was that the dead would return to lead the Native Americans to regain their lands. By dancing the prescribed dances (seen by the revivalist leaders in visions), the dancers could bring on the process. The tragic denouement was the massacre of the Lakota at Wounded Knee in 1890. The warrior spirit of the Lakota had frightened the whites, with some reason, and produced the military confrontation. No doubt it would have been useless for the Lakota to argue that their religious beliefs and traditions required them to preserve the buffalo, and other features of their native culture. During the westward expansion of the United States, white economic interests regularly rode roughshod over the rights granted Native Americans in treaties, and if they were not citizens, their rights under the Constitution were dubious. So the case of Native Americans shows the intrinsic limits of the American guarantees of religious freedom. Predicated on a cultural situation in which one could distinguish between religious and secular activities, the Constitution could not meet the needs of the holistic Native-American cultures.

Asian Traditions: Islam

Presently there are perhaps three million Muslims in North America, many of them in Canada. Worldwide, Muslims are second only to Christians in population (nearing one billion). Muslims consider themselves religious relatives of Jews and Christians, who adhere to defective versions of the religion that God (Allah) has made known through numerous prophets. "Islam" signifies "submission" to Allah and acceptance of true religion. All people should be Muslims, since submission to Allah and obedience to his precepts is the natural human estate. Because of human forgetfulness and weakness, however, God has had to send prophets and make the divine will explicit. The main beliefs constituting Islam provide, first, for acknowledgment of God, who is One, and then for acknowledgment of angels, scriptural books (of which the Qur'an is paramount), prophets, the Day of Judgment, and predestination. These six articles of faith frame the Muslim worldview.

Practically, Islamic faith involves five activities incumbent on all Muslims. First, one must make the confession of faith: "There is no God but God, and Muhammad is his prophet." Second, one must pray five times each day. Third, one must give alms, to support the poor. Fourth, one must fast during the daylight hours of the month of Ramadan, And fifth, one must make the pilgrimage to Mecca, if possible. Wherever they go, Muslims are held to the practical program implied in these five "pillars" of Islam.

Muhammad (570–632 c.e.) formed the Muslim community when he left his native Mecca in 622 and took charge of a group of followers in the city of Medina. There he led his people when they went to battle, when they prayed, and when they had legal or social disputes. Muhammad's leadership reflected the holistic character of traditional Arab culture and Muslim faith. Although he tried to move the Arabs beyond their traditional clan loyalties, making Islam their deeper and broader frame of reference, he did not have to argue that religion and culture ought to be a seamless whole. His contemporaries in Arabia assumed it, so when they gave their allegiance to Allah, they accepted the implication that all of their cultural institutions ought to become Muslim.

The great authority in Muslim life has been the Qur'an, the collection of the "recitals" that Muhammad made expressing the revelations God had told him to proclaim to his people. On the basis of the Qur'an and traditions (hadith) about the practice of Muhammad himself, Islam gradually developed a code of laws (Shariah) to regulate its communal life. Despite the split of the Muslim community into two main groups, the Sunnis and the Shiites, Islam has maintained considerable behavioral uniformity the world over, due to the relative sameness of its legal codes.

The Sunnis believe that Muhammad made no special provision for succession in leadership of the Muslim community and so judge that the succession that occurred after Muhammad's death was legitimate. The Shiites believe that Muhammad expected succession to follow his blood line, and so assumed that Ali, his cousin and son-in-law, would be the second leader. The conflict between these two views sharpened shortly after the prophet's death and has continued to be significant to the present day. Shiites, who have been strongest in Iran, parts of Iraq, southern Lebanon, and North Yemen, recall each year the death of Ali, and the death of his sons, whom they consider martyrs.

In North America, Muslims now have their greatest concentration in large cities, such as New York, Los Angeles, Chicago, Detroit, Houston, Washington, and Toronto. Although worldwide Shiites comprise only about 15 percent of the Muslim population, their percentage is higher in the United States, due to the relatively high number of immigrants from such Shiite areas as Iran, southern Lebanon, and North Yemen. The majority of American Muslims are immigrants from traditionally Muslim countries. Originally almost all came in search of greater economic opportunity, but recently some have come because of political conditions in their native lands. The first instance of Muslims congregating for prayer in North America probably was a community that met in Ross, North Dakota, in 1900. The willingness of Henry Ford to employ Muslims, many of them from Syria, led to Muslim communities in Michigan. By 1919 Muslims in Highland Park had acquired a building for a mosque. During the 1930s Muslims became populous enough in the South End of Dearborn to impart a Muslim character to the area: coffee houses, grocery stores, and restaurants of Arab-Muslim cast. Prior to World War II Arabs were the largest group of Muslims in the United States. Since World War II Palestinians, Egyptians, Pakistanis, Indians, Yemenis, and Iranians have immigrated in significant numbers.

The majority of American converts to Islam have been African Americans, some to sects such as the Nation of Islam led by Elijah Muhammad and others to the American Muslim Mission (a more orthodox group) led by his son Warith Deen Muhammad. Since 1952 the Islamic Center in Washington, D.C., has given Islam visibility in the nation's capital and among embassy personnel. The Muslim Students' Union, founded in 1963, has created a network of U.S. and Canadian Muslim students. Alumni have formed such further groups as the Association of Muslim Scientists and Engineers, the Association of Muslim Social Scientists, and the Islamic Medical Association. There is also a Muslim Communities Association. In 1982 all these organizations federated to comprise the Islamic Society of North America.

As their numbers have grown, Muslims in the United States have taken advantage of American religious liberty to associate for worship, buy land and build mosques, publish periodicals, and promote both a better understanding of Islam and conversions to Islam. The majority of such conversions have been undertaken by women who have married Muslims. (According to Muslim law, Muslim men may marry non-Muslim women, but Muslim women may not marry non-Muslim men.) The better understanding has involved explaining Muslim beliefs about the oneness of God, Muslim history, and such practices as abstaining from alcoholic beverages, from pork, and from meat not properly butchered. The modest dress of many Muslim women has also required explanation, as has the Muslim notion that men and women are designed for different spheres, women's being mainly the home.

To date the potential conflict between traditional Muslim ideas about the relation between the religious and secular zones and American traditions has been only hypothetical. In principle, Islam does not recognize the distinction between the secular and the religious, nor between religious and secular authority. All of reality comes under the sway of Allah, the Creator. On the one hand, this has created a relatively lay religion: Islam has had no priesthood, no celibate monasticism, and no canon law (precepts applying only to the religious community). On the other hand, it has created religious warfare and religiously based criminal sanctions, including capital punishment.

Islamic art has been secular in that it has shaped public buildings and mosques similarly. Because of the prohibition against representations of God, or (strictly) the human person, Islamic art has tended toward the geometrical or abstract. The calligraphic decoration of Qur'ans, and the arabesque decoration of mosques, have been among its main art forms, as has lyrical recital of passages of the Qur'an. Muslim poetry, often oral, has taken up Arab traditions and infused them with Qur'anic motifs.

In government, modern Western notions made a great impact from the mid-nineteenth to the mid-twentieth centuries, but with the resurgence of Islamic fundamentalism in recent decades has come a call to return to older legal codes and remove the secularism begun in Turkey, Iran, and some other countries. Muslims have accommodated somewhat to modern science, but their approach to literature has been complicated by convictions about the propriety of censorship. The explosion over the publication of Salman Rushdie's book *The Satanic Verses,* and the Iranian Ayatollah Khomeini's call for Rushdie's assassination, suggest the intensity of feelings among fundamentalist Muslims about literature they consider blasphemous. They also suggest the difficulties that American Muslims may have to negotiate, as they strive to become more influential in American culture.[8]

Sectarians: Pentecostals

Pentecostals—Christians convinced that baptism must be succeeded by a further transforming event called "baptism in the Holy Spirit"—form a loose group of churches on the fringes of evangelical Protestantism (there are Roman Catholic Pentecostals, but they tend to be charismatics within the Catholic church). Pentecostals trace their origins to the late nineteenth century. Their one hundred years or so of history in the United States present a bewildering sequence of disparate starts and divisions, but many have developed the ideas of John Wesley about the need for ongoing sanctification and the possibility of achieving it. (Other Pentecostals repudiate Wesleyan influences, viewing Wesley as too optimistic about the possibility of overcoming the sin inbred in human beings.) Some Pentecostals speak of three stages in Christian growth: conversion, entire sanctification, and baptism in the Spirit. Others speak of a "four-square" gospel, summarizing Christianity in four missions or functions of Christ: saving, baptizing, healing, and returning to rule as King. Many Pentecostals associate baptism in the Spirit with speaking in tongues, in effect making speaking in tongues the sure sign that such baptism has occurred. Faith healing has played a large role in the ministry of some of the most popular Pentecostal leaders, including recent ones, such as Oral Roberts, who have adapted their work to television.

Historians and sociologists tend to locate the beginnings of Pentecostalism in a general interest in holiness that peaked in southeastern and south-central states in the second half of the nineteenth century. Different Pentecostal churches arose in different areas, but Appalachia, the area at the intersection of Kansas, Missouri, and Oklahoma, and Los Angeles are three especially important locales. Many accounts of American Pentecostalism point to an assembly of African-American Christians in Los Angeles in 1906 as the dramatic beginning of the movement. Using an abandoned warehouse on Azuza Street, these early Pentecostals distinguished themselves by the fervor of their singing, shouting, and speaking in tongues. Although Pentecostalism has shifted toward the middle classes in recent decades, and assumed a soberer behavior, in its early years it laid great emphasis on high emotion and dramatic occurrences: healings, fits of ecstatic prayer, swooning, and more. Such behavior has continued to characterize some African-American and Hispanic Pentecostal churches. More prominent groups, such as the largely white Assemblies of God, still promote an emotional faith much interested in experiences of the Spirit and healing, but they are sensitive to charges of antinomian (disorderly) behavior and so promote proper decorum.

During the years when Pentecostalism was gaining momentum, Protestant church life was shifting toward liberalism and even the smallest American towns were changing because of industrialization. For example, the long-standing rhythms of Appalachia changed as mining and logging operations intruded. No longer were farming, hunting, and fishing easy and leisurely. The Liberal ideas about the historical and literary makeup of the Bible, about the arbitrary nature of many social arrangements (including the place of women), about evolution, and about social reform were further sources of anxiety to many poorly educated, low- and middle-class people. Some analysts of Pentecostalism therefore hypothesize that the movement, like fundamentalism, sought a new basis for security. In focusing on the experience of the Holy Spirit, Pentecostals could offer something they considered incontrovertible on which to ground one's life.

Originally Pentecostals used the freedom of religion guaranteed all Americans to congregate as they wished and remain apart from mainstream American politics and culture. They considered the latter corrupt or distracting. The central value, in their eyes, was the work of the Holy Spirit they had experienced or witnessed. By the time that one earned a living, nurtured the life of the Holy Spirit in one's own person and family, and worked for the church to spread the good news, one had used most of the hours of the week. As they sought to consolidate their gains and achieve greater respectability, however, the majority of Pentecostals shifted their sense of church-state relations. Whereas most had been pacifists during World War I, Pentecostals by and large supported American efforts in World War II. After World War II, as their affluence grew, they moved away from their original lack of interest in secular affairs toward considerable patriotism and support of right-wing politics. Criticized for being uninvolved in the civil rights movement, they tended to support the U.S. presidents during the Vietnam era, and to promote vigorously the conservative agenda of Ronald Reagan and the Moral Majority during the 1980s. A Pentecostal interpretation of Christian faith recently has come to mean intense personal concern with religious feelings and healings, along with a concern for "traditional" or "family" values on matters such as homosexuality, women's rights, and abortion.

The charges of financial fraud that bedeviled Pentecostals in the first half century of their existence have continued in recent times. The charismatic character of many of the early leaders, such as Aimee Semple McPherson and Charles Fox Parham, created an atmosphere in which bizarre behavior was frequent. (McPherson favored opening worship in her Angelus Temple by riding in on a motorcycle.) Preachers were more energetic in urging their flocks to contribute generously than in accounting for their use of funds. The recent scandals surrounding Jim Bakker and Jimmy Swaggart have given Pentecostalism a black eye. In Bakker's case they have even led to a long jail sentence. The huge amounts of money that Bakker and Oral Roberts have raised, and the financial crash of both empires, have focused the question of church-state relations on the government's obligations to safeguard religious donors from misrepresentation and fraud.

Some aspects of this matter have been technical: for example, the use of public media such as television and irregularities in reporting or paying federal taxes. But the more difficult question has been where to draw the line between the free exercise of religion and the protection of citizens against criminal fraud. People should have the right to donate money and time to religious causes, as they should have the right to believe and act as their consciences dictate. But they also should have the right not to be deceived or bilked by people using religion as a cover for personal profit. The plight of a few prominent Pentecostal preachers, along with the public's fears of sects such as the Eastern groups that enrich dubious gurus, has produced a widespread cynicism about religious fundraising. Church leaders enjoying enormous houses and a luxurious lifestyle have sometimes defended themselves by claiming that the gospel promises to the faithful a hundredfold reward in this life as well as fulfillment in the life to come.

That defense has not been well received by most Christians, who have pointed to the poor and simple lifestyle of Christ himself. The U.S. government has had to separate credulity on the part of simple believers from preachers' abuse of that trust. It has had to distinguish possibly sinful excesses on the part of leaders from actionable criminal offenses. In doing so, it has reviewed the entire area of the freedoms granted to religious people, deciding in general that religious leaders have no right to defraud their followers (make false claims or promises they know they cannot fulfill), let alone to evade their taxes or flout government laws.

The framers of the Constitution lived after the Great Awakening, so they knew about ecstatic religion. Yet their own cast of mind was the rationalism sponsored by the Enlightenment. So while they had little sympathy for ecstatic religion, the founders found it hard to legislate for gullibility on the part of laity and deception on the part of clergy. Their somewhat skeptical view of human nature (more the product of Puritan influences in the general culture, and of common sense, than of the Enlightenment) would have left them unsurprised by recent abuses of religious liberty, but they probably would not have believed the size and crudity of the scams of the televangelists. Pentecostals, and evangelicals generally, are right to claim that a few bad apples should not stigmatize their whole movement. The fact remains, however, that many Americans now view religious liberty cynically, because of the expansion of fraud made possible by the mass media.[9]

Protestant Reflections

When one goes to Protestant theology for a response to these data from the margins of American religious history, perhaps the most representative warning that sounds is the reminder that the Reformation began with a simple watchword: "The Church is always in need of reform." The deep conviction of classical Protestant theology that only God gives justification and righteousness applies to the churches as well as to outside society. In the case of the sixteenth-century Reformers, the glaring example was the abuses of religion in the fourteenth and fifteenth centuries, due to Roman authority. More recently, American Protestant theologians have been willing to turn the spotlight on their own churches and their own nation. Sensing that a false righteousness lurks in America's pride in its religious liberty, leading theologians such as Reinhold Niebuhr have taught that self-criticism is always relevant.

In 1943, when it was clear that World War II was a struggle to the death between democracy and Nazism, Niebuhr wrote an essay for the journal *Christianity and Crisis* about the responsibility of the allies. The essay combines realism about world politics with a keen sense, based on the biblical prophets, that only God is fully trustworthy: "The prophet Amos was certain of two things. One was that Israel had been particularly chosen of God; and the other was that this special mission gave the nation not a special security but a special peril. 'You only have I chosen,' he declared in God's name, 'therefore will I visit you with your iniquities.' It would serve no good purpose to try to compare the special destiny of the Anglo-Saxon peoples with that of Israel in olden times. Certainly no one would be so rash today as to claim the kind of destiny for our nations that the prophet's word 'only' implies. Nevertheless only those who have no sense of the profundities of history would deny that various nations and classes, various social groups and races are at various times placed in such a position that a special measure of the divine mission in history falls upon them. In that sense God has chosen us in this fateful period of world history. . . . Yet as soon as one has said this, one is forced to make qualifications. All historical destiny is compounded of virtue and grace. If the position that any nation or group of nations holds is attributed to the virtue of those nations alone, one has the beginning of that pharisaism which destroys virtue, whether in individual or national life. The fact is that no nation or individual is ever good enough to deserve the position of leadership that some nations and individuals achieve. If the history that leads to a special mission is carefully analyzed, it always becomes apparent that factors other than the virtues of the leader are partly responsible for the position the individual or collective leader holds. Those who do not believe in God's providence in history will call these factors 'accidents' or 'fortune.' The religious man perceives them as gifts of grace. The grace that determines the lives of men and nations is manifest in all special circumstances, favors, and fortunes of geography and climate, of history and fate that lead to eminence despite the weakness and sinfulness of the beneficiary of such eminence."[10]

Applied to American history as a whole, Niebuhr's analysis suggests that any virtue belongs to God. The providence that led the former colonists to disestablish religion and promote the religious liberty that many other nations have admired deserves the credit for the good that such religious liberty has produced. This is not to say that human beings have not been heroes on occasion. It is not to say that human nature is only filth and corruption. But it is to say that, on the basis of its performance, humanity's wisdom and goodness are not to be trusted. The abuses of religious liberty, past and present, that dot American history suggest that nothing human can guarantee that the First Amendment, or other relevant statutes, will achieve the end for which the founding fathers designed them. Similarly, the abuses of established religion, which prompted the founding fathers' convictions about the need for religious liberty, suggest that the other side of the legal coin also offers no guarantees. The valid insight of ecstatic religion is that only when God fills people's hearts are they able to live as they ought to live. The special pathos in the failures of ecstatic religious leaders is their having forgotten that no one can control God's movement in people's hearts or guarantee that the Spirit will blow.

The upshot of such a Protestant theological reflection is constant humility. Human beings have to make decisions, venture forth, do the best they can, but they should never let this necessity blind them to their fallibility. It takes enthusiasm to wage a war. It takes patriotism to fuel sacrifice. But enthusiasm of this sort easily becomes jingoism, exalting one's nation as unique in the sight of God, especially privileged and especially virtuous. Similarly, it takes enthusiasm to launch a church, preach to the masses, speak about the grace of the Holy Spirit. Enthusiasm of this second sort is no more protected against abuse than enthusiasm of the patriotic sort.

Religious liberty can only flourish when people join legal controls with religious controls. Even then there is no guarantee that a nation will be virtuous or its churches and synagogues will not house frauds. But when the laws provide cautions, restraints, and sanctions, preachers and parishioners alike are reminded that their practice of religion occurs in the midst of a wider culture, to which they have responsibilities. The abiding American temptation to adopt individualistic interpretations of religious and other liberties (such as the right to bear arms) tends to blunt the force of these responsibilities. Then greedy or power-hungry preachers can injure an entire society's ability to think well of the divine mystery that is its ineluctable challenge.

Implicit in the compact represented by the American tradition about religious liberty is the responsibility to use religious freedom for the common good. The common good includes respect for the religious sensibilities of one's fellow citizens. It includes making religion a force for justice, good citizenship, creativity in the arts and sciences, large-mindedness and fidelity in politics, excellence in education, and honesty in business. The founding fathers were wrong to limit the cultural import of "religion" to ethics, but they were right to stress the ethical obligations of all citizens, including prominently religious leaders. The nation did not establish a single moral code, any more than it established a single church. It left people free to think as they wished about ethics, as it left them free to think as they wished about God. But it could not leave them free to neglect their obligations to the truth, or to their fellow citizens. It could not separate religious liberty from the responsibility coded in each person's makeup to bow before the mysteriousness of human existence and derive from that mysteriousness a radical humility. Religious liberty guarantees only the wisdom of realizing one has to decide for oneself whence human existence derives its meaning. It cannot protect people fully from either false preachers or wanton atheists. Only a genuine desire to know the truth and follow it can do that.

Sophistication and Naiveté

It would be naive to think that the people on the margins of mainstream American religious history have not appreciated either the opportunities that American religious liberty afforded them or the myriad ways in which actual American culture failed to live up to the ideals sketched in the statutes about religious liberty. Indeed, it would be naive to think that the minorities did not use American religious liberty to vent their own frustrations and hostilities against either the Protestant mainstream or other minorities who irritated them.

In the green spaces of culture created by the freedom to express one's religious opinions, marginal groups could become sharply critical of one another's postures. For example, John Murray Cuddihy, a Catholic, has been willing to attack Jewish postures regarding anti-Semitism: "Recently the position that anti-Semitism has nothing to do with Jews and everything to do with Gentiles was formulated in its pure form: 'The notion that anti-Semitism can be, in the slightest degree, the fault of Jews,' writes Cynthia Ozick, 'is in itself—even when it crops up, as it frequently does, among Jews—a species of anti-Semitism. In three indelible sentences of irrefutable clarity,' she continues, 'Barbara Tuchman blows away this foolishness: "Anti-Semitism," she says, "is independent of its object. What Jews do or fail to do is not the determinant. The impetus comes out of the need of the persecutors." ' Not only does anything Jews do or refrain from doing have nothing to do with anti-Semitism, but any *attempt* to explain anti-Semitism by referring to the Jewish contribution to anti-Semitism is itself an instance of anti-Semitism.

"This *reductio ad absurdum* has stunning implications. It means that Jews have not been causal agents in their own history. Nothing about them has 'contributed' to the emergence of anti-Semitism. They did not act and interact causally and historically with other groups in history. Morally blameless, the Jews in this self-conception escaped the rough give-and-take of history. They were outside history, aspiring to what Lionel Trilling calls in another connection 'unconditioned spirit.' Following Maritain, let us call this 'angelism.' "[11]

This is an interesting discussion, because Cuddihy is more honest than most people engaged in ecumenical considerations usually are. In the rest of his study, he frankly admits his irritation with Jewish claims to moral superiority. Presumably he would be willing to admit that many other ethnic and religious groups have given grounds for a similar irritation, Catholics prominent among them. But by using the American tradition of free expression about religious affairs, he is able to open discussion of matters too often left to fester under vapid amiability and the desire not to offend.

In fact the matter of the causality of anti-Semitism is more complicated than either Ozick or Cuddihy here seems to allow, and the two writers complement one another nicely. Drawing usefully on Tuchman, Ozick makes the valid point that anti-Semites are fulfilling a personal need when they castigate Jews and make them scapegoats. But whereas Tuchman is careful to delimit the assertion she makes, saying that Jewish action is not the *determinant* of anti-Semitism, and leaving open the possibility that Jewish action can occasion or qualify or otherwise shape anti-Semitism, Ozick leaves all nuance behind. She is right to say that making anti-Semitism the fault of Jews is itself an expression of anti-Semitism, if she means that anti-Semites make Jews the sole or sufficient cause of anti-Semitism. But she is surely wrong to suggest that what Jews do has no bearing on anti-Semitism, for precisely the reasons that Cuddihy brings forward. Any group that lives in history (any group that we consider realistically) interacts with other groups and contributes to what other groups make of it. The further implication is that the behavior of the first group plays a role in the judgments, favorable or unfavorable, that the second group makes of it. The proposition can be turned around, so that the behavior of the second group shapes the perceptions and judgments that the first group has of it. So Catholics play a role in the judgments that Jews make about Catholics, and Jews play a role in the judgments that Catholics make about Jews. Neither group is responsible for prejudice (anti-Catholicism or anti-Semitism). Such prejudice lodges in the minds and hearts of the prejudiced, and there is a sense in which it becomes independent of what the group against whom the prejudice is directed does or says. But any realistic assessment of bigotry against Catholics in the United States has to take into account Catholic failures, and Catholic doctrines, such as those about the papacy, that could easily give offense, and any realistic assessment of anti-Semitism in the United States has to make a similar accounting regarding Jewish failures and doctrines. No group creates or justifies bigotry against it, but neither does any group escape responsibility for defects that prepare the way for bigotry. To deny this would be, as Cuddihy suggests, a species of "angelism": rejection of the flesh-and-blood conditions of actual human existence; dealing with human beings as though they were immaterial spirits, unshaped by the sights, sounds, smells, touches, and tastes their neighbors produce.

The sort of sophistication that religious liberty has produced among Americans of intelligence, honesty, and reflection has embraced the protests of an Ozick, the irritation and acute analysis of a Cuddihy, and the measured assessments of a Tuchman, moving beyond all of them to call for a climate of mutual acceptance and forgiveness. Each of the three writers in this little scenario has offered a useful perspective, but, as their statements stand, the result is more alienating than unifying. What remains to be said is that Jews and Catholics and Protestants and all other religious and ethnic groups in the United States have valid complaints to bring forward or get off their chests, and that they also have stains of prejudice and guilt on their consciences. Some may have better records than others, or be more sinned against than sinful, but none is without blame. Each has lived dialectically, interactively, with other groups, sometimes abusing American religious liberty and sometimes vindicating it wonderfully. Each probably has had ecumenical heroes, people who did reach out to those beyond its own ghetto and so prevented misunderstandings, hatreds, and even violence. It behooves none to act as though its past were simon-pure, or its present were marred by no residual pride, prejudice, or conviction that it is special in the sight of God, uniquely loved and so superior. It behooves all to put aside passions and over-sensitivities, so that study of either the past or the present of American prejudice can be calm and realistic, dealing with facts and naming all things honestly.

Sophistication therefore turns out to be a second naiveté. The best use of the religious liberty offered by American traditions probably has always been to treat other people as exact equals. The Golden Rule can seem a banal maxim, something any schoolchild can trip off the tongue. Or it can seem truly profound, expressing the exactly equal distance of all people from the holiness of God. If there is an "infinite qualitative difference" between God and human beings, as Kierkegaard thought, then all human beings stand together on the near side of a great divide. Realizing this, they might let the alienating aspects of their traditional differences become secondary and concentrate on the primary condition they all share. All are mortal, ignorant, sinful. None knows God's designs with surety. All must believe, enter on a dark night, navigate by faith. True sophistication would be to know how to hold this primary equality in tension with secondary differences, so that humanity would be to the fore but religious and ethnic variety would not be lost. True sophistication would be the ability to love the variety of religious traditions but love the sameness of human beings even more.

Disestablishment: American Wisdom

Most religious groups in the United States have made their peace with the disestablishment enshrined in the Constitution. Many groups, in fact, have realized that by its neutrality the government of the United States left them free to exercise their utmost creativity and energy. For example, the Roman Catholic response to the American situation, as summarized in the recent actions of the Catholic bishops, represents an acceptance of the separation of church and state established by the Constitution and a willingness to contribute to the dialogue among all religious groups that the constitutional situation invites. J. Bryan Hehir, studying the Catholic bishops' recent entry into U.S. politics (through their statements on abortion, nuclear arms, the U.S. economy, and U.S. policy in Central America), puts the constitutional question as follows: "The constitutional question is usually posed in terms of 'the separation of church and state.' The phrase is omnipresent in American political discourse: it is the tag line for editorial writers, the way in which 'the religious issue' is discussed in political campaigns and the shorthand used by plain citizens to define the relationship of religion and politics. The phrase refers to the First Amendment of the Constitution. Strictly speaking, the 'separation clause' is not literally found in the First Amendment, but the idea of 'separation' has served to structure the understanding of the role of the church in the political process.

"In the face of 'activism' by the largest single religious denomination in the country [Roman Catholics], the constitutional question inevitably arises. Does such activism breach the separation of church and state? Is it appropriate legally and politically? When faced with this question the U.S. bishops have responded with a blend of Catholic theology and American political theory. Their response to the constitutional question involves three steps.

"First, a working definition of the political meaning of the First Amendment; essentially it says that religious organizations should expect neither favoritism nor discrimination in the exercise of their civil or religious responsibilities. It is important to stress that the separation clause meant to protect against both favoritism or discrimination. There is little or no indication in law, history, or policy that silencing the religious voices was the intent of the First Amendment. Given this definition of the meaning of separation the Catholic response is to agree with it."[12]

The other two points in the Catholic response have been a position that the separation of church and state does not mean a separation of church and society (that is, the state is only a portion of the society), and a reliance on the American tradition supporting voluntary associations (groups, including churches, that citizens form or join freely). Together, these three aspects of the Catholic outlook on religious activity in America amount to working within well-established understandings of what religious liberty does and does not mean in the United States. There is nothing eccentric in the Catholic position. One could apply it to most Protestant churches and to the outlook of American Jews. The separation of church and state has not meant the alienation of religion from American culture at large, as even the briefest of studies of how Americans actually live will show. Religion shapes the private lives of the majority of Americans, and it has an enormous influence on politics, economics, the arts, education, and even sports. Nor is this actual situation at odds with American legal tradition. As the First Amendment has been interpreted through the past two hundred years, neither favoritism nor discrimination stands approved. The separation of church and state has been interpreted as a benign neutrality: no promotion of religion by the government, but also no suppression of the rights of religious groups to exercise their faith. Religion has been a voluntary matter, neither required by the government nor limited much by the government. The majority of religious groups in the United States have come to consider this situation wise, healthy, and good.

In the light of such an understanding of church-state relations, calls for cooperation among the major American religious bodies have had to rely on the principle of voluntary association. What ecumenical closeness has arisen has been the result of private initiative, not government policy. Still, many religious leaders have understood the American situation to require not simply the free exercise of religion but, ideally, the responsible, public-spirited exercise of religion. In other words, religious bodies have an obligation to give back to the culture at large a concern for the common good, an effort to be forces of healing and unity, that assists the work of the government and the public at large to make the United States strong both materially and spiritually.

Writing at the beginning of the 1980s, when the first presidential campaign of the decade had made it clear that religion could be a source of division, Martin Marty, one of the leading historians of American religion, made a plea for what he called "the public church." Addressing himself to the three major components of American Christianity—mainstream Protestant, Evangelical, and Roman Catholic—Marty reminded them that they had an obligation to consider the overall common good of their country and live truly public lives. Truly public lives would be those that took into account the impact of the churches' political activism, economic policies, and overall influence through business as well as worship, preaching, and theological education. In his preface, Marty explained the chief concerns motivating him to write his book: "I have written the book in a spirit of some urgency, motivated chiefly by two concerns. The first is the already mentioned listlessness in much of mainline Protestantism and Catholicism and of confusion in evangelicalism. On their present course these churchly movements could dwindle into relative insignificance, and we would see America without religious options beyond those that appeal to people in isolation from each other or that call for developing belligerent groups.

"The second concern issues from a vision of the world near the end of the second millennium after Christ as a place where people huddle together over against each other and use religion to justify their over-againstness. The decline of civility has not reached crisis proportions in North America, but there is a disturbing decline of faith in the values of civility. I believe that what I am calling the public church has distinctive if not unique resources for exemplifying to a large world a way of being faithful to the truth it knows, while showing 'counter-intolerance' toward people with whom it disagrees and from whom it remains separate."[13]

Civility is the virtue of respecting the citizenship of all others with whom one shares a commonwealth. It is implied in the notion of civil religion that Rousseau proposed in the eighteenth century and Robert Bellah resurrected in the late 1960s. A large part of traditional American wisdom about the implications of not establishing any one official religious body in the United States has focused on civility and civil religion. By and large, the Enlightenment ideal of tolerance has flourished here, because it has been buttressed by laws guaranteeing religious liberty to all. The wiser American religious groups have not abused this religious liberty but have respected their neighbors' rights and sensibilities. In the 1980s, however, voices sometimes grew more strident, frequently because of such volatile issues as abortion, which polarized people politically, morally, and religiously. The religious groups bear some responsibility for this polarization, as they bear some responsibility for the polarizations of the 1960s and 1970s generated by the civil rights movement, the antiwar movement, women's liberation, and the other social movements carrying political, moral, and religious overtones. In retrospect, it seems fair to say that the religious groups could have done a better job of tempering what they considered their prophetic responsibilities to bring society into line with God's will. They could have been better reconcilers and servants of the public peace. At the beginning of the 1990s, when abortion remains a divisive issue at home, the plight of the homeless and the drug-ridden ought to affect all Americans, and eastern Europe seems to be embarking on a cultural shift of sea-change proportions that just might free America from the incubus of nuclear militarism, the emergence of Marty's public church would be a great repayment by America's religious groups for all the benefits they have reaped from their country's tradition of religious liberty.

NOTES

1. See Deborah Dash Moore, "Social History of American Judaism," in *Encyclopedia of the American Religious Experience*, ed. Charles H. Lippy and Peter W. Williams (New York: Scribner's, 1988), pp. 294–5.

2. See Jacob Neusner, "Judaism in Contemporary America," ibid., pp. 311–323; also Jacob Agus, "Jerusalem in America," in *The Religion of the Republic*, ed. Elwyn A. Smith (Philadelphia: Fortress, 1971), pp. 94–115.

3. Richard P. McBrien, "Catholicism: The American Experience," in *American Catholics*, ed. Joseph F. Kelly (Wilmington, DE: Michael Glazier, 1989), p. 10. See also his *Caesar's Coin: Religion and Politics in America* (New York: Macmillan, 1987).

4. Elizabeth Cady Stanton, "Academy," in *A Documentary History of Religion in America*, ed. Edwin S. Gaustad (Grand Rapids, MI: Eerdmans, 1983), vol. 2, p. 69.

5. Carolyn De Swarte Gifford, "Women in Social Reform Movements," in *Women & Religion in America*, ed. Rosemary Radford Ruether and Rosemary Skinner Keller (San Francisco: Harper & Row, 1981), vol. 1, p. 296.

6. Vincent Harding, "Out of the Cauldron of Struggle," in *Religion: North American Style*, 2d ed., ed. Patrick H. McNamara (Belmont, CA: Wardsworth, 1984), p. 264; see also James H. Cone, "Black Religious Thought," in *Encyclopedia of the American Religious Experience*, vol. 2, pp. 1173–1187.

7. Ake Hultzkrantz, "Ghost Dance," in *The Encyclopedia of Religion*, ed. Mircea Eliade (New York: Macmillan, 1987), vol. 5, p. 546.

8. See Newell S. Booth, Jr., "Islam in North America," in *Encyclopedia of the American Religious Experience*, vol. 2, pp. 723–729.

9. See Grant Wacker, "Pentecostalism," ibid., pp. 933–945.

10. Reinhold Niebuhr, "Anglo-Saxon Destiny and Responsibility," in *God's New Israel: Religious Interpretations of American Destiny*, ed. Conrad Cherry (Englewood Cliffs, NJ: Prentice-Hall, 1971), pp. 304–305.

11. John Murray Cuddihy, "The Elephant and the Angels; or, The Incivil Irritatingness of Jewish Theodicy," in *Uncivil Religion: Interreligious Hostility in America*, ed. Robert N. Bellah and Frederick E. Greenspahn (New York: Crossroad, 1987), p. 24.

12. J. Bryan Hehir, "From Church-State to Religion and Politics: The Case of the U.S. Catholic Bishops," in *American Catholics*, pp. 53–54.

13. Martin E. Marty, *The Public Church* (New York: Crossroad, 1981), pp. x–xi.

Part Three

AMERICAN PRAGMATISM

Chapter 6

William James and Pluralism

The Philosophical Background

William James (1842–1910) was a key figure in the golden age of America's philosophical preoccupation with religion. Arguably, that golden age ran from the late 1870s to the 1930s, when such luminaries as Charles Sanders Peirce, Josiah Royce, George Santayana, John Dewey, and Alfred North Whitehead joined James in reflecting on the foundations of the religious aspect of American cultural life that they deemed crucial to its survival. In the far background stood the Protestant Reformation and the Enlightenment. In the near background stood such thinkers as Jonathan Edwards, the founding fathers responsible for the structure of the American republic, and Ralph Waldo Emerson, the great transcendentalist thinker who had urged a refocusing of philosophy (or spirituality) on personal experience.

The assumption of all of these American philosophers was that their work served the public life of their country. They were reflecting on the foundations of the knowledge and morality necessary for their country to be what its founders had envisioned it to be. Philosophy had begun to separate itself from theology as early as Descartes, Newton, Locke, Hume, and Kant. In reaction to these giants, all of whom pushed aside the normative influence of biblical revelation and focused on human reason, many American thinkers had conceived of religious reflection as concerned ideally with the signs of divinity in nature and the implications that religious faith bore for morality. Biblical and doctrinal theology, as they had been practiced prior to the Enlightenment, and as they are practiced again today, had little vogue. A distinction between what one did in church, to satisfy one's emotions and bind the community together, and what one did in one's study had reduced religious reflection to generalizing about the impact of religious experience on the sphere of knowledge and ethics. Few philosophers of religion dealt seriously with the traditional attributes of the Christian God, or the structures of grace and the theological virtues, or the implications of ecclesiology for politics, or the metaphysical implications of revelation.

The American philosophers who dealt with religion in the period from the 1870s to the 1930s disagreed about many particulars, but they agreed that religion was important. Charles Sanders Peirce, greatly influenced by Kant, thought that religion was crucial to the healthy functioning of the American democracy, even though he looked to physical science for his paradigms of reliable truth. Physical science was self-correcting, while religious thought had no way of testing its claims so that error might be eliminated systematically. Josiah Royce developed an idealistic view of God and human nature that made divinity the basis for human beings' ability to live together and create sustainable cultures. Like Peirce, Royce was trying to reform or rehabilitate what had become traditional (Deistic) views of religion, by working out the functions proper to religious influences. Those religious influences were more valuable for their emotional and social consequences or potential than for their cognitive yield. Like Peirce, Royce tended to think in the dichotomous terms (natural/supernatural, history/eternity) handed down by the theological tradition. However, philosophy aimed at exposing and explaining reality, conceived as something objective and independent of human beings. Physical science obviously was important to philosophy, inasmuch as physical science described the objective world. Religion and art were also important, but mainly for what they said about how people might find their existence beautiful, compelling, and so both bearable and exhilarating. For Royce, mathematics was also significant, because it revealed the spirituality of the human mind—a spirituality in which Royce found the key to the divine sustenance of the world.

Henry Samuel Levinson has described Peirce and Royce as "reformers" of the philosophy of religion they had inherited. William James, George Santayana, and John Dewey appear to him as "radicals," wanting to venture forth in significantly new directions.[1] As we shall see, James was the radical most open to religious experience, and most creative in working out the pluralistic implications of such experience. Santayana, a student of both Royce and James at Harvard, conceived of philosophy as a broadly gauged reflection on culture. The aesthetic component of culture fascinated Santayana, and his instincts took him to a naturalism that dealt with religion as a part of the human being's emotional makeup rather than as the product of divine revelation. Like the other philosophers we are treating here, Santayana was convinced that American republican and democratic traditions represented high humanistic achievements. They therefore provided the context in which one ought to consider science, art, religion and the other major components of culture. Santayana spoke of an "animal faith" that would tie religious and aesthetic emotion to a basic vitality. What helped people to find the world beautiful, and live their lives in the light of the ethical maturity that such beauty could illumine, was the truest or most valuable philosophy.

Both James and Santayana inclined to such a pragmatic view of philosophical investigation and reality itself. Their pragmatism was not crude, not simply a matter of "what works" in the sense of what makes "us" victors, or wealthy, or full of good feeling. But it was skeptical of older objectivist views of reality that seemed to separate judgments of truth and value from human experience and to be impervious to correction by the results they generated. Philosophical explanations ought to clarify the ideas and actions necessary for human beings to survive and prosper. When philosophy, or theology, or any other body of thought claiming to bear on how human beings ought to live, did not concern itself centrally with results, it ought to be suspected if not rejected outright.

John Dewey was the American philosopher who brought the naturalism of Santayana and the pragmatism of James to bear on such matters as education and democracy. Throughout his long life and distinguished academic career, Dewey reflected on the full range of significant human activity: science, art, politics, education, and (on occasion) religion. He shared with the other leading American philosophers of the period we are considering a distrust of institutional religion, thinking that institutional religion had often been a foe of honesty, intellectual curiosity, and civic freedoms. Like William James, he was interested in psychology, but whereas James was fascinated by what psychology said about human consciousness, Dewey was more interested in what it said about learning. In the second quarter of the twentieth century Dewey was the most influential American philosopher, and his lectures on such topics as "Art and Experience" and "A Common Faith" made his views of what ought to direct the human enterprise and how people ought to create the consensus necessary for a democratic society part of the intellectual mainstream.

The last American philosopher to concern himself greatly with religion (after the 1930s, academic philosophy turned toward mathematics, science, logic, and language, seeking more rigorous categories and procedures) was Alfred North Whitehead, who began his career at Cambridge University in England but taught for many years in the United States. Whitehead had collaborated with Bertrand Russell, the English logician, on the foundations of mathematics. In the second half of his career, however, he was concerned with developing a metaphysics that could account for the world that modern science was revealing. This world was above all a place of process: change, development, relationships. Whitehead saw God as the necessary foundation for such a world, but the God that he envisioned was di-polar, having a side where divinity itself changed, as well as a side that stood outside change, in an eternal self-sufficiency. Whitehead admired Jesus, but his philosophy was shaped more by Plato and modern science. He gave emotion, including religious emotion, a significant place, thinking that emotion is what moves people to their most important decisions and what gives life its tone and zest.

Overall, then, the philosophical milieu that surrounded William James was one of considerable creativity. His immediate predecessors were trying to rehabilitate the philosophical and religious traditions they had inherited, to create new visions viable for the greatly changed times in which they lived. The century since the founding of the nation had brought developments that the founding fathers could never have foreseen, so the public life of the country required a restatement of the reality in the midst of which American citizens lived. James and those who succeeded him were less sanguine about rehabilitating the older traditions. The variety, change, and empirical aspects of the world were what fascinated them. Their temper (with some qualifications regarding James) was more naturalistic than religious (concerned with the supernatural: grace, revelation, faith). They tended to join religion to ethics, when it came to evaluating social consequences, and to aesthetics, when it came to emotions. When it came to cognitive values, they tended to subordinate religion to both the physical sciences and the common sense of the average good, democratic, American citizen.

The Life of William James

The family in which William James grew up has become famous as one of the most illustrious in American intellectual history, mainly because both he and his brother, the novelist Henry James, reached the peak of their professions. Their father, Henry James, Sr., had studied theology at Princeton University but then became alienated from organized religion. He did, however, develop an abiding interest in the thought of Emanuel Swedenborg, a theosophist or mystic who described a new interpretation of Christianity, fit for the modern age and based on interior revelations. The elder James was a restless man, both physically and intellectually, wandering throughout Europe and through many different intellectual enthusiasms (but remaining indebted to Swedenborg).

William James received a somewhat irregular schooling, spending time in New York, France, and Switzerland, and being exposed to vigorous conversation at the dinner table. At the age of eighteen he studied art, but soon decided that was not his gift and turned to scientific studies at Harvard. After training in chemistry and anatomy he entered Harvard Medical School, but on a trip to the Amazon (he had interrupted his medical studies to accompany the eminent geologist Luis Agassiz on a scientific expedition) his health deteriorated. Unsettled, he left medical school and went to Germany for a year, where he studied with the eminent physicist Hermann von Helmholtz and other leading scientists. Psychology and philosophy began to attract him, most of the latter being of a neo-Kantian variety. But in 1868, at the age of twenty-six, he suffered a great despondency and apparently contemplated suicide. He returned home after eighteen months in Germany and completed his medical degree, but for the next three years he was too sick to practice medicine and had to live as a semi-invalid.

James began to heal when he read the works of Charles Renouvier, the neo-Kantian philosopher with whom he had studied in Europe, dealing with freedom of the will. His scientific training had inclined him to a deterministic outlook (the notion that human beings as well as nature are governed by inflexible laws of causality). In finding a basis for taking charge of his own life, by deciding that there was a realm of freedom that he could exploit, James accomplished a kind of self-cure and laid the foundations for much of his later work in psychology and philosophy.

In 1872 he received an appointment to teach physiology at Harvard, and before long he had turned this into a concentration on physiological psychology: empirical studies of human consciousness. Previously most psychology had been controlled by theological interests, going under the heading "mental philosophy." James led the way to making psychology a laboratory science—something one might investigate scientifically. By 1878 James's life had expanded considerably, and that year he married Alice Gibbens of Cambridge, Massachusetts. His health problems (fatigue and anxiety) virtually disappeared and he felt filled with energy. In 1880 he began work on a textbook in psychology, but by the time it was finished ten years later it had become a huge, two-volume work, *The Principles of Psychology*, which soon was recognized as a landmark in the field. The book took a functional view of mental occurrences, approaching them the way a biologist would approach physical occurrences. James defended free will, but he did not elaborate any full doctrine sufficient to warrant embracing the notion.

Although he had created the first real laboratory for psychological studies, James found that his real interests lay elsewhere. He was drawn to the bigger questions of philosophy and religion, and after 1890 they received the bulk of his attention. Such matters as the existence and nature of God, the immortality of the soul, the pros and cons of free will and determinism absorbed him. Though these were traditional questions, James determined to study them empirically, paying more attention to experiential data than to traditional arguments. From the late 1880s he had begun to study religious subjects, among them data on psychic experience. Perhaps his father's long-standing interest in Swedenborg had prepared him for this step. Certainly something deep in him was responsible for an openness that the majority of scientists, philosophers, and other academics of his age (when mechanism was still the rule) did not show. James's findings were inconclusive regarding immortality or existence after death, but he regarded the existence of God as proven by widespread testimony based on personal experience. The God so proved was not the traditional God of Western monotheism but rather a collection of saving powers, which placed pluralism and variety in divinity itself. Concerning human freedom, he found sufficient looseness in the data bearing on human choice to provide a space for free choice. Between 1893 and 1903 James wrote a variety of essays on these subjects that later were collected into such works as *The Will to Believe* and *Essays in Popular Philosophy*.

In 1901–1902 James delivered the Gifford Lectures in natural religion at the University of Edinburgh, consummating several years of preparation. Published as *The Varieties of Religious Experience*, they became a classic. Because of overwork, he had again been suffering bad health, but the triumph of his Gifford Lectures put his trials in a new light. Many people interested in defending religion against determinist or materialist attacks found the rich bank of data that James presented useful apologetically, because it seemed to establish that human beings do draw on a fund of spiritual powers beyond the realm that materialism allows.

In the final phase of his career, James devoted his energies to developing his philosophy of pragmatism. Peirce had done the pioneering work with logical studies in the 1870s, but James was the one who gave pragmatism the broad scope necessary to make it an effective philosophical movement or school. James's point was that the meaning of any idea rests in the experiential consequences that it produces. What he had done in studying the phenomena of religious experience could be extended to ideas from the natural sciences, politics, or private experience. Among the consequences that James drew were a denial that the universe is monistic, a methodological insistence on a radical empiricism (foundation of thought in experience), and an argument that reality is dynamic (processive) rather than static. His great enemy was any claim to absoluteness, which he found unverified by the pragmatic criteria of experiential consequences.

James elaborated his view of this new philosophy during his Lowell Lectures in Boston in 1906. His last essays on the subject were published after his death in a book entitled *Essays in Radical Empiricism* (1912). There James argued that not only things but also the relations among things are so real that one need not postulate underlying causes or substances to explain them—a view that attacked most traditional metaphysics (and is similar to some Buddhist notions).

From 1907 and the publication of *Pragmatism,* James became the toast of the English-speaking philosophical world. His lectures at Harvard, Columbia, and Oxford were received as the words of a new prophet, and John Dewey became his vigorous disciple. The publication of his Hibbert Lectures at Oxford as *A Pluralistic Universe* (1909) presented his ideas in more popular form, adding to his influence. His health deteriorated, but before his death in 1910 at the age of sixty-eight he had produced and collected enough material for several posthumous books. Since his death many of his instincts about the natural world and the human psyche have been vindicated, and his general philosophical style has been taken by some observers of American culture as quintessentially American: practical, flexible, antidogmatic, pluralistic, and rooted in experience.

The Will to Believe

In 1897 William James published a collection of his essays that included "The Will to Believe." In this essay he showed both the pragmatic cast of his mind (his desire to be guided by experience and consequences) and his willingness to swim against the intellectual tide of his times (which was skeptical, if not hostile to religion). Consider the following passage: "To preach skepticism to us as a duty until 'sufficient evidence' for religion be found, is tantamount therefore to telling us, when in presence of the religious hypothesis, that to yield to our fear of its being error is wiser and better than to yield to our hope that it may be true. It is not intellect against all the passions, then; it is only intellect with one passion laying down its law. And by what, forsooth, is the supreme wisdom of this passion warranted? Dupery for dupery, what proof is there that dupery through hope is so much worse than dupery through fear? I, for one, can see no proof; and I simply refuse obedience to the scientist's command to imitate his kind of option, in a case where my own stake is important enough to give me the right to choose my own form of risk. If religion be true and the evidence for it still be insufficient, I do not wish, by putting your extinguisher upon my nature (which feels to me as if it had after all some business in this matter), to forfeit my sole chance in life of getting upon the winning side—that chance depending, of course, on my willingness to run the risk of acting as if my passional need of taking the world religiously might be prophetic and right."[2]

Here James shows us both his appealing literary style and the vigor of his mind. He is not about to lose the chance to gain truth because someone else's stuffy protocols say that he ought to hold back until all the evidence for the correctness of religion (belief in God) is in. What, he asks, makes yielding to one's fear of making a mistake better than following one's hope that religion may guide one to a great truth? Religion is not concerned with the same things as science. It involves more personal matters, and so the scientist's detachment and skepticism may not be appropriate to religion's kind of quest for truth. At the least, anything so significant as one's overall sense of the meaningfulness of life, or of salvation, or of whatever else James means by "getting upon the winning side" ought to permit the individual to make a passionate choice. He or she is intimately involved, so an impersonal stance is not appropriate, does not fit.

One notes the openness James shows the religious option, his willingness to entertain the possibility that it may be prophetic: a pathway to the truth. This openness was characteristic of James's entire philosophy, and it went hand in hand with his empirical cast of mind. What mattered to James were experiential foundations and consequences. Ideas were as fertile or sterile, as true or false, as the difference they made when one embraced them and followed through upon them. One could not know, before the fact, whether or not religious belief would prove fertile. Certainly, there was sufficient testimony from believers of different kinds that belief had changed their lives for the better, to warrant entertaining the possibility that belief could be fertile. It was dogmatism of an ironic kind, therefore, for people to be skeptical of religious claims in a pseudo-scientific way, as though they could overlook the intrinsic contribution of personal involvement in the experiments of faith. James certainly was not credulous about religion, but neither was he credulous about natural science. He knew that foolishness and rigidity could thrive in either realm, so he was determined to let evidence and openness be his governing concerns.

This independent, open, practical cast of mind is much of what one implies when speaking popularly about American pragmatism. William James did not invent the characteristically American temper of testing things, prizing their active and practical side more than their contemplative and speculative side, and moving on to get things done. But he did articulate much of the American temper, and he did think through what kind of a human consciousness, and what kind of an objective world, consorted with the facts of American pragmatism. In a word, the human consciousness was empirical: concerned with experiential realities, and the objective world was pluralistic: varied, rich, not uniform, not static, hard to grasp once and for all, best appreciated by keeping oneself open to new revelations and possibilities.

The fact that America's most eminent psychologist would champion open-mindedness about religious claims has struck many students of James's philosophy, some of whom have noted the ties between religion and pragmatism at the historical beginnings of James's articulation of his philosophical views. Thus Gerald E. Myers has written: "When William James delivered 'Philosophical Conceptions and Practical Results' at the University of California on August 26, 1898, officially announcing pragmatism, no one guessed that a movement or a whole controversial literature about cognition and truth was being launched; nor did James betray any awareness that he was moving toward something momentous. He told his audience that, employing an informal notion of meaning he credited to Peirce, they might discover pragmatic reasons for choosing a tender-minded religious hypothesis even in a tough-minded era. *The Will to Believe* had been published only a year before, and James's connection between pragmatism and religion was obvious enough. There was not much reaction to his paper until an altered version was published in 1904; but by 1906–07, his lectures in Boston and New York (which he published as *Pragmatism* in 1907) often attracted audiences of a thousand or more. Added to the fact that James was America's foremost psychologist and the spokesman from Harvard of a new philosophy called pragmatism, he was an intriguing apologist for religion; the combination had an immediate attraction. Unquestionably, a movement was underway and was arousing popular curiosity."[3]

It turned out that James was no orthodox Christian believer, and that the movement attracted such naturalists as John Dewey, who used religion more as an instrument than out of any personal conviction that religion itself revealed special truths. James himself was convinced, for autobiographical reasons, that a sense of freedom, including the freedom to open oneself to the world as though it had mysteriously healing or saving powers, was an ingredient for health. He had discovered something essential to the human spirit, its need to honor the experiential evidence presented to it and not be bound by dogma or convention. Speaking about the roots and implications of this discovery, he could defend those fellow explorers who had followed religious pathways, noting that their boldness and courage had considerably expanded his prior sense of reality, showing him more things than a mechanistic philosophy deemed possible.

Religious Experience

When James described the feelings that led him to insist that the religious option be given a chance to show its merit, he spoke in terms of a need to consider the universe as having a personal form and calling upon human beings to honor this form. Note the connection between James's convictions about human freedom or autonomy and this obligation to serve the universe: "The more perfect and more eternal aspect of the universe is represented in our religions as having personal form. The universe is no longer a mere *It* to us, but a *Thou*, if we are religious; and any relation that might be possible from person to person might be possible here. For instance, although in one sense we are passive portions of the universe, in another we show a curious autonomy, as if we were small active centres on our own account. We feel, too, as if the appeal of religion to us were made to our own active good-will, as if evidence might be forever withheld from us unless we met the hypothesis half-way. . . . This feeling, forced on us we know not whence, that by obstinately believing that there are gods (although not to do so would be so easy both for our logic and our life) we are doing the universe the deepest service we can, seems part of the living essence of the religious hypothesis."[4]

This description is hardly a specimen of Christian orthodoxy, locating divinity as it does as an aspect of the universe and speaking of "gods" in the plural. On the other hand, if one grants the rejection of religion regnant in the academic circles in which James moved as either a psychologist or a philosopher, it is remarkably courageous. James is willing to speak about the obligations that religious feelings create, and the way that they make any veto on responding to the overtures of the personalized universe illogical. Because the overtures are experiential (many people have reported them or their equivalent), and responding might open new vistas of truth, it would go against people's best interest to discourage or even ridicule their interacting with the universe with reverent expectancy. Finally, we should note that James's description provides the equivalent of the traditional conviction of Christian theology that one must believe in order to understand: "evidence might be forever withheld from us unless we met the hypothesis half-way." To meet the hypothesis halfway is to cast aside one's methodical doubt, one's doctrinaire skepticism, and make an act of faith or trust that the solicitations of the universe, the calls to follow up on the intimations that its more perfect and eternal aspect might have a personal form, could prove revelatory and true.

The description of James's lecture at the University of California in 1898, "Philosophical Conceptions and Practical Results," mentioned "pragmatic reasons for choosing a tender-minded religious hypothesis even in a tough-minded era." James developed the empirical basis for these reasons in his Gifford Lectures, and it seems to have caught for him the pathos of the modern believer. The tough-minded, practical, commonsensical world of business and technology, of science and the other academic disciplines desiring to be scientific, had little place for what it considered religious claims, because these latter inevitably involved feelings, emotions, intuitions—things hard to cast into material, measurable, empirically verifiable terms. Moreover, as we noted, in the nineteenth century religion had become "feminized" and relegated to the domestic sphere. It was what ladies did, along with bringing up children, patronizing the arts, and helping the unfortunate. While it put some color and grace into an otherwise harsh, ugly, even brutish world, it did not have much status among self-styled "realists," the great majority of them men of affairs. William James's achievement in *The Variety of Religious Experience* was to display the empirical basis for thinking that religious hypotheses, emotional and affect-laden though they were, had a solid claim on the attention of anyone open to the facts and concerned about pragmatic results in a wide, comprehensive sense. James called forth myriad examples of people experiencing the divine, or at least the transordinary, and, in the spirit of his essay on the will to believe, argued well that people who shut themselves off from the solicitations of the universe came away the poorer for their closure.

As an example of the reports on which James drew to establish an empirical basis for taking religious claims seriously, consider the following account. In adducing and analyzing it, the foremost American psychologist was laying the ground for arguing that there is an unseen dimension to reality: "I have on a number of occasions felt that I had enjoyed a period of intimate communion with the divine. These meetings came unasked and unexpected, and seemed to consist merely in the temporary obliteration of the conventionalities which usually surround and cover my life. . . . Once it was when from the summit of a high mountain I looked over a gashed and corrugated landscape extending to a long convex of ocean that ascended to the horizon, and again from the same point when I could see nothing beneath me but a boundless expanse of white cloud, on the blown surface of which a few high peaks, including the one I was on, seemed plunging about as if they were dragging their anchors. What I felt on these occasions was a temporary loss of my own identity, accompanied by an illumination which revealed to me a deeper significance than I had been wont to attach to life. It is in this that I find my justification for saying that I have enjoyed communication with God. Of course the absence of such a being as this would be chaos. I cannot conceive of life without its presence."[5]

James did not claim that a report such as this established the reality of God. What he claimed was that a report such as this, when found to be the product of a healthy person and joined by many other similar reports, put the responsible psychologist on notice that something significant just might be in question. If the psychology of the day had no place for such tender-minded reports and claims, so much the worse for it. By the principles of empiricism and pragmatism (the requirement that we stay close to experience and study consequences), the report deserved respectful study. It had colored a person's whole life, determined a person's deepest sense of reality. And there were many other such people, many other equivalent claims. A psychology or philosophy that wrote them off categorically was neither scientific nor fully honest.

On the other hand, to admit the effect claimed for religion in many lives was not to commit oneself to a particular religion. James never revealed the personal resonances of the questions that he pursued in his Gifford Lectures, but some biographers link his interest in mystical experience with desperate efforts to cure his own chronic depression and ill health. Although he never did become religious in an orthodox fashion, James seemed to derive some consolation from studying the accounts of those who had been healed through religious experience. On this question of the personal dimension of James's religious thought, Daniel Bjork has recently written: "James had to find religious ideals in experience, but not just in the experiences of the mystics and saints. His own life was filled with a foreboding about his physical condition, a despair that might yield a religious—that is, an ideal—meaning. And here the notebook launches into a truly remarkable discussion James calls 'the broader indifference.' The meaning of religious experience becomes intertwined with his crisis; it becomes a meaning inseparable from coming to terms with illness and impending death: 'I find myself in a cold, pinched, quaking state when I think of the probability of dying soon with all my music in me. My eyes are dry and hollow, my facial muscles won't contract, my throat quivers, my heart flutters, my breast and body feel stale and caked. Laughter and cheerfulness even about other things than my own destiny are impossible. My mind is pinned down to the continual contemplation of annihilation which fills me with a kind of physical dread, none the less positive for not being very acute. My queries revolve around myself.' "[6]

It says volumes about William James that he managed so great an objectivity about religious experience when such personal reasons for rushing either to embrace or reject religious claims churned within him. He stays sufficiently the scientific psychologist to keep the orders of evidence separate, allowing that religious claims have sufficient foundation in the wide range of human experience to warrant taking them seriously and appreciating their pragmatic import, yet in his assessments of the meaning of his own life not moving beyond what he himself has felt and become convinced about.

Pragmatism

In 1907, when he was sixty-five, James published some of his lectures under the title, *Pragmatism: A New Name for Some Old Ways of Thinking.* By that time, pragmatism had become a watchword, a movement, a fashion. This did not entirely please James, but he did his best to explain his understanding of the term and display its advantages. Among such advantages was the ability of pragmatism to serve up the kernel of religious experience and discard the husk of rationalistic thinking that much religion carried. The ghost of the German idealist Hegel was about, depicting divinity as a matter of "absolutes" and making God something quite remote. James's studies of the varieties of religious experience had convinced him that the God (or gods) people actually were moved by were nothing remote. They were palpable, as revealed by the great emotional effects they wrought. What real people needed was a divinity that dealt with the blood and dust of their actual struggles: "In this real world of sweat and dirt, it seems to me that when a view of things is 'noble,' that ought to count as a presumption against its truth, and as a philosophic disqualification. The prince of darkness may be a gentleman, as we are told he is, but whatever the God of earth and heaven is, he can surely be no gentleman. His menial services are needed in the dust of our human trials, even more than his dignity is needed in the empyrean. Now pragmatism, devoted though she be to facts, has no such materialistic bias as ordinary empiricism labors under. Moreover, she has no objection whatever to the realizing of abstractions, so long as you get about among particulars with their aid and they actually carry you somewhere. Interested in no conclusions but those which our minds and our experiences work out together, she has no *a priori* prejudices against theology. *If theological ideas prove to have value for concrete life, they will be true, for pragmatism, in the sense of being good for so much. For how much more they are true, will depend entirely on their relations to other truths that also have to be acknowledged.*"[7]

Here James expresses his own bias toward the tough-minded, that which can be nailed down and shown to make a clear difference. The divinity he finds affecting people's lives, and, no doubt, the divinity he needed in his own troubled times, was not a remote idea, not an ideal notion, but a force or function capable of engaging the brute pains and requirements of human life, capable of making a perceptible difference. It is ironic that a member of the privileged class such as James should disparage the prince of darkness as a gentleman. Much of the vigor of pragmatism came from the urgency of James's conviction that ordinary people needed curing, healing, real succor.

A sure sign of the distance between James and traditional Christianity is the move he does not make at this juncture. For the traditional Christian, the obvious nexus between human need and divine influence is the crucified Christ. The crucified Christ more than entered into the dust of our human trials. He so fully embraced human pathos that he became the great

Western symbol of pain and dereliction. But the crucified Christ was not a tragic figure. Because God raised Christ from the dead, the Christian story became a comedy, in Dante's high sense of the word. Yet neither the crucifixion of Christ nor his resurrection comes to James's aid. If he thinks of this prime Christian symbol and article of faith at all, he cannot allow himself to bring it forward. So he moves on to the generic defense of religion, on pragmatic grounds, as possibly useful to human beings in their trials. Because theological ideas may have a value for concrete life (may save people from despair, may even lead people to joy), pragmatism is willing to grant them possible legitimacy, is willing even to grant them possible truth. But James hedges this also, inasmuch as such truth will have to be joined with other truths, to see whether it squares with the pragmatic whole.

It turns out, then, that James the defender of the possibly pragmatic value of religion is careful in the ways proper to academic lecturers. Certainly, this care was probably an expression of his personal judgments, which did not allow him to affirm a traditional Christianity yet also would not allow him to discount the possible validity of religious claims, Christian ones included. So religion functions not so much as a primary value that pragmatism illumines as a primary instance of the openness that pragmatic methodology enshrines. Nothing is to be ruled out of court, unless it fails to deliver value, utility, in the concrete. If religion, or art, or science, or politics, or even an academic lecture improves someone's mental or physical estate, it can present credentials of possible truth. Truth is what people find valuable, significant, useful. None of these words need imply a low, crass, commercial sense. Each can be quite elevated, including both lofty states such as prayer and love and lofty notions such as meaning and fulfillment.

The link between concrete value, existential payoff, and ideas, beliefs, and procedures is what makes pragmatism a typically American cast of mind and philosophy. James was quite forthright: he was simply giving a new name to an old idea. But he was also too modest. Never before had the old idea that one could judge the truth of something by its experiential grounds and practical consequences received so lucid, winning, and polished a presentation. The genius of William James was to move between the data that only a scholar could marshal and the arresting arguments that only a first-rate mind could create. When one added a gift for graceful, forceful, interesting expression (the high art of the popular writer and lecturer), one had just the recipe for the success that pragmatism in fact became. It was *the* philosophical movement at the end of the first decade of the twentieth century, and ever since it has struck students of American culture, domestic and foreign alike, as quintessentially American.

The sophisticated yet still grim view of human nature bequeathed by the Puritans, and the rationalistic yet practical view of religion bequeathed by the founding fathers, bear no obvious connection to this pragmatism. Certainly, one can describe Jonathan Edwards's tests of religious experience as empirical and concerned about consequences. Equally certainly, one can argue that the main goal that Jefferson, Madison, Franklin, and the other founding fathers sought when they disestablished religion was the practical good of civil peace and fair play. But both Edwards and Jefferson would have been surprised by the analysis of such options that James and the pragmatists tended to make. Between Jefferson and James stood decades of experience, including such watershed events as the Civil War, the great waves of immigration, and the industrialization of America. American culture had changed significantly. The west that Jefferson had opened had reached the Pacific, leading to such acculturation that in 1898 there was a sturdy University of California for James to lecture at. The young, naive energy of the United States was presenting old, sophisticated Europe a curious spectacle, one that no novelist exploited better than Henry James. Americans had built, and were continuing to build, a prosperous nation. They had become significant in the world, had reached the borders of greatness, by doing, achieving, focusing on results. In William James they found the spokesperson for the viewpoint that had shaped them and, arguably, was making them the great hope of Western civilization. Pragmatism was a mirror in which many Americans saw themselves for the first time. By and large, they liked what they saw.

More precisely, the mainstream liked what it saw. As the acids of modernity ate their way into the intellectual and wealthy classes, the older philosophies, derived from Calvinism or the Enlightenment, seemed passé. Reason was the vogue, but it was less the speculative faculty studied by Kant and more the practical faculty so brilliantly deployed by engineers and captains of industry. Pragmatism was a philosophy of practical reason, and of practical emotion as well. It was a theory capable of elevating the instincts of the typical successful American of the turn of the century to the status of a coherent, persuasive worldview. In James's hands, it was neither materialistic nor idealistic. It had no bias against religion, emotion, or art, and no need to blush before science, commerce, or technology. It was an exegesis of the judgments and feelings that got most of the people in James's audiences through the day. It was a defense of trial and error, of a high-mindedness that wanted results. If atheists and evangelicals both rejected it, so much the better. It was the golden mean that both had missed.

Pluralism and Radical Empiricism

James's Hibbert Lectures, published in 1909, developed the metaphysical implications of the pluralism he had found in religious experience. To be faithful to the data that people reported, one had to acknowledge that there was great variety in the ways that individuals found religious meaning and claimed to sense the divine. No one God, or one religious system, or one pattern of effects emerged. So it was necessary to speak of gods, in the plural, and to champion a certain laissez-faire attitude. To Americanize the state of affairs, one might call it democratic. Divinity itself seemed to grant people free exercise of their liberty in the realm of religion. A psychologist certainly should do no less. James had little use for theology, as it was practiced in his day, but clearly his advice to theology was that it too ought to be flexible. In assessing either the nature of divinity or the nature of religious experience, if theology wanted to honor the facts and deal with the truths that people found viable, variety and pluralism would have to be its watchwords.

In his Hibbert Lectures, James surveyed some of the leading opinions of his day about the nature of religious experience and the character of the universe, including the universe's divinity. By now his opposition to rationalism, understood as a reliance on pure intellection that shortchanged actual experience, was well established. So was his opposition to monism, the view that the universe had ultimately to be (or reflect) a One. Both rationalism and monism seemed to him to disdain the realities by which people actually lived—the realities on which pragmatism built its case. In his own words, "Only one thing is certain, and that is the result of our criticisms of the absolute: the only way to escape from the paradoxes and perplexities that a consistently thought-out monistic universe suffers from as from a species of auto-intoxication—the mystery of the 'fall,' namely, of reality lapsing into appearance, truth into error, perfection into imperfection; of evil, in short; the mystery of universal determinism, of the block-universe eternal and without a history, etc.;—the only way of escape, I say, from all this is to be frankly pluralistic and assume that the superhuman consciousness, however vast it may be, has itself an external environment, and consequently is finite."[8]

Finitude and pluralism therefore mark the universe, the full sweep of reality, through and through. The superhuman consciousness that is the best index of what has traditionally been called divinity does not stand outside of the universe, as its Creator from nothingness. It exists within the universe, having an external environment, being one of the pieces of the entire gigantic puzzle. There is no absolute, no Hegelian divinity standing apart from the conditions that human beings find applying to all of their experiences. Everything is related, processive, limited.

This is the metaphysical world that Whitehead later elaborated with amazingly new and demanding terminology. This is the world suggested by the theories of relativity and quantum mechanics, which were soon to rewrite the physics books. Darwinian evolution had been on the intellectual scene long enough to have persuaded a scientist such as James that movement, change, diversity, selection, and the like were the essential features of life. What James wanted from metaphysicians, those who pondered the ultimate character of the universe, the basic structures of being, was an adequate fidelity to all these evidences of pluralism and finitude. The finite nearly by definition was relational and but one of many. The world being revealed to the natural scientist, and to the psychologist, was abuzz with different finite events, forces, emotions, and more. It was up to the philosopher, the one who stepped back to contemplate the ultimate consequences or implications of what experience reported, to keep faith with these data. Whether the experience in question was the common sense of the person who found great diversity when looking either without or within, or the sophisticated probings of the scientist whose telescope or microscope revealed diversity on other scales, the charge to the philosopher was the same: honor this diversity, respect this finitude.

When James analyzes how the metaphysicians who will not accept this charge try to resolve the problems that a richly pluralistic human experience presents them, he groups together in a dense cluster a number of famous ideas, apparently branding them all errors. The paradoxes and perplexities forced upon a consistent monism make him imagine such a philosophical position to be a kind of intoxication with the self that, by implication, forgets our human rootedness in the finite world. Here the reference may be to Hegel, and the notion may be that in the Hegelian dialectic the spirituality of the self takes on a life of its own. The movements of reason are projected and extrapolated, becoming currents that one can ride into the empyrean, where human spirituality loses its conditions and shows its kinship with the divine, absolute Spirit. The paradoxes that prompt this evaluation of the monistic mind include the mystery of the "fall" (apparently an illusion to the story of Adam and Eve), which James reinterprets as a matter of "reality lapsing into appearance" (a notion more congenial to Hinduism than to biblical thought). When he goes on to speak of perfection lapsing into imperfection, and then equates these several failures with the mystery of evil, he moves into Gnostic territory: the fall, the source of evil, was from a heavenly perfection and unity down into the imperfection and diversity of earthly matter. Still more equivalents follow: monism gives us the (false) problems of determinism (apparently because the Absolute must control everything) and of the "block-universe" that is eternal and has no history (more consequences of fixating on an Absolute, something that is indebted only to itself and suffers none of the conditions of creatures, including most prominently the limitations imposed by space and time).

This is a dazzling concatenation of problematic ideas and speculative referents, all of which James claims would become much less troublesome if one opted for a pluralistic view of the universe. The student of metaphysics and the history of ideas can only both marvel and be appalled. On the one hand, James has isolated quite well the difficulties of reconciling some sort of absolute, or true Creator, or self-sufficient One, with the world that human beings experience—the world that such a divine or superior entity supposedly caused and furnishes its ultimate explanation. On the other hand, James neglects the experiences that give rise to monism, absolutism, and the traditional metaphysics of a creative divinity, as well as the postulates of human reason that figure in such constructions. These experiences include the raptures of a Plotinus or an Emerson, while the postulates include the intellectual demands of an Aristotle or a Shankara. They may be less persuasive than the pragmatist's appeals to common experience, especially when the audience is composed of Americans without a sturdy idealistic or contemplative tradition, but they make a unique claim (pluralism is illusory) and have had such an influence in the history of philosophy and religion that they deserve a more sympathetic hearing. One doesn't responsibly jettison the Hindu doctrine of *maya* (illusion), or the Christian doctrine of original sin, without giving its supposed data and reasons a patient hearing.

In his posthumous work, *Essays in Radical Empiricism,* James suggested the psycho-metaphysical foundations for a pragmatism that could successfully oppose metaphysical monism. These turned out to be an interpretation of human consciousness as a continuous stream and a metaphysical conviction that one could derive the nature of reality as a whole from this fluid character of human consciousness: "I conclude, then, that real effectual causation as an ultimate nature, as a 'category,' if you like, of reality, is *just what we feel it to be,* just that kind of conjunction which our own activity-series reveal. We have the whole butt and being of it in our hands; and the healthy thing for philosophy is to leave off grubbing underground for what effects effectuation, or what makes action act, and to try to solve the concrete questions of where the effectuation in this world is located, of which things are the true causal agents there, and of what the more remote effects consist. From this point of view, the greater sublimity traditionally attributed to the metaphysical inquiry, the grubbing inquiry, entirely disappears. If we could know what causation really and transcendentally is in itself, the only *use* of the knowledge would be to help us recognize an actual cause when we had one, and so to track the future course of operations more intelligently out."[9]

One sees, then, that by the end of his life James had become a radical empiricist indeed, offering as an underpinning to pragmatism a view of philosophy, of the mind's reach for ultimate explanations, that branded as illusory or unprofitable any search beyond the flux of human experience for deeper, more permanent or abiding principles. Did that amount to a veto on divinity, traditionally understood as the first, uncaused cause? Probably so, if logic were to prevail. Perhaps not, if the varieties of religious experience were allowed to jostle, overlap, and continue on their way without sifting themselves out into a single coherent pattern.

Faith and Reason

As enunciated by William James, pragmatism puts a premium on reason and downplays the influence of traditional faith, Christian, Jewish, or any other sort. It is a philosophy, not a theology. If faith wants to seek understanding by using pragmatic categories, it is welcome to do so. But pragmatism itself is a complete worldview. By its exposition of a pluralistic universe and a radically empirical interpretation of human consciousness, pragmatism describes a world at odds with traditional Christian and Jewish faith. It has no God independent of the world, standing apart from creation. It has no Christ changing the makeup of history by his death and resurrection. And it has no Holy Spirit immortalizing people by taking them into the deathless divine life. Whether the many Americans who rushed to pragmatism with enthusiasm realized it or not, traditional religion had moved another step away.

The response that traditional theology could have made to pragmatism is succinct: Accept pragmatism and you have no certain meaning or salvation. This response remains applicable to Whiteheadean process thought, the child of Jamesian pragmatism. If pluralism reigns throughout, nothing is grounded by an independent, self-sufficient reality. Everything is contingent. Nothing is necessary. Therefore, meaning is in abeyance. No divine mystery, whole and perfect, guarantees meaning (because none made the world intelligently, diffusing its being and goodness throughout creation). Equally, there is no salvation history centering in an incarnate divinity, a divine Word that marries time to eternity. Divinity did not confront evil and embrace it in a greater good, a salvific love. There is no crucifixion, no revelatory symbol recalling divinity's historical self-sacrifice. There is no resurrection, no revelatory symbol recalling divinity's defeat of evil and immortalizing triumph by love. To gain radical empiricism, thoroughgoing process, one loses the reality described by the perennial philosophy, Western but also potent in the East, that grounded the variety of the world in the infinite perfection of God. One also loses the good news trumpeted by the Bible, Jewish and Christian alike. So the cultural consequences were momentous. In responding so positively to Jamesian pragmatism, Americans of the early years of the twentieth century showed how far they had distanced themselves from their premodern forebears. They also pointed up the cultural divide between those who wanted a new worldview and those who wanted to worship through the millennial biblical symbols. Obviously, this divide remains with us today, though most Jews and Christians who want to make such symbols transparent for divinity are more shaped by pragmatic ideas than they realize.

Valid as this analysis of pragmatism may be, it leaves out the positive space James has provided for religion, and so for faith. By showing the sympathy and openness that are among the most winning characteristics of James's thought, one can respect the beliefs that people employ to manage their lives. One can also respect the analogy between the faith that a human government requires and the faith on which successful participation in the universe depends. If one is willing to bracket the questions that the radical empiricism underpinning James's pragmatic worldview raises (the questions of ultimate meaning and salvation that we have raised), his appreciation of the holistic character of people's practical philosophies, of their need for a "faith-ladder" by which to organize their sense of how reality coheres, can seem a strong endorsement of faith. As one analyst has put it, "A federal republic simply cannot run without presumptive faith *in* its constituents *by* its constituents—without it active cooperation dissembles. If the government of the universe is like that of a federal republic, we humans must surely do our best, in spite of the if, i.e., without the certainty that there are other (unseen, more powerful) agents that can do and are doing theirs. We must provide, says James, *by our behavior,* one of the 'premises' that would generate a salvable world. But this is not to say that our trust needs to be dogmatic. Remember: our faith must remain practical and go with the search for the most probable. For we can provide only *one* of the premises; other powers must provide the rest. So James's vision stands in need of *some* evidence, some phenomena that we can look at, which will tend to support the claim that 'there may be gods, even here and now.' "[10]

The problem with this use of religious experience, of course, is that it cannot lead to any unassailable proof that the divinity experienced is the traditional Creator and Savior, who is infinite—independent of the finite universe. Faith therefore becomes a practical stance, a kind of prudence. One is willing to accredit one's feelings and even one's ecstatic moments. But they do not gain a privileged status and direct the construction of a world in which divinity guarantees full meaning. So the faith is not that hymned by the Bible and clarified in Western religious tradition, Jewish and Christian alike. There is no Master of the Universe, no fully transcendent Lord, into whose hands one commends one's spirit (amazed that those hands should be lovingly parental). What works, in James's high sense, does determine what qualifies as true. But one cannot trust the inferences of religious reason, which move from what works (what has seemed salvific) to attribute an otherworldly character to the principal Worker.

Still, James is so respectful of the idealism of Josiah Royce, so aware of its uplifting qualities, that, despite his fundamental problems with its monism, which is the antithesis of his own pluralism, he can write lines like the following: "And here again, from the very depths of the desert of skepticism, the flower of moral faith is found to bloom. Everything in Dr. Royce is radical. There is nothing to remind one of that dreary fighting of each step of a slow retreat to which the theistic philosophers of the ordinary common-sense school have accustomed us. For this reason the work must carry a true *sursum corda* into the minds of those who feel in their bones that man's religious interests must be able to swallow and digest and grow fat upon all the facts and theories of modern science, but who yet have not the capacity to see with their own eyes how it may be done. There is plenty of leveling in Dr. Royce's book, but it all ends up being a leveling-up. The Thought of which our own thought is part is Lord of all, and, to use the author's own phrase, he does not see why we should clip our own wings to keep ourselves from flying out of our own coop over our own fence into our own garden."[11]

Here one has to note that the last line establishes the difference between the idealism of Royce and traditional theism. If what is at issue is claiming our human divinity, and the garden to which we fly by spiritual ascent remains finite rather than infinite, then all of the problems about ultimate meaning and salvation remain. The idealistic option is finally no more radical than the empirical option. Neither breaks through the requirement that human experience be limited to the finite. Neither provides for a divinity not so limited, let alone for a divinity that would take humanity into the divine immortality (something unimaginable but not contradictory).

The Absence and Presence of Christ

It is remarkable how little influence Christ had on the estimable corpus of William James's writings. The leading philosopher of his day made virtually no reference to either Jesus of Nazareth or Jesus the Christ, the messiah and resurrected Son of God. William James could discourse on the will to believe, the pragmatic criteria of truth, the radical empiricism that best established the ineluctable pluralism of the universe, and even the varieties of religious experience—without confronting the founder of Christianity. Jesus did not enter into James's estimates of the build of reality or even play a significant role in James's analyses of the varieties of religious experience. Had American religious thought changed so greatly in the less than 150 years or so that separated James from Jonathan Edwards, or was James not representative of American religious thought, was he more a prophet than an exemplar?

This is an interesting question, especially if one recalls that at roughly the time that James was writing the lectures that would establish his reputation in the annals of American religious thought the Pentecostals were starting up and the fundamentalists were crystallizing their ideas. On the one hand, then, the thrust of the Enlightenment toward the disestablishment of religion in civic life and intellectual life still had momentum, so that even as tenuous a championing of religious experience as James's was eccentric to mainstream American intellectualism. On the other hand, the enthusiasm witnessed by Jonathan Edwards during the Great Awakening was raising its head again in the Christian churches, portending the evangelical movement that exploded exponentially in the second half of the twentieth century. What is one to make of this schizophrenia in early-twentieth-century American religion? How did it come about, and what does it imply, that the same culture should be both remarkably profane and remarkably concerned with evidences of the Spirit of Christ? Perhaps James's religion will give us some answers.

William James seems honestly innocent of Christology. Whatever the religious formation he received, it left no orthodox impact. No sense of the long-standing Christian conviction that Jesus Christ was both fully human and fully divine troubled James's reflections about religious experience or the ultimate construction of the world. Whereas Jonathan Edwards accepted such a proposition as foundational, and Thomas Jefferson went out of his way to deny the divinity of Christ and reedit the gospels so that they spoke only of the surely human Jesus, William James didn't feel the slightest vibrations of the problem. It is axiomatic in his writings, assumed without doubt, that dogmatic religion, as he and his contemporaries tended to call it, is the enemy or foil of healthy intellectuals. The best one could do was to show religious people the courtesy and interest by which James distinguished himself. But the fact that religious people came in so many different guises, and so frequently had little to say that illumined the worlds of science or politics, meant that at most they deserved a small corner on the map of what pragmatism considered significant.

But were the many people who continued to populate the mainstream Protestant churches, and the Catholic and Eastern Orthodox churches as well, similarly innocent of Christology—of reflection on Christ? And if they were not, how significant actually was pragmatism? In answer to the first question, one may propose that the Unitarian view of Jesus, which denied his divinity (and also denied the Trinity), did not represent the Protestant mainstream. James is not associated with Unitarianism, but its diluted form of Christianity is closer to the religious thought one finds in his writings than is traditional Christianity. In dealing with religion, then, James was not dealing with the beliefs that formed the majority of his fellow Americans who were churchgoers. They thought more highly of the Bible than he did, making it the center of their faith. With more or less clarity, they considered Jesus to be the exemplar of the virtuous life, ultimately because he had a special relationship with God. Jesus was God's "Son" in a unique, perhaps a truly divine, way. Certainly, the neoorthodoxy that grew during the 1920s and 1930s was more explicit about all of this than the liberal theology that preceded it. In the majority of Christian churches, however, a greater focus on Jesus than James found congenial or necessary distanced James from the mainstream of American religion even before the upsurge of neoorthodoxy.

Relatedly, despite his wrestling with depression, and his interest in what one might call the clinical psychology of religious experience, James did not develop anything approaching a profound doctrine of sin. The Puritans, with their almost prurient interest in the depravity of human nature, belonged to another culture, as well as another century. Thomas Jefferson was of a generation that put aside pessimism about human nature, without remaining unskeptical, and that ceased speaking much in such theological terms as sin and grace. The Enlightenment did not know what to do with such terms, laden as they were with symbols, myths, and other more-than-rational implications. The religious horror that Jonathan Edwards experienced when contemplating the foulness of human sin had passed from the cultural stage, to be replaced by a genteel recoil from bad manners or unseemly vice. William James deserves some credit for realizing that God could not be a gentleman on the Enlightenment model (though Satan could). He knew that any significant divinity had to deal with the muck of human existence, where people suffered great pain. But he did not correlate the nadir of such muck with sin and the release from it with amazing grace. He did not think that sin was a great mystery and grace (restoration, elevation to communion with God) a greater mystery still.

In fact, there is no clear sense of an incarnate mystery in the pragmatism of William James. The delineation of the final significance of the human condition in terms of its sacramentality, its being a privileged revelation of a divinity so loving that it would pitch its tent among its images, stands outside the pragmatic pale. This is more a commentary on the drift of American culture than on the movements of James's own mind, but it still bespeaks a great ignorance or disregard of classical Christian theology. No doubt the scholasticism and rationalism, to say nothing of the Hegelianism, that afflicted theology in James's day absolve him of most blame. The theologians themselves were not reading the scriptures, or the fathers, or the medievals, or even the Reformers with sharp appreciation. The theologians themselves had abandoned their birthright, as Jonathan Edwards would still have described it. Nonetheless, it is remarkable that James works so little with sin, the main category that had organized the data on human evil through the Western centuries, and it casts doubt on the degree to which his pragmatism concerned itself with history. In principle, pragmatism found history congenial, since history was the medium of change and variety, the great concommitant of pluralism and finitude. In fact, pragmatism did very little with the full sweep of the history of ideas. It knew a little about the Greeks, but then it leapt to the modern period, where the Enlightenment was the great star. Had it been more historical, pragmatism would have traced the marriage of Greek culture (Hellenism) with the Christian culture that Jesus centered, as that marriage unfolded through fifteen hundred years. Then, the significance of Christ in early American culture would have seemed normal, rather than quaint, and modernity would have been put on notice to explain its historical aberrations, which might have shown that pragmatism was both more limited and more brilliant than James and his followers appreciated.

Pragmatism and Secularism

George Santayana (1863–1952) brought a different sensibility to American culture than that of William James. Raised a Catholic, he had dropped that faith and come to consider himself a naturalist. Like William James, he opposed the idealism that tended to take people away from earthly experience. He also opposed what he called "the genteel tradition," a detachment created by Calvinism and the Enlightenment, favoring instead something more positive toward the material, embodied, sensuous existence of human beings. Curiously, this posture made Santayana more interested in the symbolism of traditional Christianity. Although he reduced such symbolism to "poetry," rather than objective truth, poetry had a high status in his view of culture, so he found traditional Christian symbolism more significant than William James had.

In an essay first published in 1900 Santayana put the matter as follows: "Let not the reader fancy that in Christianity everything was settled by records and traditions. The idea of Christ himself had to be constructed by the imagination in response to moral demands, tradition giving only the barest external points of attachment. The facts were nothing until they became symbols; and nothing could turn them into symbols except an eager imagination on the watch for all that might embody its dreams. The crucifixion, for example, would remain a tragic incident without further significance, if we regard it merely as a historical fact; to make it a religious mystery, an idea capable of converting the world, the moral imagination must transform it into something that happens for the sake of the soul, so that each believer may say to himself that Christ so suffered for the love of him. And such a thought is surely the objectification of an inner impulse; the idea of Christ becomes something spiritual, something poetical. What literal meaning could there be in saying that one man or one God died for the sake of each and every other individual? . . . The whole of Christian doctrine is thus religious and efficacious only when it becomes poetry, because only then is it the felt counterpart of personal experience, and a genuine expansion of human life."[12]

Here we find what one might call a pragmatism shaped by aesthetic, cultural, and psychological insights. Santayana is more interested in the effects of the crucifixion than in its historical foundations, and he approaches such effects in terms of symbolism. Only when the crucifixion became a symbol, standing for the pitiable human condition, did it acquire the great force that Christendom granted it. In the crucifixion traditional Christians found joined their own need and God's loving response. Santayana neglects the resurrection that fills out the symbolism of the crucified Christ, but even when we consider Christ's defeat alone, without connection to his triumph, his passion remains powerful, because it stands for all people who have had their flesh ripped or their hearts broken. Why the notion that one man's death could serve the salvation of other human beings should be meaningless on a literal level is hard to say. Santayana seems to find this judgment so obvious that he need not bother to explain it. Clearly, the apostle Paul, who made the notion of Christ's sacrifice persuasive in early Christianity, did not think the idea bereft of literal meaning. Granted, "salvation" itself is intrinsically symbolic, and perhaps Santayana is focusing on this intrinsic symbolism. But his implication that salvation could not be real, an objective factor in the domestic and political realms of culture, seems gratuitous. The people most seized by Christian salvation have been those who took the story of Christ's death and resurrection most seriously. Believing that the crucifixion had really occurred, and that it really expressed a fundamental change in the human condition, as Paul claimed, they have thought themselves made whole, justified, in virtue of this event. The event has loomed larger than the symbolism, though the event was symbolic from the beginning.

Santayana is groping after what Christian theology calls incarnationalism or sacramentality. The crucifixion has its full resonance when one admits the notion that Jesus was the divine Word enfleshed. His action then becomes the action of the infinite, the eternal, the holy, in time, for the sake of human beings, in a way that transforms history. To be sure, such an interpretation depends on a robust faith. It is reasonable only if one finds the gospels or the Christian liturgy uniquely compelling. For its sanity it depends on a delicate interlocking of faith and reason, such that when the mind works with the symbolism accepted into the heart in faith, that symbolism becomes sacramental: capable of revealing the presence of God and the true range of human possibilities. Without such faith, the crucifixion must remain either merely a sad fact or a cultural artifact deriving all of its significance from what human beings have projected into it. Without such reason, the crucifixion, like Christ himself, must remain something one embraces blindly, credulously, superstitiously, out of a need one cannot articulate or control.

The pragmatic approach to reality, as exemplified in such religious matters as the status of Christ and the significance of the crucifixion, suffers from its dependence upon the good will of its practitioners. Though he found no reason to grapple with the central symbols of Christian tradition (which, of course, lay at the foundations of his country's culture), William James would have been willing to entertain the proposition that the death and resurrection of Christ were of immense psychological significance. James's general openness justifies such a likelihood. Similarly, despite his atheism, George Santayana was willing to consider the cultural implications of the crucifixion and sharpen his appreciation of its great poetic impact. Santayana should not be considered a pragmatist, but he shared with James a conviction that the most important aspects of a matter were its effects upon the human makeup, the differences it made in physical or cultural life. But, like James, he could only admit the natural or secular side of religious claims. The properly theological side eluded him, so much so that he seldom considered the precisely divine dimension that made the life of Christ, his death, and his resurrection axial for traditional Christian cultures.

By the turn of the twentieth century, when James and Santayana were contributing mightily to the transformation of American culture, the intellectuals had become secular. Neither their science nor their art felt the need to transcend a this-worldly horizon of human existence. The openness that one rightly praises was limited. James and Santayana were open, sensitive, compared to their more dogmatically secular contemporaries, but there were great limits to the range of reality that they accredited. Certainly, James listened to accounts of mysticism and the occult, but they could be fitted into a radically pluralistic universe. Santayana had little interest in such matters. Neither thinker, though, found much to preserve in the premodern Western culture that had sought to make daily life a participation in divinity. For secular Americans, daily life obviously had little to do with divinity. The crucifix had been reduced to something one might find in churches or on the walls of religious schools and hospitals. No echo of what it had meant to the Byzantine iconographers or the craftsmen of

Chartes remained. The world had lost the presence of God. Incarnational-ism no longer carried. No perception of the present or study of the past brought the presence of divinity through the incarnation or passion of Christ within the purview of a James or Santayana. The pragmatism that could winningly focus on actual experiences and effects turned up nothing definitive when it came to such Christian claims as salvation from meaning-lessness or hell, grace for joy and heaven. Was that because such Christian claims had ceased to form Americans' lives, or because James and San-tayana lived within a "higher" secular culture at odds with a "lower" culture that remained religious?

Pragmatic Truth

Jamesian pragmatism not only captured the practical temper of the American spirit that was building a great nation, it also anticipated the holism characteristic of such later philosophical movements as phenomenology and existentialism. So, had James been more persuaded by the holistic Christian experiences and symbols that had continued in the evangelical strands of American culture, he might have made a strong contribution to their revivification and helped defend them against abuse. And then the destructive aspects of the growing American secularism, its contributions to the breakdown of consensus about the higher purposes of human existence, might have been blunted. But James found little worth championing in these evangelical strata, so his pragmatism became another voice in the general chorus of individualism, whose chant was to let each person find his or her own truth and morality.

Concerning James's holistic sense of the relations among facts, mean-ing, and action, John Wild has written: "For most people, pragmatism means that we can believe in the truth of a theory if our believing in it turns out to be satisfactory to us. This 'subjectivism' was often brought up against the theory in James' lifetime. But as he often pointed out, it rests on a misunderstanding. No belief can be justified, or verified, by merely believing in it and feeling 'satisfied.' The real test lies in working with the idea, acting on its basis, and this includes acts of understanding as well as overt dealings with the real being involved. This being must turn out to be as the theory indicates, and enable us to establish working relations with it. In so far as we achieve this, we will feel not a mere subjective satisfaction, but a real satisfaction *in* this specific fulfillment of existence. . . . [James] consistently rejected a faculty psychology, and did not believe in an isolated faculty of will. He does speak of the active phase of human life, and distinguishes it from the other two 'departments,' concerned with the recognition of fact and the elaboration of meaning. He speaks of it as the 'final' phase . . . for without it, the other two remain incomplete. We cannot act in a human way unless we make a meaningful effort in a factual situation. So James refers to it as the last phase of the mental cycle."[13]

Here is a restatement of the stress on consequences that we encountered when we dealt with James's views on the will to believe. Reality is not entirely subjective. What happens when we act upon a belief will depend on our interactions with beings other than ourselves. So what "satisfaction" an idea provides us is a function of how we have found it to work out in practice, and that working out in practice engages us with the non-ego: nature, other people, perhaps spiritual forces that are not reducible to human wishes or projections.

This still leaves much room for individual differences, however, as one discovers when contemplating the diverse experiences people report when they try to act upon certain supposed truths. Two people testing the same idea of democratic freedoms may come to quite different conclusions about the truth or wisdom of freedom of religious expression. Similarly, two people testing the idea of an incarnational presence of God in the midst of a religious assembly may come away with quite different conclusions. There remains something ineluctably personal in our positions about truths of faith, whether such faith be religious, political, or economic. James was trying to honor this personal quality, and so honor the pluralism of the human dimension of the universe. How significant is it that he never found a way to secure this pluralism against chaos, never found a way to assure it ultimate significance?

No doubt answers to this question will vary as greatly as readers' estimates of the assets and liabilities of American individualism. Determining what might counterbalance the centrifugal character of modern Western culture, American and otherwise, without imposing tyranny, remains our greatest political challenge. We may place William James alongside Sören Kierkegaard and other modern thinkers who sought relief from the tyranny of a philosophical idealism such as Hegel's. In the gropings of such thinkers for a truth that would make sense of their experience and enable them to engage the world satisfyingly, one finds a return to the personal, the existential, what ought to have been the area most amenable to vital religious thought.

James found a kinship between the pragmatic philosopher and the literary person, inasmuch as the truth that both struggled to express was

personal and tentative: "[Philosophers] must more and more ally themselves with a literature that is confessedly tentative and suggestive rather
than dogmatic—I mean with novels and dramas of the deeper sort, with
sermons, with books on statecraft and philanthropy, and social and economic reform."[14]

The bugaboo with religion, then, is its dogmatic component. When it
gropes and stays fully personal, confessing the obscurities of its venture,
a religion may be quite congenial to pragmatism. Many people in the
American churches and synagogues have sympathized with this view. To
their mind dogma has meant sterility, a kind of intellectual authoritarianism. Even many evangelicals have frequently been more interested in the
stories of Christ than in the edicts of church councils. Certainly, most
fundamentalists have been dogmatic about such teachings as the Virgin
Birth and the inerrancy of scripture. Certainly, one can speak of a moral
dogmatism that has desired an unwavering position on matters such as
pornography and abortion. But much of the American religious population
has followed the pragmatists in stressing acting, doing, and feeling more
than contemplation, detached scholarship, or doctrinal orthodoxy. The
question is whether one can have the whole loaf of religion without rooting
both action and contemplation in a truly transcendent deity.

Such a truly transcendent deity would have considerable independence
of human need and experience. Writing an appreciative study of William
James's philosophy of religion, Eugene Fontinell is still forced to point out
the limits of his master's views: "Though James in his later writings refines
his view of the human mind, he continues to the end to speak of God only
in terms of human needs. In *The Varieties of Religious Experience*, he states:
'The gods we stand by are the gods we need and can use, the gods whose
demands on us are reinforcements of our demands on ourselves and on one
another'. . . . Further, as we change, so will our conceptions of God, for
'when we cease to admire or approve what the definition of a deity implies,
we end by deeming that deity incredible'. . . . Religious experiences must
ultimately be judged on the basis of 'that element or quality in them which
we can meet nowhere else'. . . . If the universal message of religion were
to be expressed in a single phrase it would be: 'All is *not* vanity in this
Universe, whatever the appearances may suggest. . . .'"[15]

The question, for recent American culture as well as William James,
is how to coordinate the two apparent truths implied in these two quotations. On the one hand, there is the undeniable human component, the
psychological aspect of religion, which assures that as we change our sense
of God will change, and that our needs will color our theology. On the

other hand, to secure the proposition that all is not vanity in the universe, the divinity we meet has to be more than psychological, more than just a projection of our needs and satisfactions. Obviously, some higher viewpoint or lovely balance is required, such that divinity can be the beginning and the beyond, but also the enabler of all our growth in between. Rejecting the dogmatic religion of his time, William James asked implicitly for a God who would be the friend of human freedom and creativity, not the enemy. The American churches and synagogues have yet to meet that formidable request, in large part because their own pragmatism has blinded them to the unique character of the priority that a real God would have to have in all matters. Such a priority would have to be in love and being, even more than in knowledge and power, and fully appreciating it would require Americans to become theistic mystics, personally aware of how the divine mystery can be both far and near, both the only reality finally significant and the creator of an eternal meaningfulness for human beings.

NOTES

1. See Henry Samuel Levinson, "Religious Philosophy," in *Encyclopedia of the American Religious Experience*, ed. Charles H. Lippy and Peter W. Williams (New York: Scribner's, 1988), vol. 2, pp. 1189–1206.

2. William James, "The Will to Believe," in *William James: The Essential Writings*, ed. Bruce W. Wilshire (Albany: State University of New York Press, 1984), p. 324.

3. Gerald E. Myers, *William James: His Life and Thought* (New Haven: Yale University Press, 1986), p. 299.

4. William James, "The Will to Believe," in *William James: The Essential Writings*, p. 325.

5. William James, *The Varieties of Religious Experience*, in *William James: Writings 1902–1910*, ed. Bruce Kuklick (New York: The Library of America, 1987), p. 70.

6. Daniel W. Bjork, *William James: The Center of His Vision* (New York: Columbia University Press, 1988), p. 241.

7. William James, "Pragmatism," in *Documents in the History of American Philosophy*, ed. Morton White (New York: Oxford University Press, 1972), p. 363.

8. William James, "A Pluralistic Universe," in *William James: Writings 1902–1910*, p. 771.

9. William James, "The Experience of Activity," in *William James: The Essential Writings*, p. 218.

10. Henry S. Levinson, *Science, Metaphysics, and the Chance of Salvation: An Interpretation of the Thought of William James* (Missoula, MT: Scholars Press, 1978), pp. 160–161.

11. William James, "Review of *The Religious Aspect of Philosophy*, by Josiah Royce (1885)," in *The Works of William James: Essays, Comments, and Reviews* (Cambridge, MA: Harvard University Press, 1987), p. 388.

12. George Santayana, "The Poetry of Christian Dogma," in *Documents in the History of American Philosophy*, pp. 429–431.

13. John Wild, *The Radical Empiricism of William James* (Westport, CT: Greenwood Press, 1969), pp. 350–351.

14. Ibid., p. 353, quoting James's essay "The Moral Philosopher and the Moral Life."

15. Eugene Fontinell, *Self, God, and Immortality: A Jamesian Investigation* (Philadelphia: Temple University Press, 1986), pp. 138–139.

Chapter 7

American Pragmatism: Responses from the Margins

American Jews

The centrality of ethics in traditional Judaism makes it possible to speak of a Jewish pragmatism. What Jews did was more important than what Jews thought, though thought certainly was significant. The revelation to Moses on Mount Sinai was understood to be the linchpin of Jewish faith, and that revelation produced a *Torah*, a Guidance or Law. Just as Jews would only discover God's identity by sojourning with God, so they would only appreciate the rich measure of their beliefs by living them out. Like traditional Christians, traditional Jews sensed that one must believe in order to understand. In addition, they realized that "understanding" God is always tenuous. The hidden God always remains. If God is truly the Master of the Universe, the Creator of heaven and earth, human beings will never understand God fully. The response that God gave to Job out of the whirlwind stood down the centuries as a caution against wanting to understand overmuch: "Who is this that darkens counsel by words without knowledge? Gird up your loins like a man, I will question you, and you shall declare to me. Where were you when I laid the foundations of the earth? Tell me, if you have understanding. Who determined its measurements—surely you know! Or who stretched the line upon it? On what were its bases sunk, or who laid its cornerstone, when the morning stars sang together, and all the sons of God shouted for joy" (38:1–7).

188

Nonetheless, European Jews were considerably influenced by the Enlightenment, in part because it held out the hope that they might be emancipated from political discrimination and allowed into the mainstream of cultural life. In actual experience, however, emancipation and modernity proved to be more destructive than those who had first found them so hopeful could have anticipated. As Eugene Borowitz has summarized its effects, "Modernity made religion a private affair and defined religious groups in terms derived from Christianity—that is, as communities united by common faith and ritual practices. Nationality was disassociated from religion and subordinated to the nation-state, an arrangement that can still cause social unrest in multinational countries. On both counts, Judaism could not maintain itself as a religio-ethnic unity (the hybrid designation modernity has forced upon students of Judaism). As a result, an unprecedented dichotomy came into Jewish life: one group of Jews defined their Judaism as 'religious,' while another group defined theirs in secular terms, as an ethnicity."[1]

As a modern country, the American republic subordinated both religion and ethnicity to secular citizenship. In law, if not always in cultural reality, one's Judaism, either ethnic or religious, was secondary to one's citizenship. By the time that American pragmatism had appeared, generated by the intellectuals' dissatisfaction with both traditional theology and idealistic philosophy, as well as by their fascination with empirical science, American Jews had become a diverse community. The Reformed Jews, who tended to have immigrated from German-speaking countries, were liberal and had begun a thorough rethinking of traditional Jewish faith, generally making it less concerned with doctrines and more oriented toward morality. This was a natural extension of the traditional concern to hallow everyday life by following the precepts of the Torah, but for the Reformed, Torah no longer retained its traditional status as the direct expression of the divine will. Hoping to make a contribution to the democratic American culture, which could seem a competitive marketplace for religious ideas, many Reformed Jews stressed the elevated ethical outlook developed in rabbinical Judaism: a high sense of justice, honesty, and self-restraint.

The more conservative members of the American Jewish community, who tended to have immigrated later than the German-speakers and to hail from Yiddish-speaking Eastern Europe, wanted to keep the laws of the Torah. In their view, modernity was more a plague than a blessing, and they wished that the old life they had created in Eastern Europe, where the Talmud was the basic text and the rabbi was the center of the community, because he was the master of talmudic wisdom, could be transplanted to the United States. So, more than the Reformed, they faced the question of how to live in America without becoming schizophrenic. Most of them appreciated the freedoms of their new land, including above all the right to practice their faith unharassed, and most were grateful for the prosperity that hard work could bring. But they feared that their children and grandchildren would lose their Jewishness, being swept away by the Christianity or secularism of the common culture.

When it came to developing a modern philosophy of Judaism, American Jewish intellectuals were caught between the past and the present: "Judaism makes its claims upon the Jew in the name of God and the Jewish people's corporate existence—but modernity radically individualizes authority. A modern philosophy of Judaism must mediate between autonomy and tradition and do justice to each of them."[2]

Inasmuch as American Jews wished to retain their traditional senses of God and corporate existence, they had to oppose the tides of such philosophies as pragmatism. William James might have been open to the notions of divinity and selfhood that American Jews derived from their experiences at home, in the synagogue, and in the workplace, but the drift of his thought, like the drift of the secular culture at large (which he represented as well as chastened), was toward a radical pluralism that left such things as God and corporate existence problematic. The defining characteristic of the traditional Jewish call to faith had been, "Hear, O Israel, the Lord our God is one Lord" (Deuteronomy 6:4). How could one be a Jew in a land of many gods? How could one preserve the peoplehood of the Jews in a land where one's first designation, more implicit than explicit, had to be "American"?

Despite these problems, American Jews adapted well to their new land, in some cases prospering to the point that other Jews criticized the American Jewish community as having lost its soul to material success. Many commentators point out the shift in the role of the rabbi, the key religious figure, that the democratization of synagogue life created. Whereas in Europe the rabbi had been the master of sacred learning, the teacher and judge elaborating the implications of the Torah on the basis of traditional interpretations, in the United States he became a many-sided figure, modeled on the Protestant minister. He led services, was expected to preach sermons, offered religious counseling, could be responsible for overseeing a sizable physical plant (though usually lay boards controlled finances), and represented the Jewish community in public affairs, often through a genteel ecumenical friendship with Christian clergy. No longer was learning the main requisite for the rabbinate. Pastoral care had replaced scholarship, though many American rabbis still yearned to study and teach. The pragmatic thing, though, had been to adapt to the American scene and create the Jewish equivalent of a Christian religious community.

The creation of the modern state of Israel in 1948, and the gradual penetration of the implications of the *Shoah*, the Nazi destruction of six million Jews, shifted American Judaism onto new tracks. Some measure of Zionism came to shape most Jewish communities, at least pressuring them to offer Israel financial support. And a new depth entered into Jewish religious thought, as the evils of the *Shoah* demanded acknowledgment. This latter shift dimmed the success of the American Jewish movement called Reconstructionism (a native response to the question of how to adapt Judaism to the modern world, as the United States exemplified it). Reconstructionism, the creation of Mordecai M. Kaplan (1881–1983), wanted a reworking of Jewish thought and culture in the light of scientific advances and the democratic character of American culture. God became the power that gives people fulfillment (a rather Jamesian notion), and Jews were invited to become patrons of the arts and other important areas of American culture. But reflection on the Holocaust could make all of this seem superficial, so the current generation of young Jews has tended to give traditional observances and ideas a kinder hearing than Reconstructionism. As Borowitz has put it: "Experience made substituting Auschwitz for Sinai unacceptable to most Jews. Despite the mass depravity that continues to plague the twentieth century, the revelation of God's absence and of humanity's depravity in the Holocaust does not constitute the norm of human or Jewish existence. Sanctifying the routine without forgetting the extraordinary remains the Jew's fundamental obligation. The primary response to the Holocaust, Jews agree, must be an intensification of human responsibility."[3]

Roman Catholics

Catholics in the United States struggled with many of the same issues as Jews. How could they manage a twofold fidelity: to their own traditions, and to the ideals of their new homeland? Predictably, the Catholic community divided into two camps. The majority realized that accommodation to the American scene was a simple fact of life. The first rule was to survive, and survival demanded accommodation. A significant minority thought that American Catholics ought to keep as many of their old ways, and as much of their old doctrinal theology, as they could. Almost cruelly, Catholics could not win, no matter which option, progressive or conservative, they favored. If they did not accommodate to the American scene, they risked being branded by Protestants as un-American. If they did accommodate, they risked being branded by Roman authorities as unfaithful. So the Catholic hierarchy walked a narrow line, trying to work out a pastoral practice and a public profile that would balance its two loyalties.

The hierarchy itself was divided, but perhaps the more viable option was developed by the progressives, represented by John Ireland (1839–1918), Archbishop of St. Paul. Ireland was gladdened by the work of such accommodationists as Isaac Hecker (1819–1888), the founder of the Paulists, perhaps the most distinctively American group of clergy. In his preface to a biography of Hecker, Ireland argued that Hecker had rightly discerned the harmony between Catholic faith and American political philosophy: "Father Hecker understood and loved the country and its institutions. He saw nothing in them to be deprecated or changed; he had no longing for the fleshpots and bread-stuffs of empires and monarchies. His favorite topic in book and lecture was, that the Constitution of the United States requires, as its necessary basis, the truths of Catholic teaching regarding man's natural state, as opposed to the errors of Luther and Calvin. The republic, he taught, presupposes the Church's doctrine, and the Church ought to love a polity which is the offspring of her own spirit. . . . He laid stress on the natural and social virtues. The American people hold these in highest esteem. They are the virtues that are most apparent, and are seemingly the most needed for the building up and the preservation of an earthly commonwealth. . . . It will be a difficult task to persuade the American that a church which will not enforce those primary virtues can enforce others which she herself declares to be higher and more arduous, and as he has implicit confidence in the destiny of his country to produce a high order of social existence, his first test of a religion will be its powers in this direction. This is according to Catholic teaching. Christ came not to destroy, but to perfect what was in man, and the graces and truths of revelation lead most securely to the elevation of the life that is, no less than to the gaining of the life to come."[4]

Ireland and Hecker assumed that Catholics had a different view of human nature than Protestants. They thought that Catholic theology, not persuaded that original sin made human beings depraved and inclined to harmonize the natural and the supernatural, reason and faith, fit well with the assumptions of the American Constitution (despite the derivation of the latter from the Enlightenment). The natural virtues (narrowly: prudence, justice, fortitude, and temperance; broadly: any goodness not explicitly religious—honesty in business, fidelity in marriage, loyalty in friendship, and so forth) had a respected place in Catholic theology, due in large part to the high regard that Catholic scholasticism had for Aristotle. So Hecker, Ireland, and others enamored of the American venture in democracy and disestablishment considered the American scene congenial to Catholic instincts.

Ireland wrote his preface in 1891. In 1899 Pope Leo XIII wrote an encyclical letter (one to the whole Church) on "Americanism," pointing out errors that he feared might mislead American Catholics. Clearly, Leo had been listening to the conservative wing of the American Catholic church, and what he had heard jarred his Roman sensibilities, honed as they were by centuries of ruling Catholicism monarchically and stressing the primacy of the supernatural virtues (faith, hope, and charity), along with accepting the teachings of magisterium, past and present, including the instructions of the popes. It is interesting that, after insisting that much in Catholicism is immutable (cannot be changed to suit new cultural situations), Leo focuses on the matter of virtue: ". . . it is especially in the cultivation of virtue that the assistance of the Holy Spirit is indispensable; but those who affect these novelties [American aberrations] extol beyond measure the natural virtues as more in accordance with the ways and requirements of the present day, and consider it an advantage to be richly endowed with them, because they make a man more ready and more strenuous in action. It is hard to understand how those who are imbued with Christian principles can place the natural ahead of the supernatural virtues, and attribute to them greater power and fecundity. Is nature, then, with grace added to it, weaker than when left to its own strength?"[5]

Most commentators think that Leo was tilting at a straw man. No American thinker of note deprecated the supernatural virtues or made action the enemy of prayer and deep faith. But Americans had gained the reputation of being people of action (natural pragmatists), and a European pope was anxious to offer cautions. To be sure, from a traditional Catholic perspective, which Ireland and Hecker fully shared, the great treasures in life were the gifts of grace that came from the Spirit of Christ. Salvation and divine life ranked higher by far than anything human beings could attain on their own. If an American philosophy, such as pragmatism, rejected the primacy of Christ and his grace, it had to be pushed aside as not harmonious with Christian truth. William James could find no full endorsement among orthodox Catholics, any more than he could among orthodox Protestants (or orthodox Jews, whose Lord demanded a similar primacy).

On the other hand, the outlook and manner of the Roman authorities were bound to grate on the sensibilities of American Catholics, who had become schooled to democracy and pluralism. In this context, the openness of a William James, his catholicity, struck a winning contrast. American pragmatism might suffer the ultimately fatal flaw of not estimating correctly the objective primacy of the One God and his Christ, but it was lyrical about the virtues necessary for public life. As well, it articulated much of the existential criterion for truth that an active people such as the Americans required, if they were to build their land. They had to look to themselves—in frontier situations, in a pluralistic religious culture, in the face of scientific advances that their churches were slow to assimilate. Compared to the authoritarian, distant, hierarchical ways of Roman authorities, the pragmatic advice to "test the spirits" and do what seemed best on the spot was very winning. So American Catholics might develop considerable sympathy for the style or tone of pragmatism, even while their better analysts realized that pragmatism had serious flaws in its religious foundations.

Women

In asking how American women tended to respond to the pragmatic views bruited about during the first decades of the twentieth century, we come upon another suggestion that pragmatism was vulnerable to subjectivism. American women had been schooled by their religion to exemplify and advance the domestic virtues. As they began to appreciate the connection between such tasks as raising children, nursing the sick, and ameliorating the condition of poor people, and the mentality that government and business brought to their estimate of society's needs, leading American women realized that one could not rely on the good will or enlightened self-interest of those holding economic or political power. Until women had the vote, education was available to all citizens, and America's social problems gained a prominent place on the nation's agenda, the pragmatic mindset could easily become a defense of vested interests. Men, the upper classes, and the healthy could interpret the lower pragmatic criterion of "what works," and even James's higher criterion of what is rooted in experience and has desirable consequences, so as to exclude radical change.

Unless one could appeal to an objective moral order, determined by the basic equality among all human beings and tending to grant all human beings rights more precise in their economic and social entailments than what was listed in the Bill of Rights, American pragmatism might become a tool of repression.

This did not mean that American feminists were not pragmatic when it came to arguing that the emancipation of women would benefit the nation as a whole. For example, Susan B. Anthony argued in 1897 that granting women the vote would serve the interests of the entire human race: "Until woman has obtained 'that right protective of all other rights—the ballot,' this agitation [the women's suffrage movement] must still go on, absorbing the time and energy of our best and strongest women. Who can measure the advantages that would result if the magnificent abilities of these women could be devoted to the needs of government, society, home, instead of being consumed in the struggle to obtain their birthright of individual freedom? Until this be gained we can never know, we cannot even prophesy, the capacity and power of woman for the uplifting of humanity. It may be delayed longer than we think, it may be here sooner than we expect; but the day will come when man will recognize woman as his peer, not only at the fireside but in the councils of the nation. Then, and not until then, will there be the perfect comradeship, the ideal union between the sexes that shall result in the highest development of the race."[6]

Jane Addams, a pioneer explorer of the changed social consciousness that would be necessary if America were to rectify in any satisfactory way the deleterious effects of industrialization (the poverty of the industrial workers, the blighted housing in which their families lived, the alcoholism and health problems in the growing city slums), came to question the philanthropy that industrial wealth was making possible. In her view, this easily became paternalistic. If it did not feed the vanity of the people making the benefactions, it retarded the maturation of those receiving them. It also retarded the day when social consciousness would have evolved to a truly democratic state, one in which social improvements were not done *for* those needing help but *with* them. The only way to gain this improved state of affairs concerned legislation to correct the abuses introduced by industrialization: "A large body of people feel keenly that the present industrial system is in a state of profound disorder and that there is no guarantee that the pursuit of individual ethics will ever right it. They claim that relief can only come through deliberate corporate effort inspired by social ideas and guided by the study of economic laws, and that the present industrial system thwarts our ethical demands, not only for social righteousness but for social order. Because they believe that each advance in ethics must be made fast by a corresponding advance in politics and legal enactment, they insist upon the right of state regulation and control."[7]

If Susan B. Anthony was a critic of the pragmatic judgment that keeping women without the vote benefited the nation, and an advocate of the pragmatic judgment that enfranchising women would help the nation greatly, Jane Addams was a critic of the pragmatic judgment that working conditions, pay scales, housing conditions, and the other aspects of American industrialization could be left to the ethical sensitivities of the individual industrial owners. Addams was a socialist, in inclination if not full theory. Her work in the settlement houses convinced her that the individualism congenial to pragmatism, and the pragmatism congenial to individualism, had serious drawbacks. The benevolence of the individual factory owner was too fragile a repository in which to place the well-being of the factory workers. Though one could make a pragmatic argument that proper legislation would improve the lot of many American workers and soon benefit the country at large, pragmatism itself offered little basis for discriminating between that argument and the counterargument of individual owners that laissez-faire was the part of wisdom, the policy most likely to produce prosperity.

At some point one had to appeal beyond pluralistic experience and diverse consequences to an objective moral order, a transpersonal hierarchy of rights and duties, according to which one could measure the wants of the few wealthy people against the needs of the many poor people. An older social philosophy, such as the natural law theory mainly espoused by Catholics, articulated such an objective moral order and allowed one to judge between the wants of the few and the needs of the many. So did a biblically based social ethics that considered all human beings equally distant from God, because of their creaturehood and sinfulness, as well as equally beloved by God, because of God's own goodness and desire for people's salvation. Utilizing neither of these arguably more objective moral philosophies, pragmatism seemed subjective and easily abused. The sophisticated philosophy of James and others took some of these objections into account, but the perception by the culture at large that pragmatism articulated the American genius for judging things by their practical effects did not. This was especially ironic when one found de facto pragmatists who showed up in church each Sunday and nodded sagely at sermons about the golden rule, or even the Good Samaritan. Many Americans did not see the contradiction between pragmatism and the biblical religion they were professing. Many had little appreciation of the prophetic dimension of either the Old or the New Testament. In such cases, pragmatism had become stronger than the quite different ethos expounded by Amos and Jesus. Sometimes American women, sensitized by their own marginal status, saw these contradictions most sharply.

Mary Antin, herself an immigrant from Russia, spoke eloquently for the rights of immigrants to free education, and the proposition that such education would benefit the nation as a whole. As well, she was so bold as to contrast the progress of poor immigrants with the regress of poor Yankees, for the sake of arguing that immigration should be widened, not restricted: "Any sociologist, any settlement worker, any census clerk will tell you that the history of the average immigrant family of the 'new' period is represented by an ascending curve. The descending curves are furnished by degenerate families of what was once prime American stock. I want no better proof of these facts than I find in the respective vocabularies of the missionary in the slums of New York and the missionary in the New England hills. At the settlement on Eldridge Street they talk about hastening the process of Americanization of the immigrant; the country minister in the Berkshires talks about the rehabilitation of the Yankee farmer. That is, the one assists at an upward process, the other seeks to reverse a downward process. Right here, in these opposite tendencies of the poor of the foreign quarters and the poor of the Yankee fastnesses, I read the most convincing proof that what we get in steerage is not the refuse but the sinew and bone of all the nations."[8] So, Antin's pragmatic argument for widening immigration was that it would bring to the United States new vigor and talent. Behind this argument, however, lay the compassion for the suffering, the disenfranchised, that sparked the arguments of Anthony and Addams. Even when they were quite pragmatic, the American women who spearheaded social reform at the turn of the twentieth century brought to bear the "domestic" sensibility of mothers concerned instinctively for the most vulnerable of their children.

African Americans

As we have noted, African Americans were greatly concerned with justice. In their political lives (such as they could be) they sought the redress of laws and customs that kept them in slavery. In their religious lives, they sought intimations that the justice of God would punish those who had abused them and reward their long suffering. This religious orientation, usually nourished by reflection on the biblical stories of the exodus of the Hebrews from Egypt and the sufferings of Christ, made the philosophy of pragmatism alien to their instincts. Certainly, they were seeking a religion, a mythology and symbolic system, that had the practical effect of helping them survive. But their intention in their religious endeavors, the outreach that they attempted, was toward the objective reality of God. A God conceived principally as the fulfiller of human needs, and so as the expression of human needs, was not sufficient. The God depicted in the Bible as the Creator of heaven and earth, the Master of the Universe, the Father of Jesus Christ—that God, established by Scripture as the main reality in the world, could do the job. The divinity that William James found in the variety of people's religious experience was too subjective.

Though many African Americans labored for the liberation of their people, both prior to the Civil War and afterwards, it was only in the second half of the twentieth century, with the civil rights movement, that such labor came to great fruition. The leadership of Martin Luther King, Jr., had much to do with the success of the civil rights movement, and the vision that King laid out was not pragmatic. To be sure, King and the other leaders learned about raising money and counting votes. They were interested in real change, that would alter the going legal, economic, educational, and medical systems, and other key social structures. But they did not argue that their cause was right and true because it would have good effects. They argued that their cause was right and true because it was simply just. No people ought to be enslaved, discriminated against, condemned to poverty, illiteracy, and social abuse. In a country that prided itself on the Bill of Rights, the Declaration of Independence, its openness to the suffering masses of other nations crying to be free, segregation, discrimination, racism, and the other negative aspects of the condition of African Americans were scandalous. They suggested that America's vaunted idealism was a sham, a hypocrisy, something so fragile that the color of a person's skin could determine whether it held up or not.

In his famous letter from a Birmingham jail of 1963, Martin Luther King, Jr., put the burden of removing this hypocrisy on moderate whites, those who claimed to agree with the aims of African-American civil rights workers but protested their methods: "I must make two honest confessions to you, my Christian and Jewish brothers. First, I must confess that over the past few years I have been gravely disappointed with the white moderate. I have almost reached the regrettable conclusion that the Negro's great stumbling block in his stride toward freedom is not the White Citizen's Counciler or the Ku Klux Klanner but the white moderate who is more devoted to 'order' than to justice; who prefers a negative peace which is the absence of tension to a positive peace which is the presence of justice; who constantly says, 'I agree with you in the goal you seek, but I cannot agree with your methods'; who paternalistically believes he can set the timetable for another man's freedom; who lives by a mythical concept of time and who constantly advises the Negro to wait for a 'more convenient season.' Shallow misunderstanding from people of goodwill is more frustrating than absolute misunderstanding from people of ill will. Lukewarm acceptance is much more bewildering than outright rejection. I had hoped that the white moderate would understand that law and order exist for the purpose of establishing justice and that when they fail in this purpose they block social progress. . . . We who engage in nonviolent direct action are not the creators of tension. We merely bring to the surface the hidden tension that is already alive. We bring it out into the open where it can be seen and dealt with. Like a boil that can never be cured so long as it is covered up but must be opened with all its pus-flowing ugliness to the natural medicines of air and light, injustice must be exposed, with all the tension its exposure creates, to the light of human conscience and the air of national opinion before it can be cured."[9]

This is the philosophy of nonviolence that King had learned from Mahatma Gandhi. The purpose of nonviolent demonstrations was to reveal the disorders, the injustices, of a social situation, so that, once revealed, they might be corrected. King was not interested in opposing violence with violence, because that would only perpetuate the cycle of injustice. No doubt, he realized that in most situations his group had little military power, little ability to compel change by physical means. But his nonviolent tactics were not simply pragmatic. He realized that the social change the civil rights movement sought could only occur when the light shone and people became ashamed of living in the darkness. The light consisted in the imperatives of justice: what was simply fair and right. The darkness was the fears, the guilts, the enjoyment of illicit powers that created prejudice, bigotry, racism, refusal to let other Americans have a fair share of the American dream.

Could one justify this claim on the light, this protest against the darkness, on pragmatic grounds? Yes and no. Yes, it might prove more effective than simply political or legal maneuvering, let along physical violence. Yes, it might give the civil rights movement the sense of inevitability on which most ultimately successful social change depends. No, it was not obvious that provoking the reactions of the bigoted, revealing the tensions caused by great untruths, was the best way to win the battle against segregation and second-class citizenship. No, the appeal of Martin Luther King, Jr., went beyond the certainties one could find in either empirical experience or a purely reasonable estimate of consequences.

The appeal of Martin Luther King, Jr., was to justice, a quality of the human mind and heart that might require people to work against their own superficial or temporary interests. The grounding of King's work was his faith in a God who guaranteed justice, and who promised, as well, that people could be turned around, converted, empowered to make a new start, forgive one another, enter into a new, free state of affairs called "the Kingdom of God." When it came to the crunch, no calculus of likely consequences was sufficient to sustain King. Sensing that his life might soon end, a sacrifice to hatred, he had to find deeper reasons for hope. These became the figure of Christ, who had gone before him in suffering for the sake of righteousness, justice, the love of other human beings that the love of God made obligatory. A student of King might realize that William James was right: people do depend on unseen powers when they are called to accomplish great deeds. But William James was also wrong, the same student might claim, in thinking that one could be individualistic, pluralistic, pragmatic about these powers, when the call came to sacrifice one's very life. At that moment, the support one sought was the grace of a persuasive divinity like Jesus: an embodiment of God who stood, once and for all, as proof that love is stronger than death, heaven more real than earth, eternal justice more important than any temporal profit or benefit.

Native Americans

As they tried to make sense of their experience with whites, Native Americans of recent generations sometimes turned an excellent education in Western thinking back upon those who had subjected them. Thus Vine Deloria, surveying the implications of the cultural encounter between Native Americans and whites, found that white individualism had led to considerable provincialism, while more holistic Native-American views of the world might hold the key to new advances. One can question Deloria's emphasis in narrating the history of Western thought, but his analysis of Native-American views is striking: "Instead of isolating things, Indians encompassed them; togetherness, synthesis, and relatedness characterized their experiences of the universe. The ordinary distinctions between mind and matter, human and other life forms, nature and human beings, and even our species and the divinity were not considered valid ways of under-standing experience. Life was a complex matrix of entities, emotions, revelations, and cooperative enterprises and any abstraction was considered stupid and dangerous, destructive of spirit and reductionist in the very aspects that made life important. A great many non-Indians have intuited this 'togetherness' from observing Indians and reading of the 'Indian way,' but have failed to understand the remarkable system of relationships which undergirds a seemingly innocent and simple life."[10]

Here we have a sketch of a way of knowing that Jamesian pragmatism, and, even more, Whiteheadian process thought, would find quite congenial. The reason is its rootedness in experience. Whether it accounts adequately for the gains, intellectual as well as practical, that have come from the West's isolating individual phenomena for study and being willing to abstract from particulars to make generalizations, is a valid question. Without the Western philosophical outlook there would be no higher mathematics, no nuclear physics or astronomy. On the other hand, Native-American intuitions about relatedness, togetherness, seem to prefigure much that has been discovered by modern ecological studies. Inasmuch as the different elements of nature constantly interact, it is artificial to isolate them from one another, and one only gets a true picture of their natural reality when one finds ways of honoring their interdependence.

The intriguing question is how this ecological outlook shades the issue of human nature: humanity's place in reality. Native Americans did not live in an anthropocentric world. Was that because they had not developed the technology to dominate nature, or was it because they had a profound instinct that the other kinds of creatures with whom they shared the world would always be their equals in the mystery of existence? One aspect of the religious background to the Western development of anthropocentrism was the biblical teaching that human beings are the images of divinity, something closer to the form of the Creator than what rocks and plants, fishes and cattle enjoy. As it came to locate the special dignity of human beings in their reason, Western culture took the Greek discovery of the range of reason as a stimulus to speculation. When that speculation, that ability to infer possibilities, became joined with close empirical observation, the dynamo of modern science emerged. In modern science, speculation and empirical observation married to produce a highly reasoned investigation of the natural world.

Scientific research is not in itself pragmatic. It does not seek results that would benefit human beings, except insofar as discovering more about reality is always a prime benefit, an experience uniquely fulfilling. But the world that scientific research has discovered is amazingly complicated—varied even beyond the pluralism championed by William James. Technol-

ogy is the stepchild of modern science, but technology quickly became at
least as influential. The general public has been more interested in the
machinery and new products that technology could derive from scientific
advances than in the elegances of pure research.

Native Americans apparently never isolated reason, or canonized
human creations, to develop a science or technology on the modern Western models. Their goal was physical survival and spiritual harmony with
nature. To gain physical survival, they had to study the habitats in which
they lived, but such study was quite practical. To gain spiritual harmony,
they had to stress images and feelings not controlled by logic, images and
feelings that mediated a sense of participation in the living whole that all
creatures comprised. So they fasted, meditated in solitude, created colorful
myths, healing ceremonies, festive dances, and more. They found ways of
purifying their bodies and spirits, ways of venerating the sun and the
moon, the air and the water. Little of this was religious, and yet all of it
was religious. One could not discern a separate compartment of Native-
American culture called the religious domain, and yet it was pervaded by
a desire for harmony and a sense of the sacrality of all things.

Inasmuch as harmony implied a state of well-being, or the tranquillity
and pleasure that come from right order, one can call Native-American
spirituality pragmatic. It sought a desirable end, and it gauged the efficacy
of its measures by their success in gaining that end. On the other hand, the
focus of much Native-American culture was spiritual, a matter of mental
and emotional dispositions, rather than material, so the practicality that
they found among white Americans often puzzled them.

Deloria has a knack for pointing out some of the follies to which
Western ways of thinking led, and suggesting why Native Americans
made a mistake in being bedazzled by white technology: "Marvelous in-
struments and tools of iron and other metals blinded us and produced an
uncritical assumption that whatever the white man was doing must be
based upon some superior insight into the world of nature. We forgot, to
our detriment, that the first Europeans we encountered thought they were
going to sail over the edge of the world, that succeeding expeditions had
fantasies about Fountains of Youth, Cities of Gold, and northwest passages
to Cathay. Native Americans did not realize that Europeans felt a dreadful
necessity to classify us within a view of the world already made obsolete
by discovery of our continent. While we could not participate in the heated
theological discussions concerning our origins—whether we derived from
Noah's Ark or were survivors of the Ten Lost Tribes of Israel—we perhaps could have been more insistent on making the non-Indians provide

more and better arguments for their version of world history and human knowledge. Any group that frantically dug gold in the west in order to transplant it to the east and bury it cannot be quite right and their insights cannot form the highest achievement of our species."[11]

What is the highest achievement of our species? Perhaps that is the question that emerges when one takes any philosophy into the welter of human cultures and asks what it is finally worth? Pragmatism, as exemplified by William James, is a marvelous collection of insights, but does it take human beings into the richest possible appreciation of the nature of their world, the richest possible life that such an appreciation can generate? Certainly, pragmatism is not the only American philosophy, and when one speaks of the typically American cast of mind, pragmatism is not the only term one should use. But for the rough purpose of comparing Native-American and white outlooks, pragmatism can suffice to remind us that American individualism and practicality are not the only ways to construe the world. Whether the white or the Native-American way possesses a better tally of profits and losses depends greatly on the one making the tally.

Hispanic Americans

Though in recent years numerous Hispanic Americans have joined Protestant evangelical churches, the weight of Hispanic-American culture still falls on the side of Catholic Christianity. The influence of the Spanish explorers and missionaries in the New World continued long after Spanish rule ceased.[12] The Christianity cultivated from the blend of Spanish and Native-American heritages continues to shape how the majority of Hispanic Americans view the world.

The "little tradition," as anthropologists sometimes call folk religion, has been very influential in Hispanic Christianity. The cult of the saints, often accommodated to local pre-Christian traditions, has flourished, setting Hispanic Christianity apart from Protestantism. Certainly, other portions of American Catholicism—Irish, German, Polish, Italian—have also cultivated the saints, but seldom with the color and the concentration on suffering that have marked Hispanic Catholicism. The cult of the saints is pragmatic, in the sense that most people pray to the saints to obtain help. They seek cures, jobs, the alleviation of family tensions, the safety of a child venturing out into the adult world. But there is a fail-safe dimension to popular Catholic use of the saints. If one's prayers are not answered, there must be a good reason. One who finally says to God, "Thy will be done," cannot hold the saints responsible, or write them off as failures, if a petition is not heard. God may know better. The mediating powers of the saints are limited by God's knowing better. Even the Virgin Mary, unique among all intercessors because of her having borne the Son of God, must fall in with divine providence. Those praying to her with traditional faith always added the mental rider that, as their Blessed Mother, she would do for them what she knew to be best. So the most popular prayer to the Virgin, the "Hail Mary," sent forth only the most basic of petitions: "Pray for us sinners, now and at the hour of our death."

On the occasion of the 450th anniversary of the appearance of Mary that made her Our Lady of Guadalupe, outside Mexico City, the Hispanic Catholic bishops of the United States issued a pastoral message. The message reviewed the history of their people and then surveyed their present religious needs. The first paragraphs of this message suggest the central place that devotion to Mary has held in Hispanic Catholicism: "Four hundred fifty years after your apparition in our lands, we, your sons, come as shepherds of our Hispanic people in the United States of North America. We come full of joy and hope, but we also come saddened and preoccupied with the suffering of our people. We are the shepherds of a people on the march. Walking with our people, we come to you, Mother of God and our mother, so that we may receive a renewed spirit. We want to be filled with enthusiasm to go out and proclaim the wonders of God that have taken place in our history, that are taking place at this time in our lives and that will take place in the future. Although the world has often misunderstood us, you do understand and hold us in esteem."[13]

First, it bears reflection that the appearance of Mary in 1531 was to an Indian peasant, Juan Diego, and that the cult of Our Lady of Guadalupe, which has included pilgrimages to her shrine, has blended features of Spanish Christianity and Native-American culture, skillfully creating a vehicle by which Native Americans might adapt the religion of their conquerers to their own sensibilities.

Second, one notes that Mary has often functioned as the patroness of the poor and marginalized, who have recognized in her "Magnificat" (Luke 1:46–55) the cry of a poor person looking to God for justice. Whatever the historical actuality of Mary of Nazareth, the mother of Jesus, from the time that she became acclaimed as the *theotokos,* the mother of God, her words and actions partook of the same twofoldness as Christ's. On the one hand, she was fully human, so that she could understand the sufferings of ordinary people, especially the sufferings of women. On the other hand, she was so closely tied to the Son of God that, though not strictly divine herself, she played an essential role in the economy of salvation. Thus she was the most important saint, the fullest exemplar, after Jesus, of what God wanted human beings to become.

When they considered the model of Mary, or the model of Jesus, Hispanic Americans found much that contested the behavior of the Anglos ruling them, even when those Anglos professed themselves to be Christians. Jesus and Mary had been poor, as many Hispanics were. Why, then, did Anglo culture set such store on wealth? Jesus and Mary had made God their great treasure. Why, then, was so much Anglo culture concerned with success in business, developing the land, and other this-worldly treasures? Jesus and Mary had been sorely afflicted, which made their lives lessons in endurance, sermons that suffering was God's way of bringing people to Himself. Why, then, was so much Anglo culture concerned with security, pleasure, physical well-being? As Hispanic Americans gained access to Anglo education, business, government, and the professions, they felt the seductions of "success," as Anglo culture defined it. But the first generations of those moving upward felt schizophrenic, enjoying the material benefits of their advance but wondering what the spiritual costs would be.

When the Hispanic bishops surveyed their cultural heritage, they found much to praise—much that any member of their churches ought to consider before leaving behind: "In the shaping of this people, many beautiful values from different cultures have been incorporated, all of which have enriched us today. Our culture is rich in imagery, art, music, dances, food, poetry, even to the point of embodying a certain mischievousness. Our language is rich in expressions that come from the Gospel. This facilitates the transmission of the word. Our personal faith is expressed very beautifully: *Mi Padre Dios* (God my Father), *Nuestra Madrecita Maria* (Our dear mother Mary), *Nuestro Senor y Hermano Jesuchristo* (Our Lord and Brother Jesus Christ), *Mis santitos* (My little saints). A true spiritual environment is fostered in our homes and many houses even become household churches. The little altar with the crucifix, your statue, *Madrecita*, and our 'little saints' hold a special place in the home. The vigil lights and blessed palms speak to us of your most holy Son. Our culture is the expression of the Gospel incarnated in our people and is a rich form of passing on the divine teachings to new generations."[14]

This passage suggests precisely the variety of religious experience that William James found when he did his studies for his Gifford Lectures. What the bishops are describing is something that would not occur in a house on Boston's Beacon Hill. The prominent place of the *Madrecita*, more prominent here than the place of Christ, put Protestant Christians off and tended to amuse secularized Anglos. The Protestants feared idolatry, remembering the corruptions of the fifteenth century, while the secularists thought they were dealing with a quaint, primitive religious style.

Inasmuch as Jamesian pragmatism derived from these two cultural sources, Protestantism and secularism in their late-nineteenth-century forms, it had little kinship with Hispanic Christianity. Hispanic Christians still believed in a world full of spiritual presences. They were not children of the Enlightenment. Their world had not been emptied of supernatural wonders. And they were relatively innocent of modern science, often of modern technology. So they stood apart from practicality, as mainstream Americans understood it. They stood for something older, closer to the spirit of medieval Europe, closer even to the vigor of pre-Columbian Meso-American culture. Like Deloria's Native Americans, the Hispanics who mixed Native-American and Christian instincts did not configure the world as the ambitious, driven whites did. They did not dig up gold in the west and transport it to the east to be buried in bank vaults. Their treasures were their beautiful land, their children, and their God, fierce in his demands yet softened by the intercessions of their *Madrecita*.

Sectarians: Christian Scientists

An intriguing twist on the reputed American instinct for getting things done occurred in the last quarter of the nineteenth century with the rise of Mary Baker Eddy's Christian Science. Although Eddy departed from the American mainstream in repudiating the reality of matter, she stood with it in seeking from her religion quite practical effects. In an essay probably written in 1883 but only published in 1896, Eddy described her program as follows: "My first plank in the platform of Christian Science is as follows: 'There is no life, truth, intelligence, nor substance in matter. All is infinite Mind and its infinite manifestation, for God is All-in-all. Spirit is immortal Truth; matter is mortal error. Spirit is the real and eternal; matter is the unreal and temporal. Spirit is God, and man is His image and likeness. Therefore man is not material; he is spiritual.'

"I am strictly a theist—believe in one God, one Christ or Messiah. Science is neither a law of matter nor of man. It is the unerring manifesto of Mind, the law of God, its divine Principle. Who dare say that matter or mortals can evolve Science? Whence, then, is it, if not from the divine source, and what, but the contemporary of Christianity, so far in advance of human knowledge that mortals must work for the discovery of even a portion of it? Christian Science translates Mind, God, to mortals. It is the infinite calculus defining the line, plane, space, and fourth dimension of Spirit. It absolutely refutes the amalgamation, transmigration, absorption, or annihilation of individuality. It shows the impossibility of transmitting human ills, or evil, from one individual to another; that all true thoughts revolve in God's orbits—they come from God and return to Him—and untruths belong not to His creation; therefore these are null and void. It hath no peer, no competitor, for it dwelleth in Him beside whom 'there is none other.' "[15]

Eddy had been sickly, a somewhat typical victim of the neurasthenia that afflicted many women of the Victorian era. In finding a belief that seemed to quicken her spirit and restore her body, she thought she had rediscovered the key to the Christian scriptures and wisdom. How she could reconcile her antimaterialism with a religious tradition that made the incarnation of divinity the first plank in its platform is baffling. Certainly, personal need and intuition overrode any consideration of traditional faith. Yet Eddy could claim kinship with Christ the healer, and her efforts to make religion restore people's bodily and mental health followed a well-trodden path.

When Hinduism became a factor on the American scene, after the World's Parliament of Religions held in Chicago in 1893, Americans had available a vocabulary to articulate an immaterialism such as Eddy's. Prior to that, only a few intellectuals, most notably Ralph Waldo Emerson, had taken much nourishment from Hindu sources. Eddy did not generate her ideas under Hindu inspiration, but she did strike many observers as putting into new form notions discussed in spiritualist, occult, and theosophical circles. For all such groups, the visible could not be trusted. It was not the prime analogate of reality. Spirit was the prime analogate of reality, because spirit quickened the human being, and God was spirit, to be worshiped in spirit and truth.

Moreover, Eddy had stumbled into a problem with which Christianity had grappled in its patristic era. In opposition to various Gnostics, who condemned the flesh and considered matter the source of illusion and evil, the fathers of the Church, such as Irenaeus, had asserted firmly the goodness of creation, the reality of the material world, and the saving significance of Christ's flesh. But they had not affirmed the existence of evil, at least not as a reality of the same order as God's creatures. Augustine had developed the most profound reflections on this theme, trying to avoid the problem of making God the source of evil. If God was the creator of everything that existed, then evil could not exist. Evil could not be a creature, a participant in the divine font of being, something independent and self-contained like a tree or a human being. For Augustine, evil was a privation: a lack of the order, being, and goodness that ought to exist. Thus, the natural evil of a flood reposed in its disorder, its violation of the rules that rivers were supposed to follow. The evil of a cancer was the disorder of its growth. And the evil of sin was the lack of obedience to the divine will, the lack of reason involved in refusing to follow God's laws.

But these metaphysical reflections from early in Christian history, which continued to be influential as long as Christian theologians pondered the mysteries of being and nonbeing, goodness and evil, took a surprising form in Christian Science. For William James, Christian Science illustrated the religion of healthy-mindedness. Some people cultivated the mind to cure all their ills, others needed to be born again, usually out of a crisis of depression and sickness. Mary Baker Eddy seems to have bridged the two categories, being what James called a "twice-born" personality yet advocating the healthy-mindedness of the "once-born," those fortunate enough to think healthy thoughts from infancy.

Stephen Gottschalk has noted the connections among these two turn-of-the-century Bostonians, James and Eddy: "In 1901–1902, at the height of his fame and powers, James delivered the Gifford Lectures on natural religion at the University of Edinburgh. The lectures were published in 1902 under the title *The Varieties of Religious Experience* and rapidly became a classic. In them he described what he called 'the religion of healthy-mindedness,' which he saw as best illustrated in 'mind-cure'—or as it was then coming to be called, New Thought. . . . James's own guarded sympathy for the religion of healthy-mindedness has been taken by some historians to reflect harmonial tendencies in his own thought. Yet he could not but feel that there was a fundamental deficiency in any religious philosophy that 'deliberately excludes evil from its field of vision.' Mind-cure, he wrote, was so 'wholly and exclusively compacted of optimism' that its adherents never crossed the threshold of human pain and despair which great religious innovators must pass. The true religious genius, James observed, was always 'twice-born' because of radical experiences that brought about the creation of a new inner person."[16]

James went on to describe healthy-mindedness as an exploration of the potentialities of the self. Like yogins, mind-curers wanted to tap hidden powers of the human spirit. Twice-born people seemed to need to roll in the depths of human helplessness and pain, if they were to find a new level of meaning. How much Mary Baker Eddy suffered before she came to her Christian Science is not certain, but there are strong indications (principally, her sickliness and unhappiness) she spent the first half of her life feeling sundered and seeking to be made whole. Her gospel, however, seemed to stress wholeness, which she said could be gained by rectifying one's false views of matter and sickness, more than sunderedness. Like Hindus or Buddhists who tell people that multiplicity and deficiency are illusions, because in itself the human being is perfect, Eddy looked at spiritual experience as a proof that the mind could make people fully well.

That this did not sit completely well with William James suggests the rich complexity of his own character. Not only was he an experimental psychologist and learned man, doubly informed thereby about mental sufferings and the reasons for feeling pessimistic, he was also a man who himself suffered depression throughout his life. If he felt that he had gained a cure in his thirties by taking a bold, positive view of life and exercising his will to believe that health was possible for him, he realized in later years that melancholy and doubt would never leave him completely. So his pragmatism had to calculate all the effects of a religious option, the bright and the dim alike, and its basic conclusion was that people experience a wide range of happenings and moods, some justifying optimism and some justifying pessimism. Calvinistic Americans would have said, "Of course. Human nature is dark, even depraved, and the basis for hope resides in God, not human beings." They would not have endorsed Eddy's disregard of matter, however, and they would have considered her views of God heretical.

Protestant Reflections

Protestant reactions to pragmatism naturally varied considerably. The more liberal groups tended to approve of the stress on experiences and consequences that James introduced and John Dewey forwarded. The more conservative groups tended to reassert the primacy of biblical revelation and the morality they thought such revelation made obligatory. At the turn of the twentieth century, the Social Gospel movement put into practical form the long-standing Protestant conviction that power is not to be trusted. Sickened by the plight, religious as well as material, of the many urban industrial workers, Walter Rauschenbusch (1861–1918) drew from the Scriptures a stress on the Kingdom of God that made social justice imperative. Rauschenbusch offered a critique of industrialization, capitalism, big business, and the other forces he thought responsible for urban poverty—a critique similar to the critiques of socialists and Marxists. But his basis was the gospel of Christ, which he heard as calling people to a solidarity and justice opposed to the individualism driving America's entrepreneurs. Like Jane Addams, the proponents of the Social Gospel wanted practical changes: laws and social policies that would improve the lot of the poor. More explicitly than she, they linked this desire with the Sermon on the Mount, Jesus's parables about the Good Samaritan and the rich man Dives in hell, and the sociology of Christian life that one could find in the epistles of Paul. Protestants of this temper were pragmatic in the sense of searching the Scriptures, Old and New Testament, for prophetic texts that would strengthen their case that great social inequalities were wrong. They parted company with secular pragmatists in making divine revelation, rather than human experience, the norm of truth and reality.

However, the Social Gospel movement was only one of a number of developments that shaped American Protestantism early in this century. Catherine Albanese has summarized the complex situation well: "The Social Gospel would be a continuing legacy to mainstream Protestantism as the twentieth century continued. Its popularity waxed and waned with the climate of the times, but it never completely disappeared. Other turn-of-the-century movements continued, too. The Liberal-Fundamentalist split seemed a permanent feature of the Protestant landscape, while, as we have already noted, both Fundamentalist and Holiness-Pentecostal groups increased in importance. Sometimes Liberals, Fundamentalists, and Holiness-Pentecostals were organized in separate congregations. But more and more, in the later twentieth century, there were divisions *within* denominations, so that some within the same church might be Liberal and others Fundamentalist in inclination. Some might prefer traditional patterns of worship, while others in the denomination sought charismatic gifts. Even within their own denominations, the new Fundamentalist and Holiness-Pentecostals included people more affluent than many of their predecessors, and there were other differences as well. Moreover, a number of conservative and evangelical churches tried to mediate between the Liberal and Fundamentalist positions, while, outside the Calvinist tradition, Lutheranism grew in membership and importance."[17]

Those Protestants most open to pragmatism, most attuned to the pragmatists' articulation of the American temper, tended to be liberals. Later in the century many evangelicals became highly sophisticated about their methods, using the mass media very effectively, but even then few embraced a pragmatic view of truth, wedded as most were to the Bible.

Liberals were convinced that they had to translate the Bible for a new, modern period. They saw pragmatists such as John Dewey turning the nation's educational system in a new direction, and they had to admit that much in Dewey's reasoning made sense. Experience was a great teacher. Until people were personally involved in either education or faith, they did tend to be underachievers. America did have a great democratic tradition that the schools had to carry forward. Granted the pluralism of the population, it was necessary to develop a common faith, stripped of denominational peculiarities, to unite the citizenry. The more adventurous of the liberals took a largehearted view of God's presence in the world and accepted much of Dewey's naturalism. Why not say that creative work in art and science manifested the designs of the deity? Why not stress the humanistic implications of the life and teachings of Jesus, since theological implications seemed a source of division? And, most importantly, why not work with all others of good will to improve the plight of the poor, stop the decay of the cities, lessen the frictions between races and social classes? Certainly this social action could translate well Christ's call to love one's neighbor as oneself.

The leading light of the neoorthodox who questioned the depth and fidelity of this interpretation of the Christian gospel, and so tried to upset any easy marriage between Christian faith and pragmatism, was the Swiss theologian Karl Barth. Reinhold Niebuhr carried the neoorthodox colors in the United States, but Barth furnished Protestants in many countries some of their deepest insights into the transcendent, more-than-human reality of God and mediation of God by Scripture: "Barth believed—and here he was at the very root of the problem of the modern theologian—that the Bible was the sum total of the sources in terms of which Christianity could be defined. Human religious experience, and human reflection on that experience, became irrelevant if one wanted to decide what God had revealed in Jesus Christ."[18]

Barth had to struggle with the consequences of this view for systematic theology, because it left the theologian without secure access to reason and tradition. Still, he made profoundly the point that many fundamentalists made superficially: the Bible must be privileged in Christian life, a unique authority. Among American fundamentalists, few approached the popularity and influence of Billy Graham, an eloquent Baptist preacher. Graham had tremendous success preaching evangelistic crusades beginning in the 1950s. In reflecting on the evolution of his own thought during this period, Graham departed from the Baptists who felt that fidelity to the gospel demanded an ultraconservatism in both theology and politics.

On the one hand, Graham's experiences reinforced his commitment to the Bible. On the other hand, they forced him to broaden his conception of the Church and the social implications of the gospel. The following passage from his self-assessment suggests both the kinship that fundamentalists might feel with pragmatists concerning social issues, and the differences bound to remain if one made central the Christian doctrine of sin: "A fifth change: my belief in the social implications of the gospel has deepened and broadened. I am convinced that faith without works is dead. I have never felt that the accusations against me of having no social concern were valid. Often the message of the evangelist is so personal that his statements on social matters are forgotten or left out when reports are made. It is my conviction that even though evangelism is necessarily confined within narrow limits the evangelist must not hedge on social issues. . . . Yet I am more convinced than ever before that we must change men before we can change society. The international problems are only reflections of individual problems. Sin is sin, be it personal or social, and the word *repent* is inseparably bound up with evangelism. Social sins, after all, are merely a large-scale projection of individual sins and need to be repented of by the offending segment of society."[19]

Many present-day theologians would dispute Graham's understanding of social sin, reviving the notion of original sin so that it is seen as what warps institutions and so taints the whole atmosphere in which people live and work. But the relevance of the long-standing Protestant stress on sin (on something radically wrong in people's evaluations and choices) to social problems has continued to separate Protestant thought from a pragmatism determined to interpret human experience without reference to biblical revelation.

Sophistication and Naiveté

Pragmatists and biblicists both could accuse their opponents of naiveté. Pragmatists tended to judge that those who used the Bible to interpret current events, or even modern human nature, were too simple by far. Biblicists tended to judge that the pragmatic analysis of human nature was superficial, because it did not probe the mysteries of sin and grace. Let us consider what was involved in these judgments.

For the Jamesian pragmatist, truth emerges from experience. Something is true, valid, reliable when people find that depending upon it does not let them down. An idea is true when it is viable. Ideas that lead to dead ends, or that leave a problem fuzzy, or that are conducive to personal doubt or depression, may and should be discarded. By these criteria, religious ideas may or may not be true. People who claim that faith in God keeps them going find such faith, such a God, true. People who claim that faith in God puts them off, leaves them alienated or angry, find such faith false. The first thing to note about people's experiences with faith and God is the variety. Not only do people vary in the kind of divinity they embrace, they also vary in whether or not they find "divinity" meaningful—coherent, helpful, something they ought to embrace. So, if one respects what people report about faith and God, one has to make such matters subjective. People decide for themselves whether they believe in God, as they decide what sort of God they believe in. Their belief is as good or bad as the experiences upon which it is based and the consequences to which it leads. Any other assessment of religion is prejudicial—determined not by what people actually report but by convictions the assessor has already developed before confronting the data.

For a pragmatist of this persuasion, the Bible is something neutral. It may be true or it may be false, depending on the use given people make of it. Those whom the Bible helps find it truthful. Those whom it alienates find it untruthful. At the least, then, one cannot claim a privileged status for the Bible. Biblicists who insist that their theology applies to all human beings ride over the freedom and mysteriousness of human conscience. Frequently, they simply do not know what they are talking about, because the sensibilities of the nonbeliever lie outside the horizon of what they can understand.

If we move to the other side of the debate, and try to represent the judgments of a person committed to biblical faith, we find another charge of naiveté. Biblicists look at the subjectivism that pragmatism seems to require, seems even to promote, and wonder how in the world that can be squared with the revelation of God, or even with common sense. How can God be real or unreal, faith be true or untrue, depending on individuals' personal judgments or whims? How can the disclosures made on Sinai or in the death and resurrection of Christ apply for some people and not for others? On both metaphysical and ethical grounds such a subjectivism makes no sense. Reality has to be something in itself, something independent of individual human judgment or choice. Nature teaches all of us this lesson. The anatomy of the rabbit is not something that depends on our judgment or desire. We cannot have a rabbit with three hearts or hands like a human being. God has to be at least as real as a rabbit, because God made all the rabbits, and everything else in the natural world. Certainly human beings did not make them, and even if one wants to credit them to "evolution," the clearest explanation for the origins of evolution is that the Creator of the matter that evolution transforms encoded its transformations from the beginning.

Similarly, one would have ethical chaos if subjectivism on the pragmatists' model were to reign. If people can choose whether or not they believe in God, whether or not God is real, why can they not choose whether they will be honest or lie, be kind or cruel, keep the peace or go to war, bring up their children well or abuse them? The slope unveiled by pragmatic subjectivism is slippery indeed. Make the variety of human experience your ethical or metaphysical criterion and you will have a pluralism that is chaotic, a subjectivism that is vicious.

The deepest thrust of the biblicists' attack on subjectivism occurred when it came to the matter of sin. Pragmatists might provide for human error, even human evil, but they had not fathomed the mystery of iniquity. In rejecting the biblical anthropology, refusing to let biblical ideas of sin and grace be normative, pragmatists had reduced the human condition from three to two dimensions. They did not see that the deepest drama of the human vocation was the question of saying yes or no to the Lord, the holy Creator, who had made all human beings. They did not appreciate that Christ had shed his blood for all human beings, in an act of consummate love that radically changed the human situation. So they took away the most passionate romance to which human beings had been invited, the romance that St. Augustine had intuited when he exclaimed in his *Confessions,* "You have made us for yourself, O God, and our hearts are restless until they rest in You." In comparison with the human nature that Augustine appreciated, the pragmatic personality became a pygmy, a sad little runt.

It does not take great sophistication to see that these two charges of naiveté tended to pass like ships in the night. The biblicist remained open to the charge of not respecting what actually happened in people's minds and hearts, and so perhaps violating what a real God would consider most important: not acceptance of dogma but fidelity to conscience. The pragmatist remained open to the charge of not respecting the claims on the human conscience to find something objectively so, real and valuable independent of human choices. As well, the pragmatist remained open to the charge of not appreciating the depths of the human adventure, where divine mystery forced all people to contend with faith, hope, and love as the determinants of their souls.

In the middle, the ground occupied by liberal believers and pragmatists open to challenge, difficult but very fruitful questions emerged. Does human experience itself disclose and depend on a religious dimension, a set of vectors toward the Beginning and the Beyond? How can one balance the subjective and the objective in assessing either human nature or God? Does the fact that all human judgments are shaped by experience, social as well as sensate, mean that all human judgments are subjective—limited, personalized, confined by the place the judge occupies on the historical charts and the geographical maps? Or ought one to weigh more the reflective phase of judgment, where something apparently independent of the person's conditioning by space and time allows the judge to find evidence and reasoning adequate or inadequate, sufficient or insufficient for saying yes or no to a proposition?

These very difficult epistemological questions make demands on the believer and theologian as much as on the pragmatic secularist. The believer has to own up to the fact that there is no such thing as a Bible, apart from human invention and reception. The pages of the artifact marked "Bible" are only smooth sheets marked by arbitrary squiggles, unless one admits the influence of human culture and organizes them into a language, a set of propositions, a speech that can be poetic and moral as well as informative. Subjectivism is built into biblical revelation. Yet subjectivism cannot be all, if one finds the Bible so helpful, truthful, healing that one feels compelled to consider it the Word of God. The leap of faith involved in making that judgment cannot and need not be blind. That is the testimony of many savants and saints whom pragmatists would do well to study carefully.

And so it goes, the dialogue that one can construct from the instincts of biblicists and pragmatists about the adequacy and inadequacy, the sophistication and naiveté, in one another's views of either divinity or humanity. Perhaps the best thing one can say about the pragmatic temper of most Americans is that they have thought the dialogue should go on, because where it concludes just might be crucially important, not only to the welfare of individuals drawn to one position or the other, but also to the future of the whole nation.

Pragmatism: American Wisdom

We have used the philosophy of William James to articulate the concern with experience and consequences that many observers consider typical of mainstream American culture. As with Jonathan Edwards's sense of human nature, and Thomas Jefferson's sense of disestablishment, James's views have been interesting as much for their representativeness as for their inner coherence, depth, or appeal. And just as we found significant variations concerning the depravity of human nature or the need for religious liberty when we consulted those on the margins of American culture, so we have found significant variations when it came to pragmatism. Still, one could say that pragmatism more reshaped those on the margins than those on the margins reshaped it, just as one could say that skepticism about human nature and conviction about the wisdom of disestablishing religion became more accepted on the margins than changed in the mainstream.

All of these are indefensibly broad generalizations, of course, but broad generalization and provocative hypothesis have been the character of our essay. We have never denied the myriad qualifications that one would have to make, were one to trace down the degree to which specific subpopulations of Americans embraced the Edwardsian thesis about the depravity of human nature, or the Jeffersonian thesis about religious liberty and so disestablishment, or the Jamesian thesis about the variety of religious experience and the pluralism of the universe, including the universe's deity. Our interest has been to suggest some of the primary shadings in which Americans have painted their own religious profile. If we have suggested this well, it is now plausible that a suspicion of human nature, and a conviction that the separation of church and state is wise, and a willingness to judge the truth of a proposition, including a central theological proposition, by its experiential foundations and consequences are characteristic features of the American religious psyche. Let us reflect on the wisdom implied in this last characteristic, the willingness to be pragmatic about religion.

As noted, this willingness goes against the grain of some powerful religious currents. Still, it invaded most of the American churches and synagogues. As a result, many Protestant churches judged their success or failure more in terms of the fellowship they created or failed to create than in terms of the doctrinal fidelity, or the biblical conviction, or the mystical depth they sponsored. Similarly, many Catholic churches were more interested in building schools and hospitals than in producing theologians who might contest American secularism, or artists who might demonstrate the priority of creativity over successful results, or even moral leaders who might show the nation a new vision of business, peace, the environment, race relations, women's rights, and the other key items on the social agenda of the late twentieth century. One could say the same of most synagogues, mosques, and other religious conventicles. Doing, building, trying to have a discernible effect on the flow of money and power regularly became as important as, if not more important than, learning a wisdom that had little cash value or developing a prayer that might make one a stranger in one's own strange land. Pragmatism, the outlook that what is truly significant is what makes a discernible difference, became a strong feature of virtually all American religious groups.

Now, the more astute of such groups tended to realize that pragmatism was reminiscent of Jesus's saying that one could know the character of a preacher, a new aspirant to leadership, by the fruits that the preaching or leadership developed. This was in line with the even older notions of the Israelite prophets, who wanted mercy in such practical matters as the treatment of widows and orphans more than lovely sacrifices to God. Naturally, there are a dozen qualifications and footnotes that spring to mind for each of these assertions, but after all of them biblical religion remains significantly practical. The liberation theologians are only the latest in a long line of reformers who have argued that how one treats one's neighbor, what one actually does with the ideals of one's faith, is the crux of one's religion.

One can defend this attitude as perceptive and wise, because action does seem to sum up what people believe in the crunch, and because often only doing the truth brings one to the light. Pragmatism is amenable to the proposition that praxis has a priority over theory, even though pragmatism cannot be reduced to this proposition. On the other hand, American wisdom about pragmatism, American good sense in wanting ideas to have significant effects, has seldom gone as deeply into the fascinating matter of the relationship between theory and practice as one who treasures the conversions that religion can create would wish.

For the fact is that the horizon in which most Americans, including most religious Americans, have made their assessments of the truthful and the valuable has seldom been stretched so as to give all the priority to God. This is the sort of stretching that Jonathan Edwards attempted, and a good summary of the failure of American pragmatism is the small degree to which Americans have appreciated the vision of the divine glory that Edwards, or virtually any other solid representative of traditional religious wisdom, enjoyed. In the turnaround, the metanoia, that the prophets and mystics cannot cease examining, all of human doing turns out to be reactive. Human beings do not furnish themselves the conditions of their action, the milieu in which they have their experience, test what has happened to them, and then set themselves up to judge, on the basis of what has happened to them, what is true and what false in the concepts handed down to them as tools for determining the human condition. All of human action is a latecomer on the evolutionary scene. If life began something like 3.8 billion years ago, even the earliest human beings depended on incalculable numbers of events to supply the backdrop for their judgments and choices. What was the Beginning of this entire process of antecedent action and causality? And what will be its End? How can one estimate the real contours of the human condition, if one does not wonder one's way out of the realm of here and now results, into the genuine mystery of creation? Human beings seek knowledge of a Beginning and a Beyond, an Origin and a Destiny, that would frame all of their thinking and doing. If they cannot even approach such a frame without surrendering their pragmatic claims to be masters of the significance of their actions, where will they find the challenge, the shock, necessary to make them drop their constant concern with doing and having, make them take up as their primary concern their human being—what they are as creatures most stirred by a pure desire to know and love the Source of their existence, the foundation and whole that makes them what they are?

These are the sorts of questions from which American wisdom about pragmatism has tended to back away, and from that backing away has come the relative superficiality that has made American religion patronized by many older cultures. To be sure, such patronizing has often been cynical and self-serving, but it has also expressed a sorry truth. The truth is that the pragmatic is no surer a touchstone of a person's worth than the non-pragmatic prayer or creativity or objectless love that the person may sometimes enjoy. The truth is that there is no sure touchstone, no way for human beings to usurp the judgment of God, to oust the silence of the mystery that virtually all traditional cultures have considered divine. In our view, American pragmatism will not be fully wise until it tries to take the measure of this impractical, nonutilitarian truth, and so finds doing to be less the judge than the judged.

NOTES

1. Eugene Borowitz, "Judaism: An Overview," in *The Encyclopedia of Religion*, ed. Mircea Eliade (New York: Macmillan, 1987), vol. 8, p. 141.

2. Ibid., p. 144.

3. Ibid., p. 147.

4. John Ireland, "Preface," in *A Documentary History of Religion in America*, ed. Edwin S. Gaustad (Grand Rapids, MI: Eerdmans, 1983), vol. 2, pp. 387–388.

5. Pope Leo XIII, "Testem Benevolentiae," in *Documents of American Catholic History*, ed. John Tracy Ellis (Wilmington, DE: Michael Glazier, 1987), vol. 2, p. 543.

6. Susan B. Anthony, "The Status of Woman, Past, Present, and Future," in *The Annals of America* (Chicago: Encyclopaedia Britannica, 1976), vol. 12, p. 148.

7. Jane Addams, "Industrial Amelioration and Social Ethics," ibid., pp. 490–491.

8. Mary Antin, "In Defense of the Immigrant," ibid., vol. 13, p. 457.

9. Martin Luther King, Jr., "Letter from Birmingham Jail," ibid., vol. 18, p. 146.

10. Vine Deloria, "Civilization and Isolation—An Indian View," ibid., vol. 21, p. 110.

11. Ibid., p. 107.

12. See Lino Gomez Canedo, "Religion in the Spanish Empire," in *Encyclopedia of the American Religious Experience*, ed. Charles H. Lippy and Peter W. Williams (New York: Scribner's 1988), vol. 1, pp. 187–199.

13. See "Pastoral Message of the United States Hispanic Bishops," in *Documents of American Catholic History*, vol. 3, p. 764.

14. Ibid., pp 767. For further background, see Edwin E. Sylvest, Jr., "Religion in Hispanic America Since the Era of Independence," in *Encyclopedia of the American Religious Experience*, vol. 1, pp. 201–222.

15. Mary Baker Eddy, "Christian Science," in *The Annals of America*, vol. 10., pp. 556–557.

16. Stephen Gottschalk, "Christian Science and Harmonialism," in *Encyclopedia of the American Religious Experience*, vol. 2, p. 901.

17. Catherine L. Albanese, *America: Religions and Religion* (Belmont, CA: Wadsworth, 1981), p. 107.

18. John H. S. Kent, "Christian Theology in the Eighteenth to the Twentieth Centuries," in *A History of Christian Doctrine*, ed. Hubert Cunfliffe-Jones (Philadelphia: Fortress, 1980), p. 584.

19. Billy Graham, "What Ten Years Have Taught Me," in *A Documentary History of American Religion*, vol. 2, p. 515.

Chapter 8

Conclusion

E Pluribus Unum?

The grand task of any political or social body is to balance unity and plurality, the one and the many. If a social body does not attain sufficient unity, it lacks definition and identity. If a social body does not honor plurality, it restrains human freedom and limits its creativity. In the best of all situations, those responsible for the definition and welfare of the body maximize the members' freedom to be themselves, to contribute their diverse gifts. They do this by creating and then administering the laws, the constitution of the body, so that loyalty is assumed and generosity encouraged. Ideally, those in the ranks, the general membership, respond by thinking more of the common good than of their individual profits. Ideally, when the individual members make significant choices the overall welfare of the whole community bulks larger than the goods that might enrich them personally.

This is the optimal situation, and it would require the wisdom of the best social scientists to determine the optimal size for a community to have a solid chance to achieve it. The nuclear family would seem to have a good chance, and perhaps the extended family as well. The small tribe has lived this way in many periods of history, and the city-state knew some golden hours, but the modern nation-state has had difficulties. The remarkable thing about the mega-states of recent years (the United States, the Soviet

Union, Japan, India, China) has been the fact that they have functioned at all. The Soviet Union and China did so by imposing tight controls. The United States did so by creating an immense network of communications and economic ties. Whether India in fact created something more than the sum of its individual states often seems hard to determine. Japan has used a remarkable ethnic self-consciousness to elicit generosity and impose many implicit controls. As Europe moves toward unification, following the lead of its Common Market, the dramatic experiment should rivet the attention of all who discourse about the global future. Still, in all of these cases, the old metaphysical problem of the one and the many remains soberingly relevant.

One might offer the thesis that the features of the American religious profile that we have developed have shaded it toward pluralism rather than unity. The consequent thesis then might be that the major problem in the future is how to develop sufficient unity, sufficient national consensus, to accomplish the demanding agenda set by problems such as high drug use, AIDS, the loss of the nation's competitive edge in international business, racism, sexism, a decline in educational standards, homelessness, the abuse of children, the growth of the population of elderly citizens, and much more.

These theses can be extended to the international community, to see how the data seem to configure when one hypothesizes that democratization, such as that implied in the recent breakup of socialist regimes in Eastern Europe, complicates the attack on problems such as environmental degradation, barriers to free trade, terrorism, incompatible political philosophies, arms sales, and the like. Granted, totalitarian tactics have not succeeded, and have often been the source of brutality and oppression. Still, as the model of freedom pioneered in the United States becomes the best candidate for a new global political philosophy, what lessons ought Americans to offer the world, based on the American experience of trying to make one out of many?

The first lesson, dear to the hearts of civil libertarians and members of the National Rifle Association, is that one cannot compel responsible citizenship. No laws are going to ensure that people put the common good before their private profit, so one does better maximizing individual liberties and trying to educate people to generous citizenship. The economic failures of socialism seem to point in this direction, but so do the less publicized failures of socialism: the lack of creativity, joy, pride, and enthusiasm that results when people are forced into molds, ideological restraints, they have not developed and do not believe in.

From the history of American religious experience, one might say that the great lesson in this area is the primacy of the individual conscience. The Protestant roots of American religion made this result likely, if not certain, and at its most profound the lesson demonstrated the coincidence of fidelity to conscience with obedience to God. One cannot compel people's consciences, because conscience is the great sensorium of the divine will. Even when people's consciences lead them to acts that have to be outlawed and punished, for the sake of public order, the sanctity of individual conscience remains, showing the limits of any state's ability to render all of its citizens full justice. The primacy of the individual conscience for the moral life of the individual reminds us that in the healthiest relationship between the secular and the religious realms the state uses its limitations, its status of being much less than God, to relativize the significance of its actions. Even in imposing capital punishment, it says, "God may judge otherwise. We wish you well on Judgment Day." One may say much the same for religious bodies. Even when churches and synagogues have to take actions that limit the rights of individuals and so seem to infringe on their consciences, they ought to confess that their own status is much less than divine, leaving final judgment to God.

The second lesson that we find in the history of American religious experience is that without "God," an Ultimate to whom both individuals and the various social bodies can refer final judgment, a culture lacks the room it needs to maneuver well along the line between individual rights of conscience and the social demands necessary for the common good. One sees this from the top in the atheistic totalitarian regimes, where individuals can be trampled at will because nothing in them is an image of God demanding respect and fair treatment. One also sees this from the bottom in the secularized democracies, where nothing restrains the individual conscience to think more of the common good than its private pleasures or profits. The greatest such restraint, historically and metaphysically, is the call of a transcendent divinity to look beyond the ephemeral and consider Judgment Day. On Judgment Day, people will be asked whether they loved their neighbors as they loved themselves. They will be asked what they did for the poor, the sick, the ignorant, the lonely—all the people in their community who needed help. And they will even be asked about their citizenship: whether they helped to build their community up or were a problem, a source of hurt, injustice, or responsible for other people's finding it hard to be productive.

Is this to say that all of the lessons that one can extract from American religious experience fall on the side of excess individualism? By no means.

There is a herd mentality, an unwillingness to think hard, challenge the status quo, create better ways of doing business or achieving justice or beautifying the common culture, and this herd mentality has inflicted many losses on Americans, perhaps especially since the development of the mass media. The narcotic potential of television, radio, and popular music seems to have helped many to abuse tobacco, alcohol, and drugs. The constant glitter of advertising seems to have induced many to put their hopes in things, merchandise with which to surround themselves, rather than in children, education, art, science, or any of the other prime expressions of the creative, spiritual life. Democracy has the unhappy tendency to dilute standards and make elite achievement a thing of reproach. It remains the most likely guarantee of the liberty necessary for great creativity, but regularly it lacks the reverence for tradition and discipline that is equally necessary. It is no compliment to be thought of as the people who have started to fill the world with fast-food outlets. It should be a stinging disappointment to be considered the great example of mammon. American religious history offers numerous resources for sifting out these various judgments and coming to a new sense of national purpose, but the very difficulty of getting people to use those resources and agree on what granting priority to the holiness imaged in each human being implies politically shows the knottedness of present-day American religion. On this point abortion is the obvious illustration, suggesting the equal folly of religious fundamentalism and secular individualism. The task of creating a unified national policy that would remove the divisions created by abortion suggests the immense difficulty of realizing the American motto, *e pluribus unum*.

The Ambiguities of Human Nature

If we ask how the suspicion of human nature nurtured in the Protestant mainstream and somewhat accepted on the margins has influenced the problem of making unity out of the diversity of America's subcultures, we find ourselves led into the ambiguities of the data relevant to understanding human nature. Grossly, there are a few saints who stand out for their wholeness and love, while there are many sinners who tempt us to condemn human nature. More subtly, theories about human nature themselves become factors in the problem of gaining community consensus, so one has to think hard about the implications of an optimistic or a pessimistic view of the typical human character. Any responsible view admits that human beings do things that are admirable and things that are abominable, but few theories have known how to encourage people to activate their better potential.

Consider, for example, the view of human nature with which we associate Jonathan Edwards. Describing people as depraved, without any moral health in them, an Edwardsian faces the problem of finding ways to help people overcome their depravity or at least lessen its effects. He or she easily recurs to the grace of God provided by Christ, and when ecstatic movements like the Great Awakening provide apparent instances of dramatic change, the grace of God can seem present sufficiently to make the human venture possible. When the Spirit offers aid, people can be what they ought to be, what their living together well requires of them, and so the wickedness of human nature loses its fangs. However, because the operations of the Spirit seem to be out of human beings' control, the situation remains precarious. Let the fervor raised by the ecstatic movement flag and once again pessimism about human affairs seems necessary.

The political consequence of such pessimism would seem to be a discouragement of democracy and an opening to rigid community controls. This was what had happened in Puritan New England before Edwards, as it had happened in the Geneva of John Calvin. However, the general citizenry is seldom so logical or theological as to make any consequence of an idea inevitable, and one seems to find that the many calls to doubt human instincts, including one's own, worked in favor of the individualism that Americans have prized and against a robust sense of community. In other words, most people doubted the goodness of the others with whom they were invited to bond even more than their own goodness, so most people decided to trust to their own resources. To be sure, many other factors were at work, including the diversity of the people who immigrated into the colonies, and then into the republic, and the vastness of the American land, which encouraged distinctive local traditions to develop. But there was also the cautionary warning of the typical Sunday sermon, which told people to be suspicious of human intentions and not fall into the trap of forgetting the pervasive influence of sin.

Were one to counter this pessimism, by a different reading of the biblical data, or by a rejection of the biblical data altogether, one might encourage community by showing other people greater trust, but this in turn risked disillusionment when one's trust was violated, and so perhaps a greater discouragement than a puritanical suspicion alone would have created. The Enlightenment ran this risk. By neglecting the biblical teachings about sin, and encouraging people to think wholly positively of human intelligence and autonomy, the Enlightenment thinkers prepared the way for the disgust if not despair that followed in the wake of modern Europe's failures to create sound civilizations. The Marxism that Lenin and Stalin turned into sources of horror, and the perversions of Nazism, struck many people as the ultimate consequence of the Enlightenment's break with traditional bases for respecting both the dignity of human beings and their tendency toward sin. Those traditional bases were religious: the gifts and laws of God. Inasmuch as the Enlightenment led the way to rejecting them, its estimates of human nature seemed pernicious as well as superficial.

The United States avoided this evolution of Enlightenment thought, in good part because a potent evangelical strain always counterbalanced the rationalism of the Jeffersons and Madisons. But inasmuch as they opened the door to secularization, the Enlightenment foundations of the Constitution contributed significantly to the problem of cultural and religious unity. Not feeling that a sense of a transcendent God was necessary for civic concord and depth, and then feeling that though such a sense was necessary it was unachievable, the disciples of Jefferson and Madison accepted pluralism as a way of life, sometimes realizing that this entailed an individualism that easily became pernicious and a cultural drift toward meaninglessness.

The traditional Jewish and Catholic theories of human nature might have done better, but neither group was strong enough to make its theory powerful culturally, and neither produced such a distinguished group of citizens that people had to wonder what splendid ideas made them special. Both groups created their formative identities as Americans as immigrant minorities forced to put most of their energies into survival. The majority in both groups was more concerned with "making it" than with furnishing their new land communities that might spearhead dedication to the common good, the health of the whole rather than the enrichment of the parts.

The aspect of the Jewish and Catholic anthropologies that might have made them serviceable was their balance. On the one hand, they noted that sin had abounded in human history and that human nature seemed weak. On the other hand, they considered creation to be very good, grace to have abounded over sin, and the covenant of God to be unbreakable. The Lord had sworn and would not repent. In light of the goodness of God, which human beings reflected (since human beings were God's images), all pessimism became suspect as faithlessness.

One sees, then, how demanding a task it is to work out precisely the right focus on human nature, and so one is tempted to let the balance be worked by a free-market approach, in which one can hope that the different American groups will cancel out most extremes and bring the overall culture to balance near the middle, where virtue resides. Still, that sort of virtue is mediocre enough to make one wonder whether human beings are good enough to accomplish what is necessary if they are to live together in justice and peace. Do we, as a species, have the wherewithal to avoid the slaughter and infliction of pain that have soiled so much prior history? Or are the pessimists right when they tell us to expect little, guard our flanks, and hope that things will be rectified in an afterlife?

The problem with this advice becomes clear when one wonders where we get our judgments about what should be so among human beings, and what these judgments ought to tell us. Why have justice and peace so often risen up from the depths of people's spirits and told them that their circumstances of injustice and strife ought not to be, were unnatural? If one finds that each generation produces people (often called prophets or sages) who say things should be otherwise, and demonstrate how they have made things otherwise in the areas of their lives they could control, does that in itself give the lie to pessimism about human nature? Is it enough that some human beings, among them many Americans, have seen how and why things could be otherwise? A pragmatist might not think so, but that may only reveal the inadequacy of pragmatism. For how much ought vision, *theoria,* to count, and how much could a new appreciation of vision do to shift American culture away from its slide into emptiness and triviality? Because these quickly become religious questions, one can argue that pursuing them might help the next generation of Americans get a better handle on the matter of the ambiguity of the basic material they have to work with, their own human nature.

The Profits and Losses of Disestablishment

The disestablishment of religion in the United States greatly helped the exercise of individual religious liberty, but it complicated the task of forming consensus and community. Many of the colonists had fled the tyrannies of crown and crozier. They were determined to establish religious liberty (the right to exercise the faith they thought true) at the heart of their ventures in the New World. The founding fathers took this individualistic instinct, stripped it of the dross that establishing Puritan, Anglican, Quaker, or other orthodoxies had created, and placed it at the heart of the republican venture. Naturally, they hoped that people would agree about civil matters sufficiently to allow the new nation to flourish. Generally, they assumed that the ethical outlook nourished by the Enlightenment and the Deistic vestiges of biblical religion would continue, making honesty, patriotism, hard work, respect for the rights of others, and the like the national ethos. But they did not reflect adequately on the fissiparous character of Protestantism. They assumed that Protestantism would be the religion of the American majority, but they failed to contemplate the political effects of a majority religion that had no effective protection against endless splintering. As the national culture moved farther and farther away from the culture of the founding fathers, this fact of American religious life became more and more significant. The principles established originally to guarantee religious freedom applied almost equally well to ethical freedom. They applied analogously to political freedom. So in the name of the individual conscience that the mainstream American culture had canonized, nineteenth- and twentieth-century America allowed people more and more to act as they wished, provided their actions did not damage other people. Similarly, it allowed people to be political or apolitical as they wished. The result was a centrifugal expansion of individualism. The ties to the general community became harder and harder to define. The eccentricities of individuals became more and more tolerable.

The good side to this centrifugal pattern was the freedom and creativity it allowed. Certainly, people continued to be molded by social trends, and great crises like the Civil War and the two world wars in this century reasserted a larger consciousness. But in the main individuals found more and more opportunities to express their technological or artistic or religious genius. Those with vision and drive had a clear field in business (though for marginal groups the field was not level). Those with especially strong material or spiritual needs could strike out to satisfy them. This produced considerable personal fulfillment, and considerable innovation useful to others. It even produced some strong sentiment to the effect that the United States was the greatest of nations because it was where individual freedoms were greatest.

On the other hand, the habits of the American heart were devolving toward the pernicious individualism that Robert Bellah and his fellow researchers found rampant by the mid-1980s.[1] The civil religion that had filled the gap left by nonestablishment was no longer potent enough to make community-mindedness, common cause, the counterweight to individual liberty. Probably people had always been narcissistic, overly concerned with what might prove therapeutic for themselves, but affluence and leisure had become such that now many could indulge their narcissism, making self-satisfaction the grand cause of their lives. Social patterns were often such that large segments of the population had no need or occasion to deal with one another, at least not as equals. Ghettoes of various kinds— racial, economic, sometimes sexual—militated against consciousness of something larger than one's own self or immediate group. The sacrality that had traditionally hung over the tribe or city-state, or even the medieval to early-modern kingdom, was no more. In its place, the most that one could find was a woolly sense that "The United States" defined one's patriotic borders.

The institutions that might have worked against so debilitating an individualism proved more impotent than effective. The political parties and elected officials seldom galvanized the nation to a spiritual consensus. The churches and synagogues sometimes built up ecumenical communities, but nearly as often they had private agendas to pursue. So the feeling grew that the country was simply too large to constitute a real community. Despite the centripetal influences of the mass media and many economic trends, people did not know what to make of such capital notions as "American," "Christian," and "Jewish." During the twentieth century the novels one would place under each of those headings spoke more of alienation and confusion than of a sure identity. And by the last quarter of the twentieth century the community people had to try to find was shifting from the national to the international. Nationalism was becoming outdated. A global culture was on the horizon.

What sort of religion might be an antidote to the thinning of community that disestablishing all religious institutions helped to create? Only one considerably more radical than what most American houses of worship have seemed capable of generating. The motto of the Liberal theologians loyal to teachers such as Adolph Harnack, "The Fatherhood of God and the Brotherhood of Man," held the key, but this motto usually had little heft. Revised to eliminate any suggestion of sexism, it might meet the modern American need, though who will do the revising and how any religious program can distinguish itself from the glut on the market are discouraging questions.

The parenthood of God: a radical notion. That there should be a God, a Creator and Redeemer assuring the meaningfulness of both evolutionary nature and each individual human being, is not obvious, but it lies at the roots of Western religious tradition. To imagine what it might mean to live according to faith in such a God, one has only to chase away the (huge) portions of American culture that either bracket the question of ultimate meaningfulness or make "God" a cozy add-on (the frosting on Miss America's cake). In the great solitude such a chasing would create, perhaps the small still voice of Ultimacy might deign to speak, making all things new again. If the speech were parental—the loving kindness of a Father and/or Mother—the wonder would escalate, the real ties among human beings would emerge, and community would be as near as living faith.

Brother and sisterhood flow automatically from faith in a parental God. They are as vivid or dull as such faith itself. Whoever reflects divinity, as child to parent, becomes a sibling, and the eye of faith sees most people as reflecting divinity—in their bodies, their smiles, their insights, their ideals, their loves, their helpfulness, perhaps even their neediness and pain. The problem is that the institutional means to faith in a parental God, a Father and/or Mother near, dear, and strong, have broken down. The problem is that worship, liturgy, has failed to persuade, making God distant or missing.[2] Relatedly, social distances, alienations, have made brotherhood and sisterhood seem pious rather than profound, ideal rather than real. When people are in great pain, or feel they are being treated unjustly, or have few reasons to feel good about themselves, their circumstances, or their prospects, they are not likely to think well of strangers or worship well across economic or racial lines. The question of which comes first, an effective liturgy or the establishment of social justice, is usually misguided. Almost always, both are necessary. Indeed, the trick would seem to be to get them to work synchronically, so that one would build a sense of community back and forth, like raising two sides of a scaffolding. Can this happen in a country where religion has no guaranteed place in the national culture? Perhaps this is the hardest question the Constitution has left us—the place where the profits and losses of disestablishment come into boldest relief. On the one hand, Americans have the religious freedom to build whatever acceptance of a parental God and a brotherly/sisterly view of other people they wish. On the other hand, the legal structure of their land cannot admit that any religious consciousness is more basic or important than itself. So the price of community will include relativizing the legal structure, the official consciousness, without despising it—something that only the very mature, or the truly simple, are likely to appreciate, let alone realize.

Doing, Thinking, and Being

Without contemplation the people perish. This biblical truism applies to the problem we pursued in the last Part, the assets and liabilities of the pragmatic American temper. Recently a movement toward spirituality (prayer, meditation, spiritual reading) has taken wing among some mainstream Protestant groups that previously had tended to consider spirituality monkish. In recognition of the superficiality of much American faith, groups such as the United Methodists working out of The Upper Room in Nashville have developed programs to form people in the classical spiritual disciplines. One of the interesting yields of this renewal has been the deepening of communitarian instincts that has accompanied individual spiritual growth. The majority of the participants have felt that their growth in self-knowledge and their increased intimacy with God have primed them for deeper, more satisfying, and more ministerial relations with other people. What are the foundations for such a spirituality?

Doing, knowing, and being are three strands of what should be a single cord. Plaited together, they suggest the deeper level at which apparent dichotomies such as the one and the many may be overcome. Doing—action, practicality, making a difference—does not vanish. It remains the test of a faith, an integrity, a person's word. But doing recedes from the primacy that American pragmatists have tended to give it, accepting a lesser though still vital role. One cannot just do, accomplish, work the most important tasks of being human, such as building viable communities. One has to try, putting one's shoulder to the wheel, but if the community is to be something significant, one is going to encounter several mysteries that require changes in the way pragmatism teaches one to think and be. For example, there is the mystery that many people are recalcitrant. Beyond the rightful privacy they may claim, many people actively avoid paying their share of the price that community, commonweal, requires. For another example, there is the mystery that one's own feelings about community are ambiguous. It is wonderful when two or three or many are raised up into a higher unity, but it is also rare and demanding. Consider the Christian ecumenical movement. Not only ought it to be fired by the general need of human beings to join together, it also has the express command of Jesus (John 17) flowing from the fact that the unity of his followers is the sign of God's love for humankind. Yet Christians still hold back from a full ecumenical reunification. They still fear that life in the whole will be less gratifying than life in the part. Catholics, Protestants, and Orthodox all refuse a full generosity to the work of reunification, even as all confess that their divisions are gross sins. Admittedly, much de facto ecumenism has occurred at the grass roots, even though unification has stalled at the institutional level. But the issue still remains: when the simple doing that seems obvious does not occur, one is forced to think harder about one's whys and wherefores.

This thinking harder quickly takes one beyond the level of information, or ideas, or even theological appreciations based on an understanding of past history. It makes one stop thinking discursively and start to contemplate holistically. At that point, the whole matter of identity and difference, the value of the individual and the value of the community, becomes fascinating. There comes into play not only the will of the different Christian denominations to preserve their recent identities, which they have worked out to a large degree by treating other denominations as alien, but also the insistence of Jews that they remain distinct, perhaps even elect, and the parallel insistence of Muslims, Hindus, Buddhists, and others now making an ever greater impact on the American scene. It seems clear that only what many traditions call grace—unexpected help—is likely to build larger communities out of groups so insistent on their own specialness. Few groups are willing to die, that they may be reborn into something higher and more comprehensive. Most groups argue well that any successful unions will preserve the distinctiveness of the participant members. And yet these arguments, which can be accommodated when grace is flowing, easily become stumbling blocks when people are left on their own, or when business as usual (defined by pragmatic, political standards) takes center stage. The result of ruminations that reach this level of reflection is a real, existential appreciation of prayer. At the end of reflection that gets into religious mysteries, it becomes obvious that human beings need union with divinity even more than unity with one another. Better, it becomes obvious that any significant unity human beings achieve with one another depends on their prior, concommitant, and subsequent union with God.

This appreciation, in turn, places the spotlight on being. It is what people are, what people both manifest and become through their doing, that determines whether they are able to grasp the programs that making a commonweal requires and make progress toward implementing them. The possibility of overcoming racism, sexism, religious differences, and the other spiritual aspects of alienation depends on what the participants to the given situation are. They can only hope to outrun their flaws in the measure that they are immersed in a divinity greater than any of them and antagonistic to their hatreds. Similarly, they can only hope to imagine and commit themselves to the changes in economic, political, educational, social, ecological, and other patterns that lock them into their alienations if union with divine being has made them good. Their hopes to become radical, countercultural, and prophetic depend on their having become metaphysical and mystical.

The American temper is nothing if not antimystical, though of course, as always, some exceptions leap to mind. The main exceptions historically probably cluster around certain American attitudes toward nature, which became a great stimulant to an aesthetic spirituality based on the beauty of creation.[3] But more powerful were the Protestant suspicion of mysticism, even Christian mysticism, and the slant of the entire American culture at large away from being and toward doing. Admittedly, "mysticism" gives knowledgeable people pause, because so many debased forms of it (including the totalitarian forms that have spawned the greatest horrors of the twentieth century) have done humanity great injury. But in its proper connotation, mysticism is simply communion with God, or ultimate reality, or the holy mystery that seems responsible for the wonders of being and may be the cure for the twists in human psyches. Granted, such a communion takes one apart from what secularism considers significant, but it justifies itself quickly by showing how the human commonweal might arise. In their experiences of being united to a divinity that is All without losing their individuality, the classical Western mystics foreshadowed what an ideal view of human nature, and an ideal sense of the relationship between church and state, and an ideal appreciation of doing, thought, and being would be.

Future Prospects

What are the future prospects for obtaining the understanding of human nature, of the relations between religious bodies and society at large, and of the relations among doing, thought, and being necessary to achieve considerably better the American ideal of e pluribus unum? From this question flow most of the agenda for American religious thought.

First, the prospects are not good, as long as one extrapolates present trends. The two main sources of American religious thought, the religious bodies and the universities, are producing little that is profound or beautiful. The religious bodies seem afraid to publish the demands, and the rewards, of living in intense communion with God. Ironically, they seem afraid to press their members to be what they profess. Those in the universities who deal with religious thought seem equally afraid of personal commitment. While their objectivity, and their clear analyses of trends and ideas, may be admirable, objectivity alone has seldom brought love of God or love of neighbor alive. In the universities religion has little association with prayer, let alone with mysticism. One can sympathize with the difficulty of harmonizing the academic and the spiritual, but one still has to lament the paucity of creative theologies—understandings of God born of intense spiritual experience.

Nonetheless, the religious bodies and the university faculties of religion remain prime resources for countering the trend of American culture at large toward the material and superficial. Along with some groups committed to social justice, or protecting the environment, or controlling nuclear energy, or protecting women and children from abuse, the religious bodies and university faculties keep alive the sense of ultimate significance that materialism and superficiality seek to oust. Every time that a religious body supports preachers who really try to say something about the radical mysteriousness of human existence, or supports worship services that really try to create something beautiful enough to be worthy of God, it gives the witness that American culture most desperately needs. Every time that a university course in religion displays the deeper reasons why education should be demanding, why honing the mind and expanding the imagination and stabilizing the judgment are acts of profound obedience to God, it gives a similar witness. The same with the witness of the groups who say no to injustice or pollution or violence or abuse, because they have experienced how these things desecrate the human spirit and spit in the face of God.

The future prospects of American culture, and of world culture, and of religious thought intertwine. Religious thought is only a small portion of the human thought, or the overall human culture, that divinity is concerned about and immersed in, but it should play the role of point-man or vanguard. It should be the edge of the movement into a deeper, more demanding and more rewarding, sense of the human vocation. Without contemplation the people perish, because they are not equipped with the vision they need to make their way. Despite all the faults they may manifest when we look back in hindsight, Jonathan Edwards, Thomas Jefferson, and William James strove to equip their contemporaries with a vision. That alone should make them models for future religious thinkers.

Jonathan Edwards wanted his contemporaries to understand the great things that God was doing in New England, and the great dangers they ran when they misunderstood their human condition and thought religion something indifferent. Thomas Jefferson wanted his contemporaries to understand the great range of possibilities that opened when one allowed a citizenry maximum individual liberty and challenged it to turn its creativity into civic virtue, a rich contribution to the commonweal. William James wanted his contemporaries to understand the wonderful variety of experience and the existential rightness of holding true what actually improved people's lives. Certainly, as we have labored to show, each of these visions and desires had its drawbacks or limitations. But each also had a depth, a passion, a ring of integrity that gave it lasting value: something that later generations were bound to find improved them if they wrestled with it.

In our view, the problem with most current American religious thought is the mediocrity of the faith behind it. We have plenty of intellectual talent. We have little profound faith that can speak of divinity as the most real thing in existence. Where are we likely to get profound faith, or likely to marry intellectual talent to the experience that could make it speak of divinity as the most real thing in existence? The greatest likelihood would seem to be from small groups—grass-roots communities—of religious intellectuals. American religious thought (in contrast to American sanctity) has to become an elitist affair. Not in the sense that those aspiring to improve it should isolate themselves from ordinary people. In the sense that study, prayer, action, and criticism become the shared passion of people talented enough to digest the history and get the point, dedicated enough to live simply, freely, for their cause, like monks and nuns of old, or like some scientists and artists of the present day. In medieval times, the best and the brightest went into theology, because theology was the queen of the sciences, the place where the most significant knowledge, the most beautiful and satisfying visions, could be found. Unless God has changed, theology could still be that today. Unless human nature has changed since the time of Augustine, the greatest restlessness of the human heart continues to be to know divinity.

But what about the people who say that God has changed, or that human nature has changed, or that history has produced a new situation regarding both? Usually, one has to say, yes and no, with a greater need to make plain the no. After Auschwitz, can we consider God to be what God was before? No, in the sense that we have to deepen the depths of the divine mystery that evil exposes. Yes, in the sense that Auschwitz, *pace* some passionate nay-sayers, is not a unique revelation of evil, nor a unique raising of the question of God's justice and goodness.

After industrialization, secularization, the findings of modern physics, geology, biology, psychology, and the rest, can one still think that God is

God? No, in the sense that the infinity of God has become more daunting, the nearness of God more subtle, the religious balance needed to discern God more acute. Yes, in the sense that by definition God is always greater, and by experience nothing modern or scientific solves our basic moral and religious problems: we still have hearts of darkness, and we still hunger for an unearthly light and love.

Do human beings still find God possible? Do they still hunger and thirst for a Righteousness that could be parental, a Power that could be gentle as well as infinitely explosive? Can they still reach out to God in good conscience when their guilty consciences bring them to the border of mental disease, or when they have to own up to unspeakable inhumanities? No, if one has in mind the God of the childhood catechism, or the average Sunday sermon, or the typical religious session available on television. Yes, if "God" continues to name the unnamable, to stand duty for the truly ultimate, to be someone only conveyable by such images as speech out of the whirlwind at the end of the mind's desperate search for justice, or by the crucifixion of Christ, where God becomes twisted to our pain, or by the in-dwelling of the divine Breath, God is more intimate to us than we are to ourselves.

The problem is not with God, or with human nature, or with our difficult moment in history. Each of these certainly is problematic, but none makes a profound American religious thought impossible. The problem is with ourselves, as Shakespeare understood. We are the reasons our lives are dissatisfying, our culture abides so much trash, our science and art do not thrill us, our low estimate of the mystical. And so, there is great reason to hope. Any one of us can change, if grace and courage should marry. Any one of us could shift from the debit column to the assets, if we chose to take an Edwards, or a Jefferson, or a James as the paradigm for our search. The new order of the ages that America has wanted to suggest by its currency is not something apocalyptic. It is a matter of what we choose to be, collectively. In the future the best American religious thought will make itself dialectical with the choices the nation makes in face of the newness held out by God.

NOTES

1. See Robert N. Bellah, Richard Madsen, William M. Sullivan, Ann Swidler, and Steven M. Tipton, *Habits of the Heart* (Berkeley: University of California Press, 1985)

and *Individualism and Commitment: Readings on Themes of Habits of the Heart* (New York: Harper & Row, 1987).

2. See Bernard J. Cooke, *The Distancing of God* (Minneapolis: Fortress/Augsburg, 1990).

3. See William A. Clebsch, *American Religious Thought* (Chicago: University of Chicago Press, 1973).

Index